Man of the Century
A Churchill Cavalcade

Man of the Century

A Churchill Cavalcade

Compiled by Editors of

The Reader's Digest

With illustrations

Little, Brown and Company

Boston   *Toronto*

The Editors would like to express their thanks and
appreciation to the British Information Services in
the U.S.A. for permission to use all photographs,
except as otherwise credited, appearing in this book.

Published simultaneously in Canada
by Little, Brown & Company (Canada) Limited

PRINTED IN THE UNITED STATES OF AMERICA

Foreword

NO one in our time has held a greater claim to the title Man of the Century than Sir Winston Churchill. He was born in the sunset of an age when there were no electric lights, no radios or telephones, no cars or airplanes; he died at the dawn of the Age of Space. The ninety-one years of his life might well be called the Age of Churchill, for history now bears imperishable marks of his mind and spirit.

The list of his careers alone is Olympian: statesman (he served under six sovereigns, and held every cabinet post in England except one); orator (his speeches rank with Demosthenes and Cicero); artist (he was a member of the Royal Academy); soldier (he rode in one of the last cavalry charges, and later fought in trenches); sportsman (he played championship polo); author (he was a war correspondent, novelist, biographer and Nobel Prize–winning historian). His life seemed superhuman, and yet there has never been a more human figure in history.

When the *Reader's Digest* began to prepare this biography (which appeared in a condensed version in the December 1964 and January 1965 issues) the Editors realized that no one author had captured Churchill in words, that no single book held the many measures of the man. The best life of Churchill, they believed, would be a compilation of the best of all that had been written about him and by him—excerpts from the sweeping prose of his own volumes of autobiography, as well as selections from newspaper accounts, magazine articles, memoirs and books. The task was assigned to Mary Coburn, a former Associate Editor of the *Digest,* and it was through her careful selection and editing that the final manuscript was fashioned.

"Anecdotes are the gleaming toys of history," Churchill once wrote, and the stories about Sir Winston and his achievements are among the most colorful and shining of all. Assembled here from scores of sources, they present a unique portrait of an uproarious, irrepressible, great-hearted man.

Contents

CONTENTS

PART 3

PART
1

1

Born to Rebellion

ONE summer afternoon, nearly a hundred years ago, the seventh Duke of Marlborough received a perplexing letter from his son Lord Randolph Churchill.

Randolph was twenty-four. He had been educated at Oxford and had since spent his time traveling. The letter announced that during a visit to the Isle of Wight he had met an American girl whom he wished to marry forthwith. Her name was Jennie Jerome.

He had known her, Lord Randolph admitted, a bare forty-eight hours, and knew little about her family. "Mr. Jerome," he wrote, "is obliged to live in New York to look after his business. I do not know what it is."

He was soon to find out. Leonard Jerome was a great American freebooter who, besides winning or losing millions with aplomb, had founded the first two great American racecourses and built his own private opera house. He had also been the American consul at Trieste and was part owner of the New York *Times*. His daughter Jennie was a young woman of striking beauty. Her dark, flashing eyes, her charming wit and poise were invariably admired in fashionable society. She was an excellent pianist and a talented painter. She was also, on her mother's side, the great-granddaughter of a lithesome Iroquois Indian girl.

Lord Randolph's letter disturbed the Duke, who hoped his son would stand for Parliament and feared that an ill-considered love match might extinguish his interest in politics. Thus he counseled delay.

But Jennie and Randolph were not to be discouraged. When elections were announced in the spring of 1874, Lord Randolph dutifully stood as a candidate. He was elected with an overwhelming majority, and that April he and Jennie Jerome were married.

The young couple lived in London, but often visited the Duke and Duchess at the Churchills' ancestral home, Blenheim Palace, where Randolph had been born. A titanic castle of three hundred and twenty rooms set in twenty-seven hundred acres of parks and gardens, the palace had been the gift of Queen Anne to John Churchill, the first Duke of Marlborough, one of England's greatest soldiers.

On the night of November 30, 1874, Lady Randolph, against her doctor's advice, insisted on attending a ball which was held at Blenheim Palace. Suddenly, at the height of the festivity, she felt that her hour, still reckoned to be several weeks away, was rapidly approaching. She left the ball at once and hurried "through the library, the longest room in England, toward the longest corridor in the world, along a quarter of a mile of dark red carpet" which led to her bedroom.

She never reached it. She got only as far as a small room which that night served as a ladies' cloakroom. Here, amid velvet cloaks, muffs, furs and feather boas, she gave birth to her first son, Winston Leonard Spencer Churchill. [5]*

He was born into a world so distant in time and spirit as to be almost beyond recapture. Old yeomen of the district who admired the red-faced, squalling baby in his carriage—and tugged their forelocks in the Victorian gesture of respect—were veterans of Nelson's fleet and Wellington's victory at Waterloo. In the United States, North and South still mourned their dead in the wake of the Civil War.

* All bracketed numerals refer to original sources, which are identified in the Key to Contributors beginning on page 309.

The two powerful winds—nationalism and socialism—that would shake and transform the world had already begun to blow. Karl Marx's masterwork was twenty-six years old. Italy and Germany were already proud and ambitious. But for a while, for the quarter of a century during which Winston Churchill would grow to manhood, it was an age of *Pax Britannica,* of kings and sweatshops, tycoons and *laissez-faire*—a world already dying, but with a splendid grace. [10]

The baby raised a terrific din. Her Grace the Duchess of Marlborough shook her head and observed: "I have myself given life to quite a number of infants. They were all pretty vocal when they arrived, but such an earth-shaking noise as this newborn baby made I have never heard!" [34]

His earliest memories were of Dublin. He was not quite two years old when his father quarreled with the Prince of Wales and the Duke accepted the position of Viceroy of Ireland in order to remove Randolph from the wrath of London society.

Churchill did not see much of his parents. His father was engrossed in politics and his mother caught up in a busy social life. The recipient of his confidences was Mrs. Everest, his nurse. Once Mrs. Everest started to take him to a theater to see a pantomime, but they were stopped by a crowd of people who said the theater had burned down. All that was left of the manager, they were told, were the keys that had been in his pocket.

Winston asked eagerly to see the keys, but this request, he wrote years later, "does not seem to have been well received." [4]

The child was red-haired, sturdy and not handsome. He had a mop of curls, a short and roundly compact face, freckled and with a snub nose. There was also a distinct impediment of speech, a combination of stammer and lisp.

He was uncommonly self-assured, obstinate, bumptious and arrogant. [5]

Modern psychologists and pedagogues would call his childhood far from ideal. Early arithmetic lessons from a governess came hard. "The figures were tied into all sorts of tangles and did things to one another which it was extremely difficult to forecast," he wrote. "You had to borrow one or carry one, and afterwards you had to pay back the one you had borrowed. These complications cast a steadily gathering shadow over my daily life."

At seven he was sent to St. James School, at Ascot in England. [56]

There discipline was rigidly strict. The headmaster delighted in beating the boys until they bled. Winston rebelled. He was beaten often and freely, nevertheless he refused to write Latin verses which he said he could not understand. Once he even kicked the headmaster's straw hat to pieces, which made him the hero of the school.

Winston nursed such a grievance against this man that for years after he brooded on revenge. He planned to return one day, denounce the master before all his pupils, then subject him to the same punishment he inflicted on his helpless charges. At the age of nineteen he actually drove to Ascot, but found that the school had been abandoned and the hated headmaster had disappeared. [4]

At the age of twelve, he was sent to Harrow. There, too, he was far and away the worst pupil. In four and a half years he never rose above the bottom of the school. "That lad couldn't have gone *through* Harrow," a contemporary remarked. "He must have gone *under* it." [5]

He consistently broke almost every rule, and had an unlimited vocabulary of "back-chat."

"Churchill," the headmaster once said to him, "I have very grave reason to be displeased with you."

"And I, sir," replied the boy, "have very grave reason to be displeased with you." [21]

6

Nevertheless, it was at Harrow that he acquired his love for the English language. He wrote: "Mr. Somervell—a delightful man to whom my debt is great—was charged with the duty of teaching the stupidest boys the most disregarded thing—namely, to write mere English." It was a lesson which, to the world's advantage, he learned thoroughly.

"Naturally," he wrote, "I am biased in favor of boys learning English. I would let the clever ones learn Latin as an honor, and Greek as a treat. The only thing I would whip them for would be for not knowing English. I would whip them hard for that." [48]

He was quite fearless. He did not mind being the laughing-stock of the school when his nurse, Mrs. Everest, came to visit him in her old-fashioned bonnet. He embraced her, kissed her, and walked arm in arm with her in the full view of everyone.

One day a great swordsman came to exhibit his skill before the assembled school. He offered to cut in half an apple balanced on the head of a boy and asked for volunteers. The pride of place was offered to the football captain, but he was not anxious for the honor. Instead, an unknown red-headed boy—young Winston—suddenly ran from the benches and knelt before the swordsman.

His memory, too, was astonishing. He won the Elocution prize by reciting twelve hundred lines of Macaulay's *Lays of Ancient Rome* without a single mistake. He could also quote whole scenes from Shakespeare's plays and had no hesitation in correcting his masters if they misquoted. [5]

He demonstrated his critical talent one day during a visit to his aunt's house, where he met H. Rider Haggard, author of *She* and *King Solomon's Mines*.

"What do you mean by this passage in your new book?" asked the boy. "I don't understand it."

Mr. Haggard examined the passage and did not understand it either. [34]

Still, he hated school and refused to absorb anything that

7

didn't interest him. His father, Lord Randolph, was then Chancellor of the Exchequer, and visitors at Harrow looked for Winston among the students who were lined up according to their scholastic achievement. He overheard a visitor say: "Why, he's the last of all!" [30]

Lord Randolph was one of the most spectacular men of the day. His career flashed like a meteor across the late Victorian sky while he advanced from the political back benches of Commons to leader of the House. He revitalized a defeated and dispirited Tory party, led it to victory, and reached the pinnacle of success when he was only thirty-six.

Then suddenly, in a moment of arrogance and folly, he resigned his position of Chancellor of the Exchequer over a minor budget dispute. The news created a sensation throughout Europe. Could the Tory administration continue, deprived of the support of its most glittering figure?

The Government staggered, and then quickly righted itself. Practically no voices were lifted in Lord Randolph's defense and no one mourned his going. [4]

Even his young son sensed the impact of the shattering blow. "One could not grow up in my father's house without understanding that there had been a great political disaster," he wrote.

Tormented by bitterness, Lord Randolph, who had hitherto devoted little attention to his son, began to worry when Winston was fifteen. He had no conception of what went on inside the disappointing boy. All he could see was that he was untalented; that there was no prospect of his going to Oxford, that he was not even good enough to become a lawyer. What remained? [5]

"My cousin Winston was a large schoolboy when I was still in the nursery," wrote Clare Sheridan. "He filled me with awe. His playroom contained from one end to the other a plank table upon which thousands of lead soldiers were arranged for battle. He organized wars. The lead battalions were maneuvered into action, peas and pebbles committed great casualties, forts were stormed, cavalry charged, bridges were destroyed—real water tanks engulfed the advancing foe. Altogether it was a most impressive show, and played with an interest that was no ordinary child game." [50]

One day Lord Randolph went into Winston's room while the boy was engaged in carrying out a large-scale operation with his soldiers. He watched him for twenty minutes. Then he asked bluntly whether he would like to go into the army. The son answered "Yes," and was taken at his word. At Harrow he was now placed in the army class to prepare him for the Royal Military Academy at Sandhurst.

"The toy soldiers turned the current of my life," he wrote later. [5]

The visionary gift that was later to distinguish him more than any other quality must already have been developed at least in rudimentary form by this time. Quite independently, he went to a throat specialist about his lisp. "Cure the impediment in my speech, please," he said. "I am going into the army first. But as a Minister later, I can't be haunted by the idea that I must avoid every word beginning with an *s*." [34]

But he flunked the entrance examinations to Sandhurst twice and probably would have failed them again had he not, in a daring maneuver in a game of tag, jumped thirty feet off a bridge into a chasm. He did not recover consciousness for three days, and during the months of convalescence that followed he boned up on just enough math to squeak through. [10]

The schoolboy who was bored to tears because he had hardly ever been asked to learn anything which seemed to be of use to him found life transformed at Sandhurst. Gone was the tedium of Latin and Greek. In their place were the enchantments of military studies. As a cavalry cadet, he now had to study fortification, topography, military law and administration. [2]

He learned how to blow up masonry bridges, construct breastworks, make road reconnaissances and contoured maps. But horses were his greatest pleasure. Besides the riding instruction he received at Sandhurst, his father arranged for him to take an additional course with the Royal Horse Guards. He spent all of his money on hiring horses, and much of his time in organizing steeplechases.

During his last term at Sandhurst, Churchill made his first public speech. The circumstances were unusual and comic. In the summer of 1894, a certain Mrs. Ormiston Chant launched a Purity Campaign. The chief object of her attention was the promenade of the Empire Theater—a large lounge containing several bars which were usually filled with professional ladies. It was a favorite place of many of the Sandhurst cadets, and they were indignant at Mrs. Chant's allegations of immorality. The *Daily Telegraph* ran an article against the lady titled "Prudes on the Prowl," and the battle was on. [4]

An Entertainments Protection League was formed. Winston became a member, and he pawned his gold watch to aid the league's finances. But Mrs. Chant was successful in getting a light canvas screen erected between the offending bars and the promenade. Shortly afterward, Churchill and his friends visited the theater. Many sympathizers were present. Comment led to action, and a crowd of some two hundred persons stormed the barricades and tore them down. At this moment of triumph, young Churchill mounted the debris and made his maiden speech. [2]

The American author Richard Harding Davis was given a version of the speech by Winston's fellow officers and preserved a portion of it for posterity.

"Where does the Englishman in London always find a welcome?" cried Churchill. "Where does he first go when, battle-scarred and travel-worn, he reaches home? Who is always there to greet him with a smile and join him with a drink? Who is ever faithful, ever true? The ladies of the Empire promenade!"

Luckily this incident was not brought to the attention of his commanding officer. [4]

"At Sandhurst I had a new start," said Winston. He started, and finished, with a vengeance. Entering at the bottom of his class, he graduated eighth in a class of one hundred and fifty, and was ready to whip the world. "Come on now, you young men all over the world," he wrote, recalling his feelings at the time. "Raise the glorious flag again! Don't take no for an answer. Never submit to failure. You will make all kinds of mistakes, but as long as you are generous and true, and also fierce, you cannot hurt the world or even seriously distress her. She was made to be wooed and won by youth."

But it was a gloomy house that Winston came home to from Sandhurst. [10]

For some time after his fall from office, Lord Randolph had seemed confident that he would be able to fight his way back to power. No one cherished these hopes more than his son. For years Winston had read every word his father had spoken or the newspapers wrote about him. "I hoped that I should grow up in time to come to his aid," he wrote.

But he could not get close to the nervous and irritable man. "If I ever showed the slightest idea of companionship, he was immediately offended; and when once I suggested that I might help his secretary to write some of his letters, he froze me into stone."

Only once did Lord Randolph "lift his visor in my sight." After a sudden outburst of temper, he confided to Winston: "Remember things do not always go right with me. My every action is misjudged and every word distorted. So make some allowances."

By the spring of 1894, it became clear that Lord Randolph

was a gravely ill man. His speech was often halting, and he suffered from symptoms of vertigo and numbness of the hands. In January 1895, at the age of forty-five, he died of paralysis of the brain.

"All my dreams of comradeship with him, of entering Parliament at his side, were ended," Winston wrote. "There remained for me only to pursue his aims and vindicate his memory." [5]

Churchill was now twenty years old, and during these years his activities had been followed with mixed feelings and some disquiet at Blenheim Palace. For Churchill, after his cousin the ninth Duke of Marlborough, was next in succession to the dukedom.

In 1895, when Consuelo Vanderbilt arrived at Blenheim as the ninth Duke's bride, Winston's grandmother, the old Dowager Duchess, said to her: "Your first duty is to have a child, and it must be a son, because it would be intolerable to have that little upstart Winston become Duke!"

Fortunately, Consuelo did give birth to a son, and thereby she did Winston Churchill an inestimable service, for had her marriage remained childless he would never have become Prime Minister. Upon the death of the ninth Duke in 1934, he would have inherited the styles and titles of his great ancestor. At that time it was impossible for the heir of a peerage to forego his predestined seat in the House of Lords, and since 1902 no Prime Minister has been a member of that House.

So, in the hour of their greatest need, the British people would have looked in vain for the man to lead and save them. Isolated in Blenheim Palace, he would have been compelled to watch history take place instead of shaping it from Downing Street. [5]

He was now in the army—Queen Victoria's and Kipling's army. He received his commission as a lieutenant and was gazetted to the 4th Hussars. He went to Aldershot sporting the gold lace, striped pantaloons and tiny pillbox forage cap accorded to the Queen's mounted troops.

There he learned the last refinements of military equitation. He enjoyed "the stir of the horses, the clank of their equipment, the thrill of motion, the tossing plumes." And he savored "that greatest of all cavalry events—the charge." [26]

But it was difficult to find any young officers who had thrilled to the thunder of a real charge or who had actually been under fire. Talk in the mess seldom concerned anything more warlike than "spit and polish." In fact, the army seemed to provide a playground for young gentlemen in fancy dress, and in the 4th Hussars five months of each year were devoted to leave. The problem confronting most of Churchill's brother officers was how best to fill the time in the social round, in hunting, shooting and travel. But Churchill longed for personal danger as passionately as many men long for the first crisis of love. [54]

The young soldier scanned in vain the horizon of the British Empire lying peacefully in the dying glow of the Victorian era. All over the world, war seemed to have become extinct—except in Cuba, where Spanish soldiers were trying to suppress a rebellion of native guerrilla fighters. It was not a real war, but there was some sharp fighting, and that was what mattered.

The English public was not much interested in the Cuban rebellion, but Churchill convinced the *Daily Graphic* of its importance, secured a commission as war correspondent, and set sail for Havana. [5]

"When in the dim light of early morning I saw the shores of Cuba," he wrote, "I felt as if I sailed with Captain Silver and first gazed on Treasure Island. Here was a place where real things were going on." [3g]

13

2

The Brash Warrior

HE was attached as a privileged observer to leading Spanish troops whose role was to seek out and destroy the Cuban guerrillas, masters of ambush. [54]

Guerrilla fighting was a type of warfare for which no training had been provided at Aldershot. It required another half century to demonstrate how exceedingly modern it was. Yet it is clear from Churchill's descriptions that he grasped its character in three days. [5]

"We did not see how the Spanish could win," he wrote. "Imagine the cost per hour of a column of nearly four thousand men wandering round and round this endless jungle. And what of the enemy?

"In the mountains and forests were bands of ragged men, supplied with rifles and ammunition, and armed with a formidable chopper-sword called a machete, to whom war cost nothing except poverty, risk and discomfort.

"November 30 was my twenty-first birthday, and on that day for the first time I heard shots fired in anger and heard bullets strike flesh or whistle through the air." [3g]

A horse was shot within a yard of him as he relaxed outside his hut. The bullet could not have missed Churchill's head by more than inches and was probably meant for him. [54]

"All the next day we pursued the trail, and halted for the

night near a rude cabin. We dined undisturbed and retired to our hammocks. I was soon awakened by firing. A bullet ripped through the thatch of our hut, another wounded an orderly just outside. I should have been glad to get out of my hammock and lie on the ground. However, as no one else made a move, I thought it more becoming to stay where I was.

"I fortified myself by dwelling on the fact that the Spanish officer whose hammock was slung between me and the enemy's fire was a man of substantial physique; indeed one might almost have called him fat. I have never been prejudiced against fat men. Gradually, I dropped asleep." [3g]

The following day brought another skirmish. Churchill rode beside the Spanish general who led an infantry attack. The rebels let the Spanish troops come within three hundred yards; then white puffs of smoke began to go up all along the edge of the woods. The first casualties fell around Churchill, but he remained in the first rank. Eventually the rebels fled. Further pursuit in the impenetrable jungle was impossible, and Churchill's Cuban adventure came to an end. [34]

In the fall of 1896, Winston's regiment was posted to Bangalore in India. Churchill fitted smoothly into the exotic life of a British officer in the Indian army, with batmen and servants and a social life revolving around the polo field. [1]

But an unending cycle of morning parade followed by polo and mess conversation was not enough. Lieutenant Churchill resolved to educate himself. [26]

At school, when they had handed him Aristotle's *Ethics*, his only comment was, "It is extraordinary how much of this I had already thought out for myself." Now he suddenly realized he had only the "vaguest knowledge about many spheres of thought." He therefore wrote his mother asking for books on history, philosophy and economics. [30]

During the interminable stifling afternoons at Bangalore, the ambitious hussar read and stored away in his phenomenal memory the great literature he had missed at Harrow and Sandhurst—Plato, Aristotle, Darwin and Macaulay. He also steeped himself in *The Decline and Fall of the Roman Empire,* and here, in Gibbon's prose, he found the model for the sweep and resonance of the Churchillian prose style. [44]

Then, to Churchill's delight, there began to be some trouble in the world. The Pathan tribesmen rose in revolt on the Indian Frontier in 1897, and Churchill wangled a spot with the field force dispatched under Sir Bindon Blood to crush them. He got ambushed near the Khyber Pass, fought off Pathans at point-blank range with his revolver and got mentioned in dispatches. [10]

He could communicate with the native troops with only three words: *"Maro"* (kill), *"Chalo"* (get on), and "Tally ho!" which, he said, "speaks for itself." His men watched him carefully. When he grinned, Churchill noted, they grinned— so he grinned often. Between grins he described the campaign for two newspapers. He wrote:

"Yi! Yi! Yi! Bang! Bang! Bang! A lot of bullets whistled around us. One man was shot through the breast and pouring with blood. The British officer was spinning around just beside me, his face a mass of blood, his right eye cut out.

"Yes, it certainly was an adventure." [30]

Churchill was now recalled to his own regiment in Bangalore, where his colonel insisted he must settle down and accept the obligations of service with the 4th Hussars. But he still itched to be on the frontier. Accordingly, he neglected no means, including intrigues and flagrant violations of the army code—even risking punishment for being absent without leave—to get back to the fighting. [13]

He was as cheeky as ever. Lord Sandhurst, the governor of Bombay, once entertained him at dinner. "His Excellency was good enough to ask my opinion on several matters,"

Winston wrote, "and I thought it would be unbecoming not to reply fully. There were indeed moments when he seemed willing to impart his own views; but I thought it would be ungracious to put him to so much trouble; and he very readily subsided."

But although he was unpopular with generals, he won the loyalty of his subordinates. Mr. Hallaway, a sergeant major, recalled: "Mr. Churchill was easygoing and always ready for a joke. Not at all stuffy like some of the other officers. He hated to see chaps punished. The officers used to inspect the stables every day, and we never knew when they were coming. But Mr. Churchill would whisper to me: 'leven-thirty, Sergeant major.'

"But the great thing about him was the way he worked. He was busier than half the others put together. I never saw him without pencils sticking out all over him. Once, when I went to his bungalow, I could scarcely get in what with books and papers and foolscap all over the place." [4]

At Bangalore he wrote *The Story of the Malakand Field Force*, a bright, lively account of the frontier campaign in which he did not hesitate to criticize certain aspects of British military tactics. But Winston had cause to regret the book. The biggest British force in years was building up in Egypt under General Sir Herbert Kitchener to invade the Sudan and attack an army of Dervishes. Every officer clamored to be included in the expedition, Churchill among them. Unfortunately, Kitchener had read his book and had decided views on what he thought of cheeky young subalterns. He refused point-blank to have Churchill in his expedition even after Lord Salisbury, the Prime Minister, had been persuaded to use his influence. It became a battle of wills between England's unbeatable and most distinguished soldier and Lieutenant Winston Churchill. Winston won. [1]

Later he received a message from the War Office informing him of his attachment to the 21st Lancers and ordering him to report "at once" to regimental headquarters. There he saw his great antagonist, Kitchener, for the first time on September 1, 1898, at the decisive moment of the Sudan campaign. [5]

Churchill had been sent on patrol, ahead of the British advance, to reconnoiter a rocky ridge. [2]

From a black spur of rock he observed a great mass advancing over the plain, a black tide shot through with the glint of spears—an immense thunder cloud, turbulent and terrible and made of one hundred thousand men dedicated to death by the sword. He rode back with the news to Kitchener's side. [54]

They were face to face, at last, but the interview was brief. Churchill reported that the Dervishes were advancing, and a clash was inevitable. The Charge of the Light Brigade was still fresh in many people's memory; it belonged to the romantic tradition to which, at the end of the Victorian era, young soldiers still clung with enthusiasm. Now the romance of nineteenth-century England was to end in a last cavalry charge, in which Churchill would take part. In history it is called the charge of Omdurman. [13]

"In the distant plain thousands of men advance," wrote Churchill, "ordered ranks bright with glittering weapons, and above them dance a multitude of gorgeous flags. As they descended the long smooth slopes which led to the river and their enemy, our batteries opened an intense fire. Down went the bright flags by dozens and their men by hundreds, but none turned back. Almost at the same moment the trumpet sounded 'Right wheel into line,' and the regiment broke into a gallop on the hard crisp desert.

"Suddenly Dervishes, a great gray mass gleaming with steel, rose up from a dry watercourse where they had hidden. Straight before me a man threw himself on the ground, his curved sword drawn back for a hamstringing cut. Leaning over I fired two shots into him. As I straightened in the saddle

18

I saw another figure with uplifted sword. I fired, and man and sword disappeared behind me. My comrades, stabbed at and hacked at by spear and sword, were dragged from their horses and cut to pieces by the infuriated foe.

"I pulled my horse up and looked about me. I could not see a single officer or man of my squadron, only Dervish riflemen crouching and aiming their rifles at me. For the first time I experienced a sudden sensation of fear. I felt myself absolutely alone. These riflemen would hit me and the rest devour me like wolves. I spurred my horse into a gallop and drew clear of the mêlée; three hundred yards away I found my troop already faced about and formed up. We moved off at a trot towards the enemy and compelled the Dervishes to retreat. In the space of two or three minutes the regiment had lost nearly a quarter of its strength." [3g]

The Battle of Omduran lasted five hours. The Dervish army, mowed down mercilessly by the rifle fire of trained infantry, supported by heavy guns, lost nearly ten thousand dead, sixteen thousand wounded and five thousand prisoners. British losses were twenty-five dead and one hundred thirty-six wounded. At sunset, Churchill rode into Omduran with the victorious Kitchener, where he learned that all of the special correspondents of *The Times* had been killed or wounded. Perceiving a professional opportunity, Churchill, in a long telegram to *The Times,* gave a detailed description of the battle. But the story never reached *The Times.* Laying it down that serving officers were not permitted to work as war correspondents, Kitchener stopped its transmission. [5]

Within a week of the battle the 21st Lancers started for home, and Lieutenant Churchill went with them. Four years in the army had shown that his expenditures were permanently in excess of his receipts and likely to remain so. [26]

"I saw that the only profession I had been taught," he wrote, "would never yield me even enough money to avoid getting into debt. On the other hand, the books I had written and my war correspondence had brought in about five times as much as the Queen had paid me for years of assiduous and sometimes dangerous work. I therefore resolved to return to India, win the Polo Tournament, leave the army, relieve my mother from paying my allowance, write my new book about the Sudan Campaign (which I decided to call *The River War*) and look out for a chance of entering Parliament." [3g]

Churchill at once asked the Central Office of the Conservative Party about the prospects of finding a constituency. He was assured that naturally they would procure one for the son of Lord Randolph; it was mainly a matter of finance. A "safe" seat would require up to a £1,000 a year; "risky" seats were cheaper and so-called "forlorn hopes" very cheap. Meanwhile they would welcome him as a speaker at their rallies and garden fetes. [5]

"I surveyed this prospect with the eye of an urchin looking through a pastrycook's window. I had always wanted to make a speech, but I had never been invited or indeed allowed to do so. Finally we selected a gathering of the Primrose League (founded by my father) in a park in Bath for my maiden effort. I spent hours preparing my discourse, learning it so thoroughly that I could have said it backwards in my sleep. I licked my chops over one sentence: 'England would gain far more from the rising tide of Tory Democracy than from the dried-up drainpipe of Radicalism.'

"The day arrived. The audience cheered a lot at all the right places when I paused on purpose to give them a chance, and at the end they clapped loudly for quite a long time. So I could do it after all!" [3g]

The *Morning Post* gave the speech a whole column and in a short leading article drew attention to "the arrival of a new figure upon the political scene."

Fighting wars. Writing books. Making speeches. Churchill had found the three main forms which he needed for the expression of his personality. [5]

In high good spirits he set off for India, in November 1898, to rejoin his regiment. The inter-regimental polo competition would be played the following February at Meerut, fourteen hundred miles north of Bangalore. Never before had a regiment stationed in the south of India won the event. The day before the match, however, he dislocated his shoulder. He had his right elbow tightly bound to his body with stirrup leather, galloped onto the field at the head of his team and managed to score three out of the four goals. The victory of his team was his personal victory. He left India, the 4th Hussars and the army in a blaze of glory. [13]

No longer subject to military discipline, Churchill was now able to write what he thought about Kitchener. *The River War*, composed when Churchill was twenty-four, is bubbling with personality and sizzling with temperament, an authoritative work valued today. Scandalized by Kitchener's "desecration of the Mahdi's Tomb and the barbarous manner in which he carried off the Mahdi's head in a kerosene can as a trophy," Churchill called it a "foul deed" and concluded: "Such was the chivalry of the conquerors!"

"The best and worst that can be said of Mr. Winston Spencer Churchill's historical account," wrote *The Times*, "may be summed up in the observation that it contains materials for two good books and one bad one. Probably the bad one would be the most entertaining of the three. He is certainly fearless, if occasionally impertinent."

Writing now began to give him artistic pleasure, the sign of the professional taking over from the amateur. "I affected a combination of the styles of Macaulay and Gibbon, the staccato antitheses of the former and the rolling sentences of the latter; and I stuck in a bit of my own from time to time." He studied the inborn structure of this thing called a "book" as an artist would study anatomy; he compared the fashioning of it to building a house, planning a battle, or painting a picture. "The materials are different, but the principle is the same. The foundations have to be laid, the data assembled, and the premises must bear the weight of the conclusions." [5]

G. W. Stevens, the *Daily Mail* correspondent and Churchill's shipmate when he was returning to England, had been astonished to find that Churchill knew so much at the age of twenty-four, but only about the things that would be useful to him. His prophetic article, "The Youngest Man in Europe," began:

"In years he is a boy; in temperament he is also a boy; but in intention, in deliberate plan, he is already a man with a precocious, almost uncanny judgment as to the efficacy of the means to the end. From his father he derives the hereditary aptitude for affairs, the grand style of entering upon them. From his American strain he adds to this a keenness, a natural aptitude for advertisement, and happily a sense of humor. He is calculating but never in cold blood, and that is his saving grace. He may or may not possess the qualities which make a great general but, if they exist, they are overshadowed by qualities which might make him a great popular leader, a great journalist. He has not studied to make himself a demagogue. He was born a demagogue and he happens to know it. At the rate he goes there will hardly be room for him in Parliament at thirty or in England at forty. Already he holds a vast lead over his contemporaries." [13]

In June 1899 there was an election in Oldham, and the Conservative party persuaded Churchill to run for a seat in the House of Commons. He lost by eighteen hundred votes. Recriminations came fast. [30]

"A young man cannot expect to get very far in life without getting some good smacks in the eye," he said after the result was declared, and, turning to his victorious opponent, added, "I don't think that the world has seen the last of either of us." A few days later Arthur Balfour, leader of the House of

Commons, wrote to him: "Never mind, it will all come right; and this small reverse will have no permanent ill effect upon your political fortunes."

But the man who had the most immediate effect upon Churchill's political fortunes was not Balfour, but Joseph Chamberlain, the Tory Colonial Secretary and father of Neville and Austen Chamberlain. Churchill was to struggle and grapple with the Chamberlains throughout his life, from South Africa to Munich. Churchill had inherited "Great Joe" from his father. "He was sometimes a foe in my father's days of triumph, and sometimes a friend in his days of adversity; but always there had subsisted between them a quarrelsome comradeship and a personal liking." Churchill had met Chamberlain several times at his father's home. Now he met him again. South Africa was the main topic. [5]

When gold and diamond mines had been discovered near Johannesburg, they had naturally attracted a rush of British pioneers and businessmen. The Dutch, or "Boer," farmers who had settled in South Africa one hundred fifty years before and established the Orange Free State and Transvaal republics bitterly resented these newcomers. When Chamberlain demanded that British subjects in the Transvaal be granted full rights of citizenship, the Boer President reluctantly agreed. But when his concession drew further demands from the British, he sent an ultimatum to London and a few days later war had begun. [4]

Chamberlain was sure the war would be quick and painless. Smiling superciliously, the Olympian expounded this theory to young Churchill while the two were rattling in a hansom cab from Chamberlain's house at Prince's Garden to his desk at the Colonial Office. In reply to Churchill's "What about Mafeking?" he admitted it might be besieged. "But if they cannot hold out for a few weeks, what is one to expect?" In actual fact the Boer War lasted three years and devoured £200,000,000.

The Boer ultimatum had been known in London for less than an hour when Churchill put in his pocket a contract with the *Morning Post* for £250 a month—a record for the time—with four months' guarantee, all expenses paid and full discretion as to movements and opinions. [34]

"Preparations occupied my few remaining hours at home," he recalled. "Mr. George Wyndham, Under Secretary of State, dined with me one night. He alone seemed to appreciate the magnitude of the task. The Boers, he said, were thoroughly prepared, had large quantities of munitions. The British forces might be attacked in detail, surrounded and pounded to pieces. I thought it quite sporting of the Boers to take on the whole British Empire, and I was much relieved to learn that the war would not be entirely one-sided.

"Never, never, never believe any war will be smooth and easy, or that anyone who embarks on the strange voyage can measure the tides and hurricanes he will encounter. Always remember, however sure you are that you can easily win, that there would not be a war if the other man did not think he also had a chance." [3g]

Churchill sailed for Capetown on the *Dunottar Castle* October 11. J. B. Atkins, correspondent of the *Manchester Guardian*, was also on the ship. "I had not been many hours on board before I became aware of a most unusual young man," he wrote in his memoirs. "He was slim, slightly reddish-haired, pale, lively, frequently plunging along the deck with neck outthrust, as Browning fancied Napoleon; sometimes sitting in meditation folding and unfolding his hands, not nervously but as though he were helping himself to untie mental knots. Soon we conversed. It was obvious he was in love with words. He would hesitate before he chose one or changed one for a better. When the prospects of a career like that of his father excited him, then such a gleam shot from him that he was almost transfigured. It was as though a light were switched on inside him which suddenly shone out through his eyes. He compressed his lips; he contracted himself as though gathering himself together to spring; the whole illuminated face grinned."

Atkins and Churchill agreed to knit their fortunes together and try to get through to Ladysmith, where the heaviest fighting would take place. When they reached the town of Estcourt, Ladysmith had already been cut off. [4]

Twelve thousand Boer horsemen occupied the terrain around the little British garrison there, but the commanding general had a novel idea: send out an armored train to reconnoiter the terrain. [34]

Captain Haldane, whom Churchill had known in India, was put in charge of the operation; he asked Churchill if he would like to accompany him. Churchill enthusiastically said yes and hurried off to extend the invitation to Atkins. But Atkins thought it was a crazy idea. "Perfectly true," said Churchill. "But I have a sort of intuition that if I go something will come of it."

His instincts were right, for the journey on the armored train was the beginning of a journey to fame. [4]

3

The War Correspondent

FOURTEEN miles from Estcourt, the Boers lay in wait for the train. Suddenly it was deluged with pom-pom shells. The engineer speeded up. Then there was a tremendous shock. The engineer had hit a curve at forty miles an hour; the train was derailed. The engine was still on the rails, the front truck somewhere to one side. The next two blocked the track; the three attached behind were unharmed.

In the rain of Boer bullets a splinter hit the engineer. He was about to make off, when Churchill grabbed him by the shoulders. "Don't you know a man can never be wounded twice on the same day?" he shouted. The engineer agreed to stay and try to push the two front trucks out of the way with his engine. [34]

Churchill helped load the wounded from the six derailed coaches onto an engine car and got it going, while the others provided covering fire. "Keep cool, men," he told them. "This will be interesting for my paper." [30]

Under persistent fire, the train steamed slowly towards Estcourt, while Haldane made his men run alongside, hoping, if possible, to get them back too. The fire was too hot. To save the wounded, the engine increased speed. Shortly before the last bridge Churchill jumped down and ran back to Haldane's men. They were no longer there. [5]

"Two figures in plain clothes appeared upon the line," he

wrote. " 'Platelayers!' I said to myself, and then with a surge of realization, 'Boers!' I turned and ran back towards the engine, the two Boers firing as I ran between the metals. I flung myself against the bank of the cutting. It gave no cover. Movement seemed the only chance. I darted forward: two soft kisses sucked in the air. I jigged to the left and scrambled up the bank and into a tiny depression, where I lay struggling to get my breath. Two hundred yards away was the rocky gorge of the Blue Krantz and plenty of cover. I determined to make a dash for it. Suddenly on the other side of the railway I saw a horseman galloping furiously, a tall, dark figure, holding a rifle in his right hand. He shouted a loud command. I put my hand to my belt; my pistol was not there. Getting in and out of the engine I had taken it off. The Boer horseman, still seated on his horse, covered me with his rifle. The animal stood stock still, so did he, and so did I. If he fired he would surely hit me. I held up my hands and surrendered myself." [3g]

Churchill argued with the Boer authorities that he should be released because he was a civilian press correspondent. But the Boers had no intention of letting him go. "It's not every day that we catch the son of a lord." Besides, he had forfeited his noncombatant status by the part he had taken in the train fight. [4]

At the officers' prisoners-of-war camp at Pretoria "the hours crawled like paralytic centipedes." After three weeks Churchill decided to escape. On the evening of December 12, 1899, he hid in the latrine. "Through a chink I watched the sentries. All of a sudden one turned and walked up to his comrade. Their backs were turned. I darted out of my hiding place, ran to the wall, seized the top with my hands and drew myself up. Then I lowered myself silently down into the adjoining garden and crouched among the shrubs. I was free!" He had £75 in cash and four slabs of chocolate in his pocket, but neither a map nor a compass. He was in the heart of the enemy's country, three hundred miles from the Portuguese frontier and without a word of Afrikaans. [5]

"The streets were full of burghers," he wrote, "but they paid no attention to me. I walked on leisurely, humming a tune and choosing the middle of the road until I reached the suburbs. A cool breeze fanned my face and a wild feeling of exhilaration took hold of me. I formed a plan. I would find the Delagoa Bay railway, board a train in motion and hide under the seats. After two hours I perceived the signal lights of a station and hid in the ditch two hundred yards beyond the platform. Suddenly I heard the whistle and the approaching rattle. The great yellow headlights of the engine drew near, the rattle became a roar. The dark mass hung for a second above me; clouds of steam rushed past. I hurled myself on the trucks, grasped some sort of handhold, was swung off my feet. It was a goods train filled with empty coal bags. I crawled to the top, burrowed in among them until I was completely buried. The sacks were warm and comfortable.

"How long I slept I do not know, but I woke suddenly. I must leave the train and find some hiding place while it was still dark. I crawled from my cozy place to the couplings, seized an iron handle, pulled with my left hand and sprang. My feet struck the ground in two gigantic strides and the next instant I was sprawling in the ditch, shaken but unhurt. I set out for the hills and entered a small grove of trees to wait till dusk." [3g]

That night Churchill walked back to the tracks with the idea of taking another train. But he saw lights in the far distance which he thought were Kaffir fires, and some instinct bade him approach them. As he drew nearer he realized it was a coal mine and decided to chance his luck. He knocked on a door, and a tall man with a pale face answered and eyed him with suspicion until he gave him his name.

"Thank God you have come here," the man said. "It is the only house for twenty miles where you would not have been handed over." [4]

John Howard, manager of the Transvaal Collieries, had been allowed by the Boers to remain to keep the mine in order. His foreman, Dewsnap, hailed from Oldham, of all places. Howard showed Churchill a warrant of arrest, three thousand copies of which had been distributed over the land. It offered £25 for Churchill "dead or alive." [5]

The description was not flattering: "Englishman, twenty-five years old, about five feet eight inches tall, indifferent build, walks with a forward stoop, pale appearance, red-brownish hair, small and hardly noticed moustache, talks through his nose, and cannot pronounce the letter s properly." [2]

At great risk to themselves, Howard and Dewsnap hid Churchill at the bottom of the coal mine. There he read Stevenson's *Kidnapped,* with white rats keeping him company, while Boer patrols overhead searched the district. Eventually Howard managed to smuggle him, concealed among bales of wool, on a goods train which crossed the frontier into Portuguese territory.

His escapade was the sensation of the newspapers on two continents. "Churchill is back," wrote Atkins, "pale and emaciated after his escape from Pretoria. He is at this moment sitting beside me in my tent with a new and lively conviction of the military genius of the Boers."

Churchill took the next boat to Durban, where he was acclaimed as a popular hero. The crowd, nearly tearing him to pieces, thronged the quay and carried him on their shoulders to the Town Hall, where he had to make a speech. Telegrams from all over the world poured in on him. One gentleman invited him to come shooting in Central Asia. "Young ladies sent me woolen comforters. Old ladies forwarded their photographs." Back in England T. E. Dunville, the music hall comedian, sang:

You've heard of Winston Churchill
This is all I need to say—
He's the latest and the greatest
Correspondent of the day. [5]

The Boers were on the run now and the British thought —again wrongly—that the war was all but over. Churchill rode with Roberts's victorious armies first into Johannesburg and then into Pretoria. He was wildly received at the prison camp from which he had escaped almost a year earlier. The Boers scattered and settled down grimly to a guerrilla warfare which was to last another two years. [1]

"The 21st Lancers started home," wrote Churchill. "In Cairo I found Dick Molyneux, a subaltern, who like myself had been attached to the 21st. He had been seriously wounded by a sword-cut above his right wrist. While we were talking, the doctor came in to dress his wound. The doctor, anxious that the horrible gash be skinned over as soon as possible, said something in a low tone to the nurse, who bared her arm. They retired into a corner, where he began to cut a piece of skin off her to transfer to Molyneux's wound. The poor nurse blanched, and the doctor turned upon me. 'Oi'll have to take it off you,' said the great raw-boned Irishman. I rolled up my sleeve. 'Ye've heered of a man being flayed aloive? Well, this is what it feels loike,' he added genially. He cut a piece of skin and some flesh about the size of a shilling from the inside of my forearm. I managed to hold out as he sawed the razor slowly to and fro until he had cut the precious fragment which was then grafted on to my friend's wound and remains there to this day. I for my part keep the scar as a souvenir." [3g]

The Conservatives, flushed by apparent victory in South

Africa, had called a snap election and Churchill, determined to take part in it, returned home. He had left England in the nineteenth century and he returned to it in the twentieth, twenty-six years old and the most famous young man in England. [1]

When last year's defeated candidate marched into Oldham with a procession of ten landaus, the streets were packed with enthusiastic operatives and mill-girls. "See the Conquering Hero Comes," the band played over and over. Oldham had every reason to be proud of capturing Churchill for the coming political contest. Eleven constituencies had offered themselves to him. Nevertheless he remained faithful to Oldham. "Because he is our adopted son," said the constituents in a pub. "Because I want to wipe out my black eyes!" Churchill explained his own constancy. [34]

London papers sent reporters to cover the campaign. "Young Churchill," wrote Julian Ralph of the *Daily Mail*, "finds it easier to vault out of a landau than to open the door when he is getting out to address his electors. He will not hesitate to admonish the Government in a newspaper letter and will calmly differ from a bishop on a point of ecclesiastical law. But he is electric in brilliance and dash. People rush to see and hear him, wring his hand, and shout God's blessing after him."

The election was fought largely on the issue of the Boer War. The radical Liberals, bitterly opposed to the conflict, thought it had been engineered by Chamberlain as a commercial venture. Churchill was bound to defend the Government and the campaign grew in violence as the climax neared. [4]

"Great Joe" Chamberlain himself came to Oldham. He spoke for over an hour telling his audience that "Lord Randolph's son has inherited some of his father's great qualities—his originality and his courage." All the same the fight was tough. When some two hundred Liberals switched their votes to Churchill "out of personal goodwill and war feeling," he won by the modest margin of two hundred thirty votes.

As soon as the election was over Churchill started on a lecture tour throughout England in which he unfolded his adventures and escape. The remuneration was high, even by present-day standards. He hardly ever earned less than £100 a night and often more, as at Liverpool where he received £300 for a single lecture. Having toured little more than half of Great Britain, by November he was able to bank safely over £4,500. He immediately crossed the Atlantic for a lecture tour in the United States and Canada. [5]

Major Pond, the American agent who had engaged him, announced his star with the poster: "Winston Churchill, twenty-six years old, author of six books, hero of four wars, Member of Parliament, forthcoming Prime Minister of England." Churchill, horrified, insisted that the poster be withdrawn. [34]

Mark Twain served as host at Churchill's first lecture in New York and introduced him by saying, "By his father he is an Englishman; by his mother, an American. Behold, the perfect man!" [30]

"Mark Twain, most of whose books I had read, was now very old and snow-white," Churchill recalled. "I was thrilled by this companion of my youth. Of course we argued about the war, but I think I did not displease him; for he was good enough to sign every one of the thirty volumes of his works. In the first he inscribed the following, intended, I daresay, to convey a gentle admonition: 'To do good is noble; to teach others to do good is nobler, and no trouble.'

"I was surprised to find that many Americans thought the Boers were in the right. In Chicago the Irish showed themselves actively hostile. However, when I paid a sincere tribute to the courage and humanity of the Boers, they were placated. On the whole I found American audiences cool and critical, but also urbane and good-natured." [3g]

The news of Queen Victoria's death, on January 22, 1901, reached Churchill in Minneapolis. She had reigned for sixty-four years. It was the end of a whole age whose face she had shaped and dominated. Churchill had passed his early youth in the Queen's service and the Queen's wars; this youth was now over. He returned home and completed his tour of the British cities. "The results were substantial." Five months in which he had spoken almost every day and often twice a day had yielded nearly £10,000. "I was entirely independent and had no need to worry about the future, or for many years to work at anything but politics."

On February 15, 1901, Edward VII opened the first Parliament of the century and of his reign. In it the Member for Oldham took his seat on the Government back benches. [5]

Ten minutes after he had been sworn, Churchill was settled comfortably on the bench, his silk hat well down over his forehead, his figure crouched in the doubled-up attitude assumed by Mr. Balfour and the other Ministers, both hands deep in his pockets, eyeing the place and its inmates critically as if they were all parliamentary novices. [4]

His maiden speech was on the Boer War. He had prepared it well and it already smacked of his father's liberal "Tory Democracy." "If I were a Boer," he announced at one point, "I hope I should be fighting in the field." [10]

This, Joe Chamberlain said cynically to a neighbor, was "a good way to throw away seats." Churchill finished his speech with a nice tribute to his father, thanking the House for its kindness and patience, "which have been extended to me, I well know, not on my account, but because of a certain splendid memory which many honorable Members still preserve."

Some of his remarks made Conservatives feel uncomfortable. The Liberals were intrigued. Listening with more care than most to the speech was the tremendous little Welshman David Lloyd George, eleven years Winston's senior and already the most brilliant of a brilliant assembly. "You are standing against the light," he told him admiringly, when he was introduced to him after the speech. A memorable if checkered friendship was taking place. [1]

If anyone at this period had asked the two men why they had entered Parliament, both might have answered: "In order to become Prime Minister." And why Prime Minister? Lloyd George would have said: "To help the people and achieve social justice." Churchill would have answered: "In order to *be* Prime Minister." Lloyd George saw a task and expected himself to be big enough to master it. Churchill saw himself and expected the task to be big enough for him. [5]

As a back-bencher Winston was one of the most hardworking young men in England. Although he shared a flat in Mayfair with his brother Jack, he had no time for frivolity and rarely made a social engagement. On a weekend visit to friends he brought his work with him. The American writer George Smalley, once a co-visitor with Winston at the vast mansion of the Duke and Duchess of Sutherland, was invited to Winston's room and was astonished at the sight that greeted him. "He had brought with him a tin box, some three feet square, divided into closed compartments. A large writing table was covered with papers, loose and in docketed bundles, but all in exact order for ready reference. When we left Dunrobin, Winston reserved a compartment in the railway train for himself and his big tin case of papers and shut himself up there during that long, long journey and wrote and worked."

He took infinite pains with his speeches, sometimes working on them for six weeks. "In those days and indeed for many years," he wrote, "I was unable to say anything (except a sentence in rejoinder) that I had not written out and committed to memory beforehand." He practiced his speeches by reciting them aloud. Wrote a newspaper editor: "All day he might be heard booming away in his bedroom, rehearsing his facts and flourishes to the accompaniment of resounding knocks on the furniture." Once a speech was ready he took care that the newspapers received a copy in advance, and editors often were surprised to see that the author had confidently punctuated his script with "cheers."

As the months passed Churchill became increasingly rebellious within his own party. He organized a group of backbenchers known as "The Hughlighans," in imitation of Lord Randolph's Famous Fourth Party, all high-spirited young politicians who discussed their burning questions over the best dinner and brandy that could be procured. Churchill laid down the policy: "We shall dine first and consider our position afterwards. It shall be High Imperialism nourished by a deviled sardine." He promptly led his small group into spirited attacks against the Government's proposed army scheme. [4]

St. John Broderick, the Conservative Secretary of War, wanted to reorganize and extend the army on the continental model, three army corps to be kept ready for expeditionary purposes. Churchill was the first to attack the scheme, an act of insubordination that was not pleasing to the Conservative party. It prompted an official motion of opposition by the Liberal leader, Sir Henry Campbell-Bannerman. "One corps," said Churchill, "is quite enough to fight savages and three are not enough to begin to fight Europeans."

Then he warned the House with remarkable prophetic insight: "A European war cannot be anything but a cruel, heartrending struggle, which must demand, perhaps for several years, the whole manhood of the nation, the entire suspension of the peaceful industries, and the concentrating to one end of every vital energy in the community. A European war can only end in the ruin of the vanquished and

35

scarcely less fatal commercial dislocation and exhaustion of the conquerors."

"And," he went on, "without a supreme navy, military arrangements must be utterly vain and futile. With such a navy we may hold any antagonist at arm's length and feed ourselves in the meantime, until, if we find it necessary, we can turn every city in the country into an arsenal, and the whole male population into an army." [1]

The speech displeased the Government benches as much as it delighted the Opposition. Henry William Massingham, distinguished Liberal publicist, called it "uncompromising, most daring," and prophesied in the *Daily Chronicle* that "its author will be Prime Minister—I hope Liberal Prime Minister—of England." [5]

The Broderick plan was abandoned, Mr. Broderick moved to the India Office and a new Secretary for War appointed. This was a great triumph for the young back-bencher. [4]

Churchill was, as his father had been, a believer in free trade. But under the influence of Chamberlain, the Tories were moving steadily in the direction of protection. Angry at this policy, Churchill attacked Chamberlain in his speeches, and Balfour and his supporters walked out. When Churchill rose to speak he was howled down. In 1904 his constituency at Oldham, though they could not turn him out until the next election, disowned him. Churchill refused to be silenced.

In May 1904, amid the deafening howls and catcalls of the Tories and the countercheers of the Liberals, Winston walked across to the other side of the chamber. Lloyd George with alacrity moved across the bench to give Churchill space next to him. Two years after his defection the nation went to the polls. The Liberals won by the smashing majority of four hundred and one to one hundred and fifty-seven, and Henry Campbell-Bannerman, the new Prime Minister, made Churchill Under Secretary for the Colonies. [1]

Not long after his collision with Chamberlain, Churchill,

deep in his biography of his father, wrote Chamberlain asking for copies of letters of Lord Randolph in Chamberlain's possession. "We were at that time in full political battle and I had attacked him face to face in Parliament." Chamberlain sent no letters, but to Churchill's surprise he invited him to come and stay with him at Highbury. They dined alone. With the dessert Chamberlain produced a bottle of '34 port. Only the briefest reference was made to current controversies. "I think you are quite right," Chamberlain said, "feeling as you do, to join the Liberals. You must expect to have the same sort of abuse flung at you as I have endured. But if a man is sure of himself it only sharpens him and makes him more effective." That was all.

They sat up together until two o'clock in the morning, the man of sixty-eight and the man of thirty, Chamberlain producing not only the letters required but diaries and memoranda of the '80's. "I doubt," wrote Churchill later, "whether the English tradition of not bringing politics into private life has often been carried much farther."

The two-volume biography of his father—a good deal of it was written in the House of Commons during uninteresting debates—begun in 1902 and published in 1906—is one of the great masterpieces of English biography. *Lord Randolph Churchill* earned about £8,000, and the time for writing was over, at least for a while. But the time for action in the "supreme affairs of the nation" had begun. [5]

The late Conservative administration had conducted the war in South Africa to a successful conclusion. The new Liberal Government had to provide for South Africa's future. Churchill, as Under Secretary for the Colonies, found himself in charge of the South African Constitution Bill, which carried out the pledge in the peace treaty that "as soon as circumstances permit, representative institutions leading to self-government will be introducd." [2]

The Tories insisted that the right conditions did not yet

prevail. Churchill was not only wholeheartedly in favor of the bill, but his emotions were involved as well. Shortly after the war ended, several Boer generals had visited London to ask assistance for their devastated country, and Winston was introduced at a luncheon to their leader, General Botha. [4]

"We talked of the war," he wrote, "and I briefly told the story of my capture. Botha listened in silence; then he said, 'Don't you recognize me? It was I, myself, who took you prisoner,' and his bright eyes twinkled with pleasure. Botha in white shirt and frock coat looked very different from the wild, wartime figure I had seen that rough day in Natal. An almost unbelievable introduction ripened into a greatly valued friendship. I saw in this grand, rugged figure, the Father of his country, the wise statesman, the farmer-warrior, the deep, sure man of solitude." [3g]

Churchill's friendship with Louis Botha strengthened his already firm faith in the Boers. He answered the Conservatives in uncompromising language: "If our counsels of reconciliation should come to nothing, the resulting evil would be trumpeted forth all over the world wherever despotism wanted a good argument for bayonets, wherever an arbitrary government wished to deny or curtail the liberties of imprisoned nationalities. But if the near future should unfold a tranquil, prosperous Afrikaner nation under the protecting aegis of the British Crown, then the cause of the poor and the weak all over the world will have been sustained and everywhere small peoples will get more room to breathe, and empires will be encouraged to step forward into the sunshine of a more gentle and more generous age."

The experiment was entirely successful. The Constitution Bill transformed the Boer Republic into staunch supporters of the British Commonwealth. [4]

In September 1907, Churchill, accompanied by his secretary, Edward Marsh, set out on a four months' tour of inspection of the African territories. The ship's officers were Tories to a man and they resented having to ship a Liberal. Churchill was much upset. To be met without provocation on his part by unconcealed hostility he found quite unbearable. But he discovered a way to overcome this. "Dining with two of the officers at a time each night," Marsh wrote, "and putting forth his powers of seduction, he had them all at his feet by the time we landed at Mombasa."

At Aden, Churchill found that the army viewed the Radical Minister with an equally jaundiced eye and was as uncooperative as the navy. A noncommissioned officer named Calvert was in charge of the main guard. One morning the telephone rang. Calvert tells the story himself. "A voice said: 'This is Mr. Churchill. I shall be here for a day or two and would be glad if the camel battery could lend me a camel to ride.' I said 'Certainly' and called the B.S.M., who said: 'Tell them to saddle No. 51.' I was surprised because No. 51, as we all knew, was a kicker and very bad-tempered. In the evening when the Somali boy brought back the camel, he arrived grinning and held out his hand showing me five rupees. 'Him very good man, sahib.' I asked about the camel. He replied: 'Sahib camel kick Churchill, Churchill sahib kick camel. Him very good camel now, sahib.'" [5]

Members of Churchill's African safaris said afterward that he was the most undisciplined man on a hunt it had ever been their misfortune to attend. He often refused to obey even the ordinary rules of safety. Once, advised to give a movement of army ants a wide berth, he investigated, was surrounded, fell down, and, in escaping in the nick of time, abandoned a prized walking stick, which was devoured. Behaving with caution, Churchill shot a white rhino, and he was with difficulty disuaded from trying to photograph crocodiles while floating down the Nile on a log. [8]

Contemplating the issue of the Nile at Jinja, in Uganda, Churchill stood for three hours thinking all the time of a way to make the river drive a turbine. "Nowhere in the world could so little masonry hold such vast masses of water," he wrote in *My African Journey* on his return to England. "Jinja is destined to become a very important place in the economy of Central Africa." The scientific age took nearly half a century to catch up with him. The "little masonry" which Churchill visualized for three hours in 1907 became a reality in 1954 when Queen Elizabeth II pressed the button which started the first two of the ten giant turbines of Owen Falls Dam, 2,725 feet long and 85 feet high. On that day the Queen telegraphed from Jinja to Sir Winston Churchill: "Your vision has become reality."

Churchill's reference in his speech on the Boer Bill to "the cause of the poor and the weak" had not been made by accident. With the European situation "bright and tranquil," the time had come to concentrate attention on affairs "within our own island" because "the gravest problems lie at home."

"I look forward," declared Churchill in a revolutionary speech at St. Andrew's Hall, Glasgow, "to the universal establishment of minimum standards of life and labor. I do not want to see impaired the vigor of competition, but we want to draw a line below which we will not allow persons to live and labor, yet above which they may compete with all the strength of their manhood."

Said fifty years ago, this was a bold conception. "More than any man of his time," wrote A. G. Gardiner in his 1908 "profile" of Churchill, "he approaches an issue without mental reserves. He is not paralyzed by the fear of consequences, nor afraid to contemplate great changes. He is out for adventure. He follows politics as he would follow the hounds. With the facility of the Churchill mind he feels the pulse of Liberalism with astonishing sureness and interprets it with extraordinary ability." His contemporaries in the Liberal party recognized with admiration and not a little envy that this novice argued their case more effectively than they had been able to do themselves.

Churchill charged enthusiastically into this fresh field, not so much because "these ideas born of our age," as Massingham put it, were in tune with his own or his father's but because they offered material with which to build, shape, create. [5]

Churchill was always reminding the House of his father. When he was speaking he could be observed fingering the plain gold signet ring which Lord Randolph had worn. Those who had known the father were startled by the reincarnation of his mannerisms and attitudes in the son: the same stoop, the same gait, the same lurching movement in his walk. When he spoke he grasped the lapels of his coat as his father had done. [2]

Both had the same habit of throwing back their heads and laughing loudly at anything that amused them—even their voices, resonant with a touch of asperity, were similar. [30]

During a visit to Manchester, Churchill had seen the slums. He was fascinated and horrified. "Fancy living in one of those streets," he said, "never seeing anything beautiful—never eating anything savory—*never saying anything clever!*" [7]

Once the idea of social reform caught Churchill's imagination, it dominated his thoughts. He could talk of nothing else. Wrote Charles Masterman to his wife in February 1908: "Winston swept me off to his cousin's house and I lay on the bed while he dressed and marched about the room, gesticulating and impetuous, pouring out all his hopes and plans and ambitions. He is full of the poor whom he has just discovered. He thinks he is called by providence to do something for them. 'Why have I always been kept safe within a hairsbreadth of death,' he asked, 'except to do something like this? Sometimes I feel as though I could lift the whole world on my shoulders.' He is getting impatient." [4]

Others too were aware of this impatience. Lloyd George wrote to his brother: "Dined with Churchill last night alone.

Very ambitious. The applause of the House is the very breath of his nostrils. He is like an actor. He likes the limelight and the approbation of the pit."

Now with a change in the premiership approaching, Churchill began to strain after a bigger part. Campbell-Bannerman was nearing his end. On March 27, 1908, he sent for Asquith and told him without fuss that he was dying. His letter of resignation went to the King. Nine days later Asquith became Prime Minister and Lloyd George, now forty-five, succeeded him as Chancellor of the Exchequer. Asquith suggested the Admiralty for Churchill, but Churchill pooh-poohed it. The Board of Trade, though its president did not rank high in the scale of Ministers, was precisely what he required: closely linked to Lloyd George's office, it placed him in the center of things and gave him Cabinet rank. This was what really mattered. Asquith agreed.

At thirty-three Churchill had achieved everything that could be achieved—for the time being: he possessed, after an exhausting and hard-fought campaign, a safe parliamentary seat as representative from Dundee; he was a Cabinet Minister, able to exert his influence. The fight to reach the battlefield, normally long and tedious, had been short and sharp.

The moment had come to consider personal matters. [5]

4

The Young Reformer

IN a world of men where women played little part, mothers of eligible young ladies had begun casting their nets at the rising young Minister. At one time matchmakers linked his name to that of Ethel Barrymore (whom Churchill greatly admired), but on August 14, 1908, Wilfrid Blunt noted in his diary: "Blanche Hozier writes from Blenheim that her daughter Clementine is to marry Winston Churchill. 'Yesterday,' she writes, 'he came to London to ask my consent and we all three came on here. He is so like Lord Randolph; he has some of his faults and all his qualities. He is gentle and tender and affectionate to those he loves, much hated by those who have not come under his personal charm.' " [5]

Of their courtship Clementine wrote, in answer to her aunt's letter of congratulations: "I cannot describe my happiness to you. I cared very much for him when he asked me to marry him, but every day since it has been more heavenly." [25]

She spoke fluent French and adequate German and at the time of her engagement lived with her mother in a small rented house in Kensington, where she gave French lessons to augment the modest family income. There was in her a great zest for life and its adventures. She possessed a swift-moving mind, a ready wit and keen sense of humor, was a radical, passionately interested in politics, openly sympa-

43

thetic to the suffragettes. And she was decidedly beautiful. "A queen she should have been. Her superbly sculptured features would have looked splendidly on a coin. 'There's a face that will last,' said everyone." [5]

Just twenty-three, Clementine Hozier indeed had a charming oval face, finely cut classic features and large, wide-set eyes. For Winston it was love at first sight. [4]

They were married a month after he proposed. It was like a royal wedding. Crowds of thousands spread from St. Margaret's to Whitehall and Parliament Square. When Winston, with his best man, Lord Hugh Cecil, arrived at St. Margaret's, the crowd gave them a welcoming roar.

The church was decorated with palms and chrysanthemums and arum lilies. The bride, in white satin and veil of Brussels net, carried a white bouquet of lilies and myrtle; on her head was a coronet of orange blossoms. Her only jewelry was a pair of diamond earrings—a gift from the groom. As she approached the chancel, Winston put out his hand and shook hers warmly.

In his address, Bishop Weldon, headmaster of Harrow in the days when young Churchill was one of the school's worst scholars, uttered prophetic words: "The sun shines on your union today. Allow me to remind you how much you may be to each other in the coming days, in the sunny hours and in the somber hours. May your lives prove a blessing, each to the other, and both to the world."

When the bride and groom left the church, the police were unable to hold back the crowd; hundreds broke through, surrounding the car to get a clearer view. As the wedding party drove past, the crowd shouted "Good old Winnie!" "God bless Winnie!"

At the wedding reception champagne flowed, presents lined the tables; the wedding cake stood nearly five feet high and weighed over two hundred pounds. Dukes and duchesses, counts and countesses, lords and ladies in the dozens were there and the even more famous plain "Misters": Austen Chamberlain, Balfour, Lloyd George.

Wedding gifts included twenty-five pairs of silver candlesticks, twenty-one ink stands, eight sets of salt cellars. A silver fruit basket came from Lloyd George. Edward Grey sent a bound set of Marlborough's dispatches, Mr. Asquith ten volumes of Jane Austen, and Sir Joseph Chamberlain two silver decanter stands. King Edward's gift of a malacca cane had a massive gold knob, richly chased and engraved "W.S.C., Turf Club."

The Churchills' wedding bells did not ring in an era of unalloyed joy, however. Winston, who had launched attacks on the House of Lords, was called a traitor to his class, and he and Clemmie were ostracized by many acquaintances. There were hostilities, too, on another flank. Churchill opposed giving the vote to women, and the suffragettes had sworn a vendetta against him. They continually harassed and attacked him at public meetings, bombarding him with rotten fruit and eggs.

It was no secret that Clementine believed in votes for women. She was with Winston when three women climbed onto the roof of a hall and throughout his address shouted demands for votes through a window ventilator. Clementine, seated on the platform, waved gaily at the demonstrators. [25]

At Cabinet councils, meanwhile, Churchill and Lloyd George sat together and acted in concert. The cause of destitute humanity fired Lloyd George with the enduring purpose of his political career: to bring relief to lowly lives and give them freedom from hunger. Under his inspiration Churchill had turned social reformer, not a role that would have been foreseen for a man who had first looked out on the spacious vistas of Blenheim Park.

The country was ripe for a step forward. After twenty years out of office, the Liberals were eager to carry through

measures of reform. But the reformers were met by unyield-
ing opposition. Through the House of Lords the Tories had
the controlling power over legislation. The Liberals could
pass their measures through the House of Commons, and the
Tories in the House of Lords, which had the controlling
power over legislation, would throw them out.

Only over money bills was the power of the peers limited:
for half a century it had been accepted that the Lords could
neither amend nor repeal the budget. As Chancellor of the
Exchequer, Lloyd George saw the budget as the instrument of
his opponents' discomfort. They must be maneuvered into a
position which would place them before the country as will-
ful obstructionists of the people's rights. With Churchill as
his coadjutor, he deliberately baited the budget with an advance in income tax to finance old-age pensions.

The Tory peers, calling it "pillage" and "brigandage," oblig-
ingly threw out the budget. Immediately there was a political
uproar against the "breakers of the constitution." [2]

In vitriolic speeches, Churchill slashed at their lordships.
"The House of Lords is a lingering relic of a feudal order. It
has invaded the prerogatives of the Crown and the rights of
the Commons. The rejection of this measure is a constitutional outrage." [34]

"The issue will be," he thundered, "whether the British
people are going to be ruled through a representative assembly, elected by six or seven millions of voters, or whether
they are going to allow themselves to be dictated to by a
minute minority of titled persons, who represent nobody, and
who only scurry up to London to vote in their own interests.
We will smash to pieces the veto of the House of Lords." [32]

Winston was immediately subjected to a steady stream of
personal abuse. Tories described him as "utterly contempt-
ible," betraying his class and belittling the institutions that
had made the country great merely to gain a sordid political
advantage. "Whenever the Churchills 'ratted,'" said A. B.

Markham, "they thought it was going to be of benefit to themselves."

One by one the doors of society closed against him, and when he attended public functions many old family friends were careful to look the other way. [4]

His face began to show the first wrinkles of responsibility rising steeply between nose and corner of the mouth. He sat in his office from daybreak until late at night. On one occasion he was so tired that he fell asleep in a corner of the House. That day he wore a pink silk shirt with his flannel suit. The following morning the papers reported he had entered the House in pink pajamas. England believed it. [34]

A general election was ordered. The Liberals promptly went to the country. Their slogan, "The People versus the Peers," returned them to power but with a reduced majority dependent on the Irish nationalists. Months dragged on. [4]

The following year a bill to limit the powers of the House of Lords was sent up to the Lords. Asquith let it be known that if the Tories persisted in rejecting it, the King would create a sufficient number of new peerages for Liberal supporters to outvote the Tories and carry the bill. The bill was passed and the Lords were forever deprived of their absolute veto. [2]

Clementine Churchill, a Liberal by instinct, regarded Conservative ostracism as something of a compliment and created an agreeable existence for herself and her husband among the small circle of intimate friends. [4]

Their house in Eccleston Square, within walking distance from Whitehall, was Churchill's headquarters, the framework which held all his activities together. Here his children were born. Here in his study he wrote his books and drafted his speeches, carefully trying them out on his wife or his friends before delivery. Here he received his friends and assembled his political associates, holding counsel with them around the open fire and arguing late into the night. If there were no guests to talk to, his wife would stay up with him playing cards.

A few months after their first child, Diana, was born, Lord Esher reported: "Yesterday I dined with Winston at his home. It was a birthday dinner. Only six people. But he had a birthday cake with thirty-five candles. And *crackers*. He sat all evening with a paper cap from a cracker on his head. He and she sit on the same sofa and he holds her hand. I never saw two people more in love. If he goes out of office, he has not a penny, but he says it is well worth it if you live with someone you love. He is ready to live in just two rooms—with her and the baby!" [5]

As they sat on the Treasury Bench together, Lloyd George offered his congratulations to Churchill on the birth of his daughter. "Is she a pretty child?" asked the Chancellor of the Exchequer.

"The prettiest child ever seen," said the president of the Board of Trade.

"Like her mother, I suppose?" said L.G.

"Not at all," said Winston gravely, "she's the very image of me." [7]

Churchill, still the most hated politician in the country, kept alive the hostility of his former associates by the pungency of his repartees. [2]

Sir William Joynson-Hicks, once defeated by Churchill, was making a speech before Commons and noticed him on the front bench shaking his head so vigorously he distracted everyone's attention. "I see my Right Honorable friend shaking his head," cried Joynson-Hicks in exasperation. "I wish to remind him that I am only expressing my own opinion."

"And I wish to remind the speaker that I am only shaking my own head," replied Churchill. [8]

His unpopularity did not prevent his advancement, however. Asquith offered him the Irish Secretaryship. Churchill declined it and took instead the Home Office.

As Churchill sat down behind his new desk he found himself responsible at one stroke for the administration of all prisons, the London police, roads, bridges, mines, agriculture and fisheries, the prevention of traffic in women and children, intoxicating liquor, dangerous drugs, explosives and firearms. Furthermore, the Home Secretary was required to be in attendance at the birth of Royal Princes and Princesses and, upon the demise of the Crown, announce the successor to the Throne. [5]

A new duty, recently transferred from the Prime Minister to the Home Office, was a daily letter to the King, reporting the proceedings of the House of Commons. The Sovereign greatly enjoyed these spirited effusions. Soon, however, they were addressed to a new monarch. [26]

On Friday, May 6, 1910, shortly before midnight, as Halley's Comet blazed in the night sky, a newspaper reporter named Hugh Martin was making a call from a public telephone box near Buckingham Palace. Suddenly, owing to a crossing of wires, he found himself listening to a conversation between a palace official and a Minister of the Crown whose voice he immediately recognized. There was only one who "talked through his nose and could not pronounce the letter s properly." The Home Secretary was at this moment being officially informed that His Majesty King Edward VII had died at a quarter to midnight. "It gave me the news fully ten minutes before any other journalist," commented Martin, a professional advantage the Home Secretary would have appreciated.

On the following Monday, the new sovereign was solemnly proclaimed. "The Great Council," Churchill wrote, "acclaimed George V as King, a man humble in the presence of the responsibilities which the hereditary lawful succession of a thousand years had cast upon him." Silver trumpets sounded and the batteries in St. James's Park thundered their salute. [5]

Churchill, throwing himself into his new job with characteristic zest, embarked at once on prison reform and made a tour of the prisons. He was moved by the number of boys in prison with nothing of the criminal type about them and scandalized that so many of them should be there, often for merely sleeping out. Where previous Home Secretaries had been content to administer the system as it was, Churchill, with his instinct for action, got powers to reform it.

That autumn he went to stay with the poet Wilfrid Blunt, who had called for a program for prison reform. "He was dressed in a little close-fitting, fur-collared jacket, tight leggings and gaiters, and a little round hat, which, with his half-mischievous face, made him look the exact figure of Puck. But," Blunt went on, "he means to arrange matters so that next year there will be fifty thousand fewer people sent to prison than this year." [7]

Nothing in the sphere of justice weighed more heavily on Churchill's mind than the death penalty and his personal responsibility for recommending or refusing a reprieve. He confessed that he "often lay awake all night before an execution, only finding sleep when the clock struck eight." He several times exercised his authority as Home Secretary to order a remission of sentences, notwithstanding the protests of the judges in the cases. [5]

In 1911 Churchill again found himself under criticism, this time over the notorious Sidney Street Affair. Some foreign anarchists murdered policemen in the course of a burglary and then barricaded themselves in a house in Sidney Street, in London's East End. Shots had been exchanged between them and the police. Winston was in his bath when he was asked by the chiefs of the police to sanction the use of soldiers. With only a moist towel around him, Winston heard the case and gave assent. [21]

Then, in fur-lined coat and top hat, the Home Secretary, unable to keep out of trouble, went down to the East End to have a look and could not resist conducting siege operations. Unfortunately he was widely photographed and even appeared on cinema reels. This was more than the conventional and respectable could stand. What, King George demanded, was a Cabinet Minister doing down there in such a position, peeping round corners among the bullets? Mr. Balfour asked sarcastically in the Commons: "We are concerned to observe photographs in the illustrated newspapers of the Home Secretary in the danger zone. I understand what the photographer was doing, but why the Home Secretary?" When he got back from the scene of action an irate civil servant chided him. "What in hell have you been doing now, Winston?" said Masterman, bursting into the room. "*Now*, Charlie," said the Minister with his inimitable lisp. "Don't be croth. It was such fun." [7]

When, later, the railway unions threatened a national strike, Churchill sent troops to many rail centers without requests from the local authorities, an action severely criticized by trade union and labor leaders. Churchill justified the show of force, claiming that it was imperative that steps be taken to maintain the movement of food and other essentials. [21]

There was a growing feeling in Parliament, however, that Churchill reveled in strong measures. He was furiously attacked by Labor Members in the House. Ramsay MacDonald reminded him in biting tones that these were not the sort of methods that the average Englishman liked, whether his party was Liberal, Tory or Socialist. "This is not a medieval state and it is not Russia. It is not even Germany. The way to maintain law and order in this nation is to trust the ordinary operations of a law-abiding people. If the Home Secretary had more knowledge of how to handle masses of men and a better instinct of what civil liberty means, we should have less difficulty in settling the difficult problem before us."

The sending of troops was so deeply resented by labor it nearly resulted in a general strike. At this point Lloyd George stepped in as negotiator and successfully brought the railway strike to an end. But the deep antagonism between Winston and the working classes was now firmly established. [4]

5

War Clouds

"BACK in the spring of 1909," wrote Churchill, "the First Lord of the Admiralty, Mr. McKenna, had suddenly demanded the construction of no less than six Dreadnought battleships. He had based this claim on the rapid growth of the German Fleet, which was causing the Admiralty the greatest anxiety. I was still a skeptic about the danger of the European situation and not convinced by the Admiralty case. I held that our margin in pre-Dreadnought ships would assure us an adequate superiority in 1912, 'the danger year' as it was then called.

"Suddenly and unexpectedly, on the morning of July 1, 1911, His Imperial Majesty the German Emperor sent his gunboat the *Panther* to Agadir in French Morocco to maintain German interests there. All the alarm bells throughout Europe began immediately to quiver. Was Germany looking for a pretext of war with France or was she merely trying by pressure to improve her colonial position? If Germany's intentions were malignant a decided word would have to be spoken before it was too late.

"For some weeks the Chancellor of the Exchequer offered no indication of what his line would be. But on the morning of July 21, when I visited him before the Cabinet, I found his mind was made up. We were drifting into war and he intended to make it clear that if Germany meant war, she would find Britain against her." [3h]

53

Winston Churchill was no longer to be found among those hampering the efforts of McKenna at the Admiralty. Hitherto Lloyd George's closest associate in social reform and economy on the services, he had not been concerned with foreign affairs or defense. Henceforth he saw the overriding necessity to prepare his country against the growing danger constituted by Germany. [7]

Through a chance conversation at a garden party for members of Parliament, Churchill learned that the magazines where the naval supplies of cordite were stored were under his, the Home Secretary's, jurisdiction. They were guarded only by a small force of unarmed policemen. He requested an admiral in charge to dispatch sailors to the magazine. The request was refused. Churchill went to the Secretary for War and demanded soldiers. Haldane gave him what he wanted.

Next Churchill signed a warrant permitting the opening of spy correspondence, a thing unheard of in peacetime, but the measure allowed the British Intelligence Service to make such complete acquaintance with the German spy ring that the latter could be rounded up down to the last man at the outbreak of war. [34]

With the gathering storm "fiercely illuminated" in his mind, he set out to learn all he could of military and foreign affairs. Throughout the hot weeks of August he remained in London, devouring documents and picking the brains of General Sir Henry Wilson, Director of Military Operations, and Sir Edward Grey, the Foreign Secretary. They often met in the late afternoon and strolled across the park to the Automobile Club for a swim.

Soon Churchill began bombarding the Cabinet with suggestions and directives signed "W.S.C." The first of these, *Military Aspects of the Continental Problem*, suggested that the War Office took too sanguine a view of the potential resistance of the French army. Winston prophesied that by the twentieth day the French would be "driven from the line of the Meuse and will be falling back on Paris and the South." He went on to say that by the fortieth day the Germans would be extended at full strength both internally and on their war fronts, and that if the French army had not been squandered the Allies should be able to execute their main counterstroke. The generals referred to the document as "ridiculous and fantastic—a silly memorandum," but events proved Churchill right; the Battle of the Marne was lost by Germany on the forty-second day. [4]

This memorandum has rightly won fame as a classical military document that ranks among the most illuminating state papers of the immediate prewar period. No other state archive possesses anything of similar vision and penetration. [5]

"In October 1911," wrote Churchill, "Prime Minister Asquith invited me to stay with him in Scotland. The day after I had arrived there, on our way home from the links he asked me quite abruptly whether I would like to go to the Admiralty. I said, 'Indeed I would.' The fading light of evening disclosed in the distance the silhouettes of two battleships steaming slowly out of the Firth of Forth. They seemed invested with a new significance to me.

"That night when I went to bed, I saw a Bible lying on a table in my bedroom. My mind was dominated by the task entrusted to me. I thought of the peril of Britain, peace-loving, unthinking, little prepared, of her power and virtue, and of her mission of good sense and fair play. I thought of mighty Germany, towering up in the splendor of her imperial state and delving down in her profound, cold, patient, ruthless calculations. I thought of the army corps I had watched tramp past, wave after wave, at the Breslau maneuvres in 1907, of the thousands of strong horses dragging cannon and great howitzers up the ridges and along the roads around Wurzburg in 1910. I thought of the sudden and successful wars by which her power had been set up. I opened the book at random and in the 9th chapter of Deuteronomy I read:

"Hear, O Israel: Thou art to pass over Jordan this day, to go in to possess nations greater and mightier than thyself, cities great and fenced up to heaven, a people great and tall, the children of the Anakims, whom thou knowest, and of whom thou hast heard say, Who can stand before the children of Anak! Understand therefore this day, that the Lord thy God is he which goeth over before thee; as a consuming fire he shall destroy them, and he shall bring them down before thy face: so shalt thou drive them out, and destroy them quickly . . . Not for thy righteousness, or for the uprightness of thine heart, dost thou go to possess their land: but for the wickedness of these nations the Lord thy God doth drive them out from before thee.

"It seemed a message full of reassurance." [3h]

The Admiralty at once felt the impact of his powerful personality. He ordered that naval officers must remain on duty all night at the Admiralty so that if a surprise attack came not a moment would be lost in giving the alarm. Secondly, he gave instructions for a huge chart of the North Sea to be hung on the wall of his room. Every day a staff officer marked the positions of the German fleet with flags. "I made a rule to look at this chart once every day when I first entered my room. I did this less to keep myself informed, for there were many other channels of information, than to inoculate in myself and those working with me a sense of ever present danger."

Churchill immediately got in touch with Lord Fisher, that explosive, astonishing old man of seventy-one with burning black eyes, rugged face and fiery temperament. Recently retired as First Sea Lord, he was regarded as "the greatest sailor since Nelson." The passion of his life was the navy, and in this field he was a genius. As First Sea Lord he had put the British fleet far ahead of all others in modern and efficient design, reorganized the navy's educational system, introduced the submarine and replaced the battle fleet's twelve-inch guns with thirteen-point-fives.

With Lord Fisher's unofficial aid and backing, Winston set about to learn his business and do his job. Eight months of every year were spent afloat on the Admiralty yacht *Enchantress*. He visited naval installations, dockyards and every important ship. At the end he knew "what everything looked like and where everything was and how one thing fitted into another. I could put my hand on anything that was wanted and knew the current state of our naval affairs." He not only worked for the navy, he lived for it.

David Beatty, Churchill's Naval Secretary, could not bear these trips aboard the *Enchantress*. He found it hard to support the unceasing battery of "Winston's 100 horse-power mind"; for he now talked nothing but the navy, forcing Beatty to think out every aspect of a naval war with Germany. Those cruises inspected Gibraltar, Malta and anything else worth inspecting—Paestrum, Spalato, Ragusa, Corfu. [7]

For there were not always important discussions on the Admiralty yacht. "Often," wrote Edward Marsh in his letters, "we were all 'a happy family.'" Asquith invented quiz games, polished Greek hexameters, discoursed brilliantly on the Peloponnesian wars. Asquith's wife, the volatile Margot, was a tremendous and fearless talker, a match for Churchill, which was not too much to his taste. Clementine Churchill remained, as always, the delightful and impeccable hostess, the soul of discretion. They all played execrable bridge, went ashore incognito like tourists when the fancy took them. While Edward Marsh declaimed amidst the ruin of Parthenon, Churchill was restrained from having the place tidied up by a party of bluejackets. [54]

The two most formidable decisions taken by the Churchill-Fisher combination were to advance from the thirteen-point-five-inch gun to the fifteen-inch and to change the entire navy over from coal to oil. The new guns led to the changeover from coal to oil. Ships run by oil gave a large excess of speed over coal, and could be refueled at sea. There was one drawback: Britain produced coal and not oil. Churchill promptly set up a Royal Commission on Oil Supply and appointed Fisher as chairman. The outcome was a long-term contract with the Anglo-Persian Oil Company which secured the necessary oil and gave the Government a controlling share in oil properties which increased their value many hundred per cent. [4]

While the British Tommies trained with bayonets, the boys at Eton practiced with their rifles. And then one day in 1914, in Sarajevo, a young Austrian prince was murdered. The game of army maneuvers became the grimness of war. It was Lord Kitchener, onetime caustic critic of a young subaltern, who came to Churchill during the difficult days of the war and said to the First Lord of the Admiralty, "Well, there is one thing at any rate they cannot take from you—the fleet was ready." [30]

Churchill's immediate action on the eve of war had been a stroke of genius: instead of the usual maneuvres in mid-July he ordered a review of the Grand Fleet, when the entire naval power of Britain was displayed in the Solent in brilliant sunshine. [54]

The King himself was present and inspected ships of every class. It took more than six hours for this armada, every ship decked with flags and crowded with bluejackets and marines, to pass, with bands playing and at fifteen knots, before the Royal Yacht, while overhead the naval seaplanes and airplanes circled continuously.

"The following Sunday," wrote Churchill, "I had planned to spend with my family at Cromer and I decided not to alter my plans. A special operator placed in the telegraph office ensured continuous night and day service. On Saturday afternoon the news came in that Serbia had accepted the Austrian

58

ultimatum. I went to bed with a feeling things might blow over. At nine o'clock the next morning I called up the First Sea Lord (Prince of Battenberg): Austria, he told me, was not satisfied with the Serbian acceptance of the ultimatum. I asked him to call me at twelve and went down to the beach to play with the children. It was a beautiful day. The North Sea shone and sparkled to a far horizon. Whatever lay beyond that line, I thought, the British navy had never been in better condition or in better strength." [3h]

In the end Serbia refused to accept the harsh ultimatum flung at her. The day after Austria declared war, the Russians began to mobilize on the Austrian frontier; three days later Germany sent an ultimatum to Russia to disperse her troops, then declared war. On the night when Churchill heard the news of the fateful act, Lord Beaverbrook had been invited to Admiralty House, to which Churchill had moved when he became First Lord of the Admiralty, for dinner and bridge.

"Suddenly," reported Lord Beaverbrook, "an immense dispatch box was brought into the room. Churchill produced his skeleton key from his pocket, opened the box and took out a single sheet of paper on which was written: 'Germany has declared war against Russia.' He rang for a servant and, asking for a lounge coat, stripped his dress coat from his back and left the room quickly with no further word. He was not elated or surprised, he exhibited no fear or uneasiness. He went straight out like a man going to a well-accustomed job. We have suffered at times from Mr. Churchill's bellicosity. But what profit the nation derived at that crucial moment from the capacity of the First Lord of the Admiralty for grasping and dealing with the war situation." [4]

"Each day," Churchill later recorded, "as the telegrams showed the darkening scene of Europe, I pulled over the various levers which successively brought our naval organization into full preparedness. On July 28, I felt that the fleet should go to its war station, at once and secretly, steaming through the North Sea to Scapa Flow. I feared to bring this matter before the Cabinet, lest it should be considered a provocative action likely to damage the chances of peace. I only therefore informed the Prime Minister, who said not a word, but it was clear from his look that he was quite content.

"We may now picture this great fleet, with its flotillas and cruisers, steaming slowly out of Portland Harbor, scores of gigantic castles of steel wending their way across the misty, shining sea, like giants bowed in anxious thought, eighteen miles of warships running at high speed and absolute blackness through the Narrow Straits.

"*August 4, 1914.* At the Admiralty a small group gathered, pencils in hand, waiting. It was eleven o'clock at night—twelve by German time—when our ultimatum to Germany expired. All over the world, every British captain and admiral was on guard. It only remained to give the signal. Along the Mall from the direction of the Palace the sound of an immense concourse singing 'God save the King' floated in. On this deep wave there broke the chimes of Big Ben; as the first stroke of the hour boomed out, a rustle of movement swept across the room. The war telegram, 'Commence hostilities against Germany,' was flashed to our ships and establishments everywhere." [3h]

Such was the pinnacle of preparation to which the navy had been brought under Churchill's care that England had command of the seas from the onset; she chased the enemy raiders off the oceans of the world in a comparatively short space, and the German fleet dared not put out from its harbors of refuge. With the war at sea so auspiciously begun, the First Lord could allow his mental vision to range over other fields: one of these was the development of the Air Force. [2]

Churchill flung himself upon what Asquith called his new "hobby"—the air army—which from the very beginning he saw as the weapon of the future. In 1911 when he took over the Admiralty, the Royal Navy had about half a dozen airplanes and the same number of pilots. [34]

The aircraft were frail, the engines unreliable, and each maneuver had to be worked out by trial and error. There had already been several accidents among the pioneer airmen of the Royal Navy, and Churchill felt a deep sympathy with the young officers who were risking their lives.

Though he had a dread of going into the air for the first time, Churchill realized that it would stimulate progress generally if he, as First Lord, learned to fly. So he commenced instruction and, fascinated, flew on every possible occasion thereafter. A very fair pilot once he was in the air, he became more than uncertain in his takeoff and landing, and his instructors usually took over the controls to make the final approach and touchdown.

Churchill's hungry bites at the air potential became so voracious that Lord Kitchener, lately made a field marshal and called to the War Office, reluctantly asked him to undertake the Aerial Home Defense. On the theory that the best defense is a good offense, Churchill directed his aircraft to proceed to Europe and win the war. The planes flew first to Cologne and Friedrichshafen, where, to the stunned astonishment of the Kaiser and his generals, they beat to a pulp the German airship sheds. Then the pilots turned their attention to Zeebrugge and the submarine bases.

When naval experts believed that aircraft were no business of the navy and not likely to be of much use to anyone, Churchill saw the possibilities of launching aircraft from the decks of battleships. Because of his encouragement, Britain became the first country to have an airplane carrying a machine gun and the first to launch a torpedo from the air. [21]

From his fertile pen there sprang such staples of our present vocabulary as "seaplane" and "flight" (of airplanes). His directives to his associates were models of painstaking composition, but he would tolerate nothing but brevity from them. "Winston made us all write what we had to say on one side only of one piece of paper," said one of them. "He wanted just the skeleton facts. He filled out the rest from his extraordinary understanding." [8]

The Naval Air Service did not exhaust Churchill's capacity for spare-time occupation. He found time to give direction to the construction of an armored car, which showed a mind groping toward the invention of the tank. He called for the construction of armored motor cars that would be provided with the means of crossing trenches. "An arrangement of planks capable of bridging a ten- or twelve-foot span quickly and easily," the instructions ran. [2]

The ordnance works produced the design, but a month later they showed Churchill a Caterpillar tractor which he decided was more suitable, the modern tank in embryo. [4]

Meanwhile, the course of the war did not go well for the Allies. Churchill has described the situation in *World Crisis:* "In their vast turning movement through Belgium in August 1914, the Germans outnumbered the French by three to two along the whole line of battle. From the ninth to the twenty-second of August the British army was crossing the Channel; they hoped, by a series of forced marches, to come to the aid of the French at Mons. With such secrecy was the whole vast operation enshrouded that on the evening of August 21, only a few hours before the British cavalry patrols were in contact with the Germans, General von Kluck, commanding the First German Army in Belgium, received from the German Supreme Command no better information than the following: 'A landing of British troops at Boulogne and their advance from about Lille must be reckoned with. It is believed that no landing of British troops on a big scale has yet taken place.' Three days later the whole British army was fighting the Battle of Mons.

"Late on the evening of the twenty-third I had a talk with Lord Kitchener. Our men had been fighting all day, but he had received no news. The map was produced. The whole movement seemed to be hinged in front of Namur.

"At seven o'clock the next morning I was sitting up in bed in Admiralty House working on my boxes, when the door of my bedroom opened and Lord Kitchener appeared, a slip of paper in his hand. He paused in the doorway. His face was distorted and discolored as if it had been punched with a fist. He looked gigantic. 'Bad news,' he said heavily and laid the slip of paper on my bed. It was a telegram from Sir John French in charge of the British troops: 'Namur has fallen. Immediate attention should be directed to the defense of Havre.'

"Namur fallen in a single day! The foundations of thought were quaking. What of the naked Channel ports? Dunkirk, Calais, Boulogne! I forget much of what passed between us. But the apparition of Kitchener *Agonistes* in my doorway will dwell with me as long as I live. It was like seeing old John Bull on the rack!" [3h]

Within a few days the fertile mind of the First Lord was engaged in the organization of the Dunkirk Circus. The vital Channel port of Dunkirk, to become the scene in World War II of the British armies, lay back from the route along which the German hordes were now pouring into France. Joffre, then French Commander in Chief, suggested that a fresh British force make a landing to create a diversion for the German troops. Kitchener appealed to Churchill to carry the thing through with marines. [2]

Immediately Churchill was in full stride. Marines and yeomen landed in France with several London double-decker buses that Churchill had ordered covered with iron plating and a few of the growing squadron of airplanes. This joyous band traveled so fast the Germans could never get anywhere near them; they were "here, there and everywhere, terroriz-

ing marauding Uhlans and inspiring French Territorials."
Like a group of wildly celebrating fans returning from a
successful football match, Winston's units rode while singing, shouting at the top of their lungs, and heaving beer
bottles into the streets. Once they impudently dispatched a
telegram to one of the Allied armies in the neighborhood,
asking details of its movements, as they wished to "cooperate." One British army officer wistfully commented in a meeting that the navy, heretofore, had always been known as "the
Silent Service." [8]

Churchill was highly delighted with the activities of his
force and made frequent visits of inspection to see how the
fun was going. The Prime Minister had been as amused as
Winston himself when the Circus opened, but while the First
Lord's relish increased, Asquith's waned. His irritation grew
when he had to take charge of the Admiralty in the First
Lord's absence. In the end he ordered the Circus wound up.
Yet, these promenaders had caused a serious disturbance of
the German plans, because German imagination saw their
flank as threatened by at least forty thousand men, and a
German retreat contributed to the salvation of the Allied
armies. [7]

Churchill was on his way to Dunkirk when desperate news
about the Belgian army was received. As he had foretold, the
Battle of the Marne had flung the Germans back from the
Marne to the Aisne and severely damaged their hope of a
speedy victory. But the immediate capture of Antwerp would
enable them to sweep to the Channel ports. The Kaiser gave
an imperative order for its capture regardless of cost. German seventeen-inch howitzers destroyed the heavy fortifications with ease, and the King of the Belgians sent out an
urgent call for aid. Unless reinforcements arrived at once,
the Belgian army might be captured intact. Churchill raced
back to London to a conference at Kitchener's house. Reinforcements, Kitchener explained, would not be ready for

three or four days; could Churchill hurry to Antwerp, and urge the King and Prime Minister to hold on with the help of a brigade of marines until further aid arrived? Churchill said yes. [4]

"I was away," wrote Asquith in his memoirs, "when Grey, Kitchener and Winston held a late meeting, and the intrepid Winston set off at midnight and ought to have reached Antwerp at about nine this morning. I do not know how fluent he is in French, but, if he was able to do himself justice in a foreign tongue, the Belges will have listened to a discourse the like of which they have never heard before. I cannot but think he will stiffen them up." [11]

At one o'clock that afternoon a big, drab-colored touring car filled with British naval officers drove down the Place de Mer in Antwerp, took the turn into the Marché-aux-Souliers on two wheels, and drew up in front of the hotel. Before the car had fairly come to a stop the door was thrown open and out jumped a smooth-faced, sandy-haired, stoop-shouldered, youthful-looking man in undress uniform. As he charged into the jammed lobby he flung his arms out in a nervous characteristic gesture, as though pushing his way through a crowd. "A most spectacular entrance," recalls E. Alexander Powell in *Fighting in Flanders*. "It reminded me for all the world of a scene in a melodrama where the hero dashes up bareheaded on a foam-flecked horse and saves the heroine.

"The burgomaster stopped him, introduced himself, and expressed his anxiety regarding the fate of the city. Before he had finished, Churchill was part way up the stairs. 'I think everything will be all right now, Mr. Burgomaster,' he called in a voice distinctly heard throughout the lobby, 'You needn't worry. We're going to save the city.' " [34, 4]

"Winston dominated the whole place," reported Lord Mottisan to Sir John French, commander on the Eastern Front, "the King, Ministers, soldiers, sailors. So great was his influence that I am convinced that with twenty thousand British troops he could have held Antwerp against almost any on-slaught."

Winston had the same belief. If only he were in command the city could be saved. He sent a message to Asquith, asking him to relieve him of his post at the Admiralty and give him the proper rank so he could take over the military command himself. Asquith gasped: an ex-subaltern of cavalry asking to command major generals. Kitchener had a more open mind. "I will make him a major general if you will give him the command," he told Asquith. The Prime Minister was ob-durate. [4]

"In the evening on October 5," wrote Churchill, "I went to General Paris's Headquarters on the Lierre road. Shrapnel burst overhead as I got out of the car, and struck down a man at my feet. As we discussed around the cottage table, the whole house thudded and shook from minute to minute with the near explosions of shells whose flashes lit the window-panes. It was two o'clock before I went to bed. I had been moving, thinking and acting with very brief intervals for nearly four days in council and at the Front in circumstances of undefined but very direct responsibility.

"At midnight on the seventh the Germans, having ad-vanced their artillery, began to bombard the city and the forts of the inner line. The forts melted under the fire, and a great proportion of the civil population fled through the night, lighted by conflagrations, along the roads towards Ghent or into Holland." [3h]

Antwerp could not be held, but the Belgians, heartened by the presence of Winston and the marines, delayed the enemy for the space of five invaluable days. And what is more, the Belgian army made a valiant recovery and got away intact. By this means the Belgian coast and the Channel ports were saved. [2]

Nevertheless, the Antwerp expedition damaged Winston's reputation badly. The Conservative Press attacked him savagely; even the Prime Minister was losing confidence in him. Things at the Admiralty were not going too well either. The Germans were sinking Allied ships, and Winston was hotly censured. Also, criticism of the First Sea Lord, Prince Louis of Battenberg, was mounting. [4]

"In the first flush of our entry upon the war," Churchill wrote, "no comment had been made upon his parentage. Now the gossip of the clubs and of the streets began to produce a stream of letters, signed and anonymous, protesting in violent terms against one of Teutonic birth filling the vital position of First Sea Lord. I was therefore not surprised when Prince Louis asked to be relieved of his burden with the uncomplaining dignity worthy of a sailor and a Prince. My mind turned in one direction only for a successor: Lord Fisher. [3h]

King George V regarded the appointment of Fisher, now seventy-four, with the utmost misgivings. He knew the distrust aroused by the volatile personality of Fisher. Churchill overrode these objections. [7]

He and Fisher agreed not to take any action without each other's knowledge. They manned the Admiralty almost the twenty-four hours around, forming what they called a "perpetual clock." Fisher rose at four in the morning and finished his work in the early afternoon; Winston began in the late morning and worked through the night. Winston wrote his minutes in red ink and Fisher in green, and both referred to them as the Port and Starboard Lights. [4]

"We had established a combination," comments Churchill, "which, while it remained unbroken, could not have been overthrown by intrigue at home or the foe on the sea." Alas, the day came when the combination ended in a fierce explosion, as was Fisher's way. It was all over the Dardanelles campaign. [7]

6

The Magnificent
Scapegoat

WHEN the old year closed a complete deadlock existed
between the great combatants in the West," explains
Churchill in *World Crisis*. "The trench lines ran continuously
from the Alps to the sea. With no possibility of maneuvre the
generals turned to a war of exhaustion and to still more dire
attempts to pierce the enemy's front, in which two and even
three British or French lives were repeatedly paid for the killing of one enemy.

"If a complete deadlock had been reached in the West,
events were moving with imperious violence in the East. In
August 1914, the Germans were concentrating practically
four-fifths of their armies against France and leaving only a
handful of divisions to guard their eastern frontiers against
Russia. High hopes were entertained that these slender
forces would be overwhelmed and that Russian masses
would be rolling forward upon Danzig, Breslau, onward into
the heart of the German Empire, thus forcing the Germans to
recall their invading armies to the defense of their own soil.
In November 1914, the Russian Grand Duke could still contemplate an advance through Silesia into the heart of Germany.

"But there came an awful change. During the first three

months of fighting Russia fired on an average of about *forty-five thousand shells a day*. The output of her factories in Russia did not exceed *thirty-five thousand shells a month*. By December, scarcely three hundred thousand shells, or barely a week's requirement, remained out of the initial reserve, and over one million out of five and a half million rifles had been lost, captured or destroyed. Though three hundred and fifty thousand Russians had been killed, wounded or made prisoners, the barracks of the Empire were full of lusty manhood: eight hundred thousand trained drafts were ready for dispatch to the front, but there were no weapons to place in their hands.

"Russia had one last supreme resource—territory, affording almost unlimited possibilities of retirement. Meanwhile the factories of the world could be set to work to supply and reequip the Russian armies and her strength be restored before the end of 1915." [3h]

On January 2, 1915, Kitchener received an urgent appeal from the Grand Duke Nicholas for a naval or military demonstration against the Turks to relieve Turkish pressure in the Caucasus. Dreading a Russian collapse, Kitchener immediately went into conference with Churchill. "The only place that a demonstration might have some effect in stopping reinforcements going East," concluded Kitchener, "would be the Dardanelles." But, he announced emphatically, he had no troops available for that purpose. And, he added, Sir John French, the French Government and High Command were all strongly opposed to any suggestion of diverting the growing military might from the Western theater. [38]

Winston began to study the possibilities of a purely naval assault on the outer fortresses of the long curving straits which led into the Sea of Marmora. If the fleet could get past the many fortresses that dotted the steep banks of the Straits and force its way into the Sea of Marmora, Constantinople might capitulate, and the Allies would be able to join hands with their Russian Allies. Arms could be shipped in and badly needed wheat sent out, the whole Balkan area would be neutralized, leaving Germany and Austria fighting alone.

"When Mr. Winston Churchill has a scheme," wrote Lloyd George in his *Memoirs*, "agitating his powerful mind, as everyone who is acquainted with his method knows quite well, he is indefatigable in pressing it upon the acceptance of everyone who matters in the decision."

On January 13 the War Council met. Winston put forward his project and all the members, with the exception of Lloyd George, agreed to it. Lord Fisher was present and made no comment. [4]

The operation began in February, 1915, with a fleet of one hundred seventy-eight British and French ships which turned their guns on the outer Turkish forts of the Dardanelles in the greatest bombardment in naval history. British Admiral de Robeck, commanding the assault group, forecast he would storm the Straits and batter Constantinople in fourteen days. But in March the British and French navies, moving in to probe the defenses, ran into a minefield which blew up five of their ships. There was chaos among the admirals. "Damn the Dardanelles!" Fisher exclaimed to Winston. "They will be our grave." [1]

To the amazement of the Turks and Germans, de Robeck broke off the action, for the Turkish gun crews were demoralized and all but out of ammunition. In London, the First Lord drew up a telegram instructing de Robeck to renew the action. It was never sent; Fisher and the other admirals refused to overrule the man on the spot. "If the orders given at that moment," wrote Liman von Sanders, the German general at the Dardanelles, "had been carried out, the course of the world war would have changed after the spring of 1915, and Germany and Austria would have been constrained to continue the fight alone." [8]

Naval operations were never resumed, and from then on

the attack became a purely military affair that ended in heartbreaking failure. Five long precious weeks were allowed to lapse between the breaking off of naval operations and the initial assault of the army; during those weeks, the Turks feverishly strengthened their defenses. When troops finally stormed the Gallipoli beaches in April the element of surprise was gone and they were unable to capture vital key points. A week later, with the increasing German submarine menace and the sinking of the Lusitania, Fisher was no longer prepared to risk the *Queen Elizabeth* at the Dardanelles and ordered her home. Kitchener was furious, accused the navy of deserting the army. Fisher announced that either the *Queen Elizabeth* left the Dardanelles that afternoon or he left the Admiralty that night. Fisher won. The dummy ship, equipped to represent the *Queen Elizabeth* at the Dardanelles, was later torpedoed.

The quarrel between the two men had now reached its climax. Fisher declared before the War Council that he had been against the Dardanelles from the start. That afternoon Winston wrote to the Prime Minister: "The First Sea Lord has agreed in writing to every executive telegram on which the operations have been conducted; and had they been immediately successful, the credit would have been his. But I make no complaint of that. I am attached to the old boy and it is a great pleasure to me to work with him. But in a matter of this kind *someone* has to take the responsibility. I will do so—provided that my decision is the one that rules. A man who says 'I disclaim responsibility for failure' cannot be the final arbiter of the measure which may be found to be vital to success."

That night Winston ordered two more E-boats sent to the Dardanelles. The following morning Fisher resigned his office of First Sea Lord. Winston, aware of the political storm if Fisher remained obdurate, wrote him a persuasive letter: "In order to bring you back to the Admiralty I took my political life in my hands—as you well know. You then promised to stand by me and see me through. If you now go and therefore let loose on me the spite and malice of those who are your enemies even more than they are mine, it will be a melancholy ending to our six months of successful administration. It will be a great grief to me to part from you."

Fisher replied: "YOU ARE BENT ON FORCING THE DARDANELLES AND NOTHING WILL TURN YOU FROM IT—NOTHING. YOU WILL REMAIN AND I SHALL GO— it is better so. No one has been more faithful to you than I have since I joined you last October." [4]

Fisher now turned traitor to Churchill: he got in touch with the Tory Opposition, particularly Bonar Law, its most dangerous opponent and Churchill's personal enemy. [7]

Bonar Law had been for some time on friendly terms with Fisher; he had a standing invitation to lunch at the Admiralty with the First Sea Lord, who had disclosed to him the hidden but deep conflict behind the apparent unanimity of the Admiralty. "Don't be cajoled privately by the P.M. to keep silence," the eccentric Fisher now wrote to Bonar Law. "W.C. is a bigger danger than the Germans by a long way in what is just now imminent in the Dardanelles. *Concentrate on the Dardanelles!*" A postscript, headed "Please burn and don't mention," added: "This evening Winston offered me a seat in the Cabinet if I would return as his First Sea Lord with him as First Lord! I rejected the thirty pieces of silver to betray my country."

Bonar Law promptly called on Lloyd George and asked him point-blank if Fisher had resigned. Lloyd George answered that he had. "Then the situation is impossible." If Fisher resigned and Churchill remained, he, Bonar Law, would not restrain the Conservatives, whatever the consequences might be, from demanding a public debate upon the issues that had provoked the crisis.

Unwilling to have an open rupture with the Opposition in such a time of crisis, Lloyd George replied: "We must have a coalition," and promptly took Bonar Law across to number 10 Downing Street to see the Prime Minister.

Asquith, who only the day before had accepted Churchill's proposed reconstruction of the Board of Admiralty, now saw that there was little chance of saving his First Lord of the Admiralty. He agreed to form a Coalition Administration, the first of the wartime coalitions.

Meanwhile the unfortunate Churchill, having "no knowledge of the violent political convulsions which were proceeding around me and beneath me," went to the House of Commons on that very afternoon to vindicate his policy and his new Board in public debate. He received a disagreeable shock when he learned from Asquith that a Coalition Government was to be formed, that no debate would take place in Parliament. [14]

The Tory Press had been hostile ever since Antwerp, but now the *Morning Post* outdid itself: THE AMATEUR ADMIRAL—POLITICIAN VERSUS EXPERT—TOO MUCH CHURCHILL ran their headlines. "Mr. Churchill sees himself as the only digit in the sum of things, all other men as mere cyphers. His instinct for the melodramatic has blossomed into megalomania." [4]

In the formation of the coalition, the Tories at last got their revenge: they insisted, as an absolute condition, on Churchill's exclusion from the Admiralty. All the experience there, all the work he had put in at that proud, cherished post, were to go by the board. [7]

"You can imagine what a horrible wound and mutilation it is for him," Edward Marsh wrote to Violet Asquith. "It's like Beethoven deaf." [54]

Lloyd George, who considered the miscarriage of the Dardanelles "due not so much to Mr. Churchill's precipitancy as to Lord Kitchener's and Mr. Asquith's procrastination," hoped to see Churchill at the Colonial Office "where his energies could have been helpfully employed in the Empire beyond the seas." But Churchill was now relegated to the Duchy of

Lancaster, "a post generally reserved either for beginners in the Cabinet or for distinguished politicians who had reached the first stages of unmistakable decrepitude, a cruel and unjust degradation." [7]

"Four thousand pounds a year for doing nothing!" Churchill commented. His tragedy was that he had to watch, and this from a ringside seat, while others ruined his work. As a member of the War Council he was still informed of the most intimate secrets, but as Chancellor of the Duchy of Lancaster he had no vote in the Council. [34]

Nevertheless, Churchill continued to press for reinforcements for the Gallipoli peninsula. [7]

Through the blistering summer, swarms of flies spread dysentery, and in the winter the coldest blizzard in forty years sank ships and froze sentries dead. [10]

For eight desperate months the army struggled on the rocky beaches overlooked by high cliffs in the hands of the enemy. In December 1915, Gallipoli was evacuated. [4]

The total British and French casualties reached two hundred and fifty thousand. One of these young unfortunates, a splendid veteran of Churchill's naval force at Antwerp, was the poet Rupert Brooke, who wrote:

If I should die think only this of me:
That there's some corner of a foreign field
That is forever England. There shall be
In that rich earth a richer dust concealed;
A dust whom England bore, shaped, made aware,
Gave, once, her flowers to love, her ways to roam,
A body of England's, breathing English air,
Washed by the rivers, blest by suns of home.

In company with Rupert Brooke, Churchill himself was among the casualties. [8]

7

"C'est la Guerre"

"THEY never fought it out to a finish! They never gave my schemes a fair trial!" Churchill cried out to war correspondent Ashmead Bartlett as he walked for the last time through the deserted offices at the Admiralty which he had graced with such promise of glory.

Clemmie, meanwhile, had moved the family from their apartments in the Admiralty to a flat at 41 Cromwell Road, Kensington. "The change from the intense executive activities of each day's work at the Admiralty to the narrowly measured duties of a councillor left me gasping," he wrote. "Like a sea-beast fished up from the depths, or a diver too suddenly hoisted, my veins threatened to burst. I had great anxiety and no means of relieving it. I had long hours of utterly unwanted leisure in which to contemplate the frightful unfolding of the war." He found refuge in painting. [34]

"During the early summer of 1915, after the failure of the Dardanelles," writes John Spencer Churchill, "my uncle withdrew to Hoe Farm, in Surrey, where we spent part of the summer. A majestic sadness hung around him. One sunlit afternoon he was browsing around the house, looking for a constructive means of filling in time, when suddenly he saw my box of watercolor paints. There and then he decided to paint a picture. He had no idea how to go about it, but he sat down and was happily occupied for the rest of the day.

"The result pleased him. And since he never does anything halfheartedly, he at once launched into painting in oils. He bought an enviable collection of equipment: an easel, palette, canvases, and tubes of every color." [17]

"The next step was *to begin*," Churchill wrote. "The sky on this occasion was unquestionably blue. Very gingerly I mixed a little blue paint on the palette with a very small brush, and then with infinite precaution made a mark about as big as a bean upon the affronted snow-white shield of the canvas: a deliberate challenge, but so halting that it deserved no response. At that moment a motor car was heard in the drive. From this chariot stepped the gifted wife of the well-known artist Sir John Lavery. 'Painting! But what are you hesitating about? Let me have a brush—the big one.' Splash into the turpentine, wallop into the blue and the white, frantic flourish on the palette—clean no longer—then several large, fierce strokes and slashes of blue on the absolutely cowering canvas. Anyone could see that it could not hit back. It grinned in helplessness before me. The spell was broken. The sickly inhibitions rolled away. I seized the largest brush and fell upon my victim with berserk fury. I have never felt any awe of a canvas since.

"Armed with a paint box, one cannot be bored, one cannot be left at a loose end, one cannot have several days on one's hands. Whatever the worries of the hour or the threats of the future, once the picture has begun to flow along, there is no room for them in the mental screen.

"I must say I like bright colors. I rejoice with the brilliant ones and am genuinely sorry for the poor browns. When I get to heaven I shall require a still gayer palette than I get here below. I expect orange and vermilion will be the darkest, dullest colors upon it, and beyond them there will be a whole range of wonderful colors which will delight the celestial eye." [3i]

When not painting at the farm, Churchill would often

amuse himself by playing games with the children. "His specialty was 'gorillas,' recalled John Churchill. "He put on his oldest clothes, crouched behind bushes and hedges, and waited for one of us to come near. Then there was a terrifying eruption, a blood-tingling roar of *Grr! Grr!* and my uncle emerged, his arms swinging limply at his sides. He chased us and made for the nearest tree. We squealed with delight and enjoyed this exclusive performance hugely. Few people can say they have seen an ex-First Lord of the Admiralty crouching in the branches of an oak, baring his teeth and pounding his chest with his fists." [17]

In November 1915, Asquith prepared to form a small War Council and then found the opposition to Churchill's inclusion too strong for him. "I do not feel able," Churchill wrote promptly, "in times like these to remain in well-paid inactivity. I therefore ask you to submit my resignation to the King. I place myself unreservedly at the disposal of the military authorities, observing that my regiment is in France." [9]

Mr. Asquith bowed him out with a lapidary tribute to "a wise counselor, a brilliant colleague, and a faithful friend" and sent him on his new career with "the universal goodwill, hopes, and confident expectations of the House and of all his colleagues." After all, the name of Churchill was not unknown on British battlefields. [26]

On the eve of his departure for France, Churchill dined with Lord Northcliffe, the newspaper magnate, owner of *The Times* and the *Daily Mail,* who found him "in great form and tearing spirits." He handed his diaries and documents for posterity to the care of his good friend F. E. Smith, who was Attorney General, then climbed into his uniform, which he topped—for no particular reason other than his own sartorial inclination—with a sky-blue French helmet. [1]

"The whole household was upside down while the soldier-statesman was buckling on his sword," recorded Lord Beaver-brook. "Downstairs his dear friend and secretary Edward Marsh was in tears; upstairs his mother was in despair at the idea of her brilliant son's being relegated to the trenches." [28]

Mrs. Churchill seemed to be the only person who remained calm and collected: she must have become used to such scenes. [7]

With two small children and an infant, a tiny income, and a husband whose rash acts were England's principal gossip, the former Miss Clementine Hozier could scarcely have been reconciled to his colorful decision. By a kind fortune, for her and the nation, his holiday amidst the bursting shells would provide an episode of high comedy in a generally bleak drama. [8]

When Major Churchill reached Boulogne in France he was whirled off in Sir John French's car to headquarters in St. Omer, where Sir John, a loyal friend, provided Churchill with a cordial reception and an excellent dinner as though he were still First Lord of the Admiralty. The next morning he asked him what he would like to do. "Whatever I am told," replied Winston. Sir John then confided that he might soon be replaced by a new Commander in Chief. "I am, as it were, riding at single anchor. But it still counts for something. Will you take a brigade?" Winston assented gladly. A brigade commander had the rank of brigadier general and the control of four thousand men. First, however, he stipulated he must have a month's training in trench warfare. The Guards Division would give him the best experience. [4]

As the 2nd Grenadier Guards plodded through the rain towards the front line, Major Churchill rode with his new commanding officer and an adjutant. For about half an hour there was complete silence. Then the Colonel observed: "I think I ought to tell you that we were not at all consulted in the matter of your coming to join us." This welcome was supplemented by the adjutant's announcement that circumstances had compelled them to reduce Major Churchill's kit to his shaving gear and a spare pair of socks. [26]

Winston was not offended. "Knowing the professional army as I did, I was amused at the elaborate pains they took to put me in my place. It took about forty-eight hours to wear through their natural prejudice against 'politicians.' " [4]

The headquarters of the battalion were in a pulverized ruin called Ebenezer Farm. A small sandbag structure behind the ruined walls of the house was the Colonel's headquarters. Here the officers ate tinned food and drank strong tea with condensed milk. Where did Churchill want to sleep—at Battalion Headquarters or with the soldiers in the trenches? He chose the trenches, but not as a matter of heroism. Liquor was served at the soldiers' dinner. Churchill could not stand the strong tea with condensed milk. [34]

Meanwhile, rumors began to reach the House of Commons that Winston was to be given a brigade. His Tory opponents, who looked upon him as a dangerous fraud, were indignant and attacked him on the ground of "privilege." While sharp questioning was going on in Parliament, Sir John French paid a visit to London and told the Prime Minister that he was giving Winston a brigade. [4]

"For God's sake," was Asquith's frenzied reply, paraphrased, "don't give him a brigade—don't give him anything more than a battalion!" Afterwards a member of the Cabinet said that Asquith was afraid Churchill might, perhaps under cover of night, march the brigade directly on Berlin. [8]

Less than a month later, French was succeeded by Sir Douglas Haig and Churchill was given, not a brigade, but a battalion in the 6th Royal Scots Fusiliers. For a month he nursed a grievance against Asquith. "A Premier," commented Beaverbrook, "may have to throw a colleague overboard to save the ship, but he should not jerk from under him the hen coop on which the victim is trying to sustain himself on the stormy ocean."

The Scots Fusiliers were billeted at Ploegstreet Village, near Armentières, known to the British as Plugstreet. Battalion headquarters were in a squalid, filthy farmhouse, half of which was still occupied by French peasants. Churchill arrived early on an afternoon, took an elevated seat in a corner of the orderly room and asked that the company officers be brought in one by one and formally introduced. "He looked uncommonly like Napoleon, with the same forward thrust in his pose, the same brooding scowl, the hand in the tunic, and even the same baldish head with its vagrant forelock."

After the presentation, during which everyone stood at attention, minutes ticked by as Churchill regarded everybody stonily. Then, without so much as a whisper breaking the tension of the room, the new commander got up and lumbered out. His first order, via the adjutant, read, "Clear the cats from the orderly room."

The next day Churchill held a second levee, as verbose as the other had been mute. When the visitors were settled into uncomfortable attention, he said: "War is declared, gentlemen, on the lice." [8]

"With these words did the great scion of the house of Marlborough," wrote Dewar Gibbs, one of the officers, "first address his Scottish captains assembled in council. And with these words was inaugurated a discourse on *pulex Europeus*, its origin, growth, and nature, its habitat and its importance as a factor in wars ancient and modern, a masterly biography of the louse that left one agape with wonder at the erudition and force of its author." [2]

When the speech was concluded, Churchill ordered the entire battalion to turn-to and get after the enemy on the double. Soldiers and officers assembled at various spots on the grounds, and, taking a few precautions to avoid the inquisitive gaze of the farm ladies, peeled off their clothes and began tossing them into pots of water. The operation took three days; when it was over the lice had thrown in the towel.

After the first shock, and resentment, the battalion began to take pride in having a former Cabinet Minister at its head. He undertook the improvement of his men with hilarious verve. [8]

Early and late Churchill was in the line. On an average he went round three times a day, no mean task with his other work. At least one of these visits was after dark, usually about 1 A.M. In wet weather he would appear in a complete outfit of waterproof stuff, including trousers, or overalls, and with his French light-blue helmet he presented a remarkable and unusual figure. He was always in closest touch with every piece of work that was going on.

"To see Winston giving a dissertation on the laying of sandbags," wrote Gibbs, "with practical illustrations, was to come inevitably to the conclusion that this had been a life-study. You felt sure from his grasp of practice that he must have served apprentice to a bricklayer and a master mason. Yet sometimes Winston was wrong about those sandbags and 2nd Lieut. Stickinthemud was right. Despite the Colonel's zeal and enthusiasm, he did not seem to be able to get into touch with the actual practical handling of those accursed sandsacks. It was a case of the 'last infirmity of noble minds.' " [2]

One morning Churchill hailed an itinerant tinker and put him to work fashioning a bathtub shaped like a giant soap dish with fluted sides, in the manner of Venus's shell. Each morning around ten o'clock the Colonel boarded this vehicle, filled with hot water by his long-suffering batman, at a spot beneath some trees in the farmyard and set up a phonograph on a beer barrel alongside, whereupon the batman was instructed to keep the records moving. As the melodies soared up into the smoke-filled air, contending with the divisional artillery, Churchill sat reading a pocket edition of Shakespeare. If the shelling was severe, he bathed with his blue tin hat on.

The 6th Fusiliers owned a battery of eighteen-pounders, which the Colonel liked to keep booming at odd hours. "We'll scramble the Hun's sleep," he told his men. What he was doing was scrambling *their* sleep, too, but they knuckled under and kept the ammunition handy. The gun crew would be bounced out of bed at 2 or 3 A.M. and told to "fire ten rounds—wake those fellows up." The firing would commence, and the enemy would shortly start lobbing shells over in retaliation. Churchill soon tired of the eighteen-pounder and made friends with the commander of the divisional artillery. From then on the nights were a perfect hell, "rendered hideous by a repeated series of shocking explosions, during which the entire division awoke from its slumbers and asked itself it this was the Great Push or only another of Winston's tunes on a borrowed fiddle."

A few days after he arrived, the entire village of Pleogstreet moved out in disgust. Helpful and good-neighborly to the end, he lent them battalion transport wagons in which to haul their household goods, and waved them down the road with many a cry of "C'est la guerre." The growls of the Ploegstreeters indicated that it was "C'est le Churchill," since, as the village midwife said, they had never had any trouble of this kind before he came. [8]

Churchill was no stranger to "Plugstreet's" daily peril from enemy shells. One day, while working on a memorandum on tank warfare, he was seated before the window at his "rest" headquarters, only a thousand yards from the enemy, when a bombardment began. He despised the protection of cellars. Shells fell closer and closer. After one burst less than fifty yards away he decided that he needed greater protection than a glass window afforded. He left his office at a pace "dignified yet decided" and entered the battalion office in the adjoining building. After the blitz died away he went to his head-quarters to find that the room in which he had been working had been shattered by a three-lb shell. [2]

He invited the company commanders to dine with him in headquarters mess, and they were astounded at the gorgeous style in which he received them: a setting more reminiscent of a London club than of a squalid French farm on the Eastern Front.

Being a celebrity, Churchill was obliged to entertain a steady queue of guests of high and low degree. It was hard for many people to believe that he actually was in Ploegstreet with a bunch of wild Scotsmen. The skeptics, if they could wangle a pass, came over to see. Churchill treated the bright spirits with punctilio. He had his couriers scouring the countryside for tasty viands, buying all the lobster and tinned fruit in Armentières, paying good prices. Once he sent a man to bespeak Hazebrouck's entire seasonal production of peach and apricot brandy. Sometimes the money came out of the Mess Treasury, presided over by the doctor, and sometimes the Colonel supplied the funds himself.

Churchill had a paternal attitude towards his troops. It grieved him to find young boys trembling in fear on sentry-go; he would quit his other duties to mount the fire step and explain in a kind and patient manner that little likelihood existed of their being hit. He lived in mortal terror of having men reported for sleeping on the job and was forever making up excuses for them in case they were caught. When some-body was wounded, Churchill was all bustle and concern. He hopped right down to the spot and carried on a learned dia-logue with the doctor, and, if feasible, with the patient. He would pad along beside the stretcher, offering medical rea-sons, conspicuously inexpert, why the sufferer would be up and around soon. The men took enormous pride in him, but the doctor became exasperated. "The confounded fellow treats me like a surgeon's orderly!" [8]

In his relationships with his superior officers, the Colonel's bearing was studiously respectful. One brigade commander, whom the battalion disliked, visited Battalion Headquarters just after that stronghold had been shelled and various protective works destroyed. He sent for Churchill and opened out about the defective condition of the protective works. "Look here, Churchill," he fussed, "this won't do. It's dangerous, you know, positively dangerous."

"Yes, sir," replied the Colonel, nettled, "but, you know, this is a very dangerous war." [2]

He used his leisure at the Front working on his memorandum for the High Command on amphibious warfare, preparing a scheme for the capture of the Frisian island of Borkum. The essence of the plan was to use tanks to run ashore from specially constructed landing craft on the beaches, methods that were to dominate the Second World War with its landings on the beaches of North Africa, Italy, Normandy and the Pacific islands. Bulletproof lighters, tanks in large numbers, flat-bottomed barges or caissons of concrete: here were Churchill's original contributions to the art of warfare. Lloyd George was so much impressed by this paper that he had it printed and circulated to the Admiralty and the War Cabinet. [7]

In May of 1916, orders came for the battalion to be dispersed and amalgamated with other units of the regiment. At the same time, a political crisis had arisen at home. The 6th Royal Scots Fusiliers held a final orderly-room session. There were refreshments. Churchill looked tired; he had spent days beating paths to all the high rank he knew, seeking good billets for his officers. The adjutant, a noted teetotaler, showed up drunk and made a speech: never again would the assembly have a commanding officer they liked half so well. "Hear! Hear!" cried the officers. Then Churchill delivered himself of a singular farewell: "Whatever else they may say of me as a soldier," he said to his men, with obvious affection, "nobody can say I have ever failed to display a meet and proper appreciation of the virtues of alcohol."

As he walked across the yard to the bus that was to take him away, both officers and men cheered. "He came to be looked on really as a possession of our own, of which we were intensely proud. And much more, he became our friend." [8]

8

"Winnie Is Back"

DARK days had descended upon England as a result of the blundering of Asquith's war government. Catastrophe followed close on the heels of calamity. [8]

Churchill had been receiving overtures from various public men, including members of Parliament, pressing him to come back to England and take part in a patriotic Opposition. With his battalion amalgamated with another, he made up his mind to follow their advice. He asked to be released from the army. His resignation was accepted on the understanding that he would not apply again for military service.

Back in London he hung about Westminster and grew pale and dispirited. "I am banished from the scene of action," he complained to his friends. "He was honestly convinced that only by his advice could the Empire be saved," wrote Lord Beaverbrook, "and he suffered tortures when he thought that lesser men were mismanaging the business." [4]

Soon after Winston's return, the one big naval engagement of the war—the Battle of Jutland—was fought in the North Sea, a confused affair because British losses were greater than those of the Germans and the enemy were allowed to slip off before getting the full hammering that could have been given them. Both sides claimed victory, but actually Britain had sustained a major defeat.

Hard on the heels of the Jutland affair, on June fifth, the

country was plunged into mourning by the loss of Kitchener aboard the H.M.S. *Hampshire*, which was taking him to
Russia for a military consultation when it struck an enemy
mine off the Orkneys. Lloyd George now inherited the War
Office and urged Asquith to appoint Winston to the vacancy
in the Munitions Ministry. But the Prime Minister refused.
Montague was moved across to Munitions. Winston was left
to paint landscapes and make occasional speeches, a soul-
shattering position for him.

The war dragged on through the summer and autumn of
1916. Then Haig launched his big Somme offensive. [9]

"The battlefields of the Somme were the graveyards of
Kitchener's army," wrote Churchill, "the flower of manhood
shorn away forever. Good, plain, straightforward frontal attacks by valiant flesh and blood against wire and machine
guns, 'killing Germans' while Germans killed Allies twice as
often, sending the wounded soldiers back three or four times
over into the shambles—such were the sole manifestations
now reserved for the military art." [3h]

Horrified by Haig's strategy, Churchill wrote a memorandum, which was circulated to the Cabinet, on the terrible
futility of these offenses against the enemy's deeply entrenched positions. A copy of this memorandum found its
way to G.H.Q. in France, where it was hotly repudiated and
its author severely criticized. [4]

On the home front the shipping and the food situations
were growing more and more serious. The Cabinet could not
decide on any topic, a babel of argument on every issue
ended in adjournment. Finally, in December, Lloyd George
could stand this aimless mismanagement no longer. He demanded of Asquith an Inner War Council, working full time,
to determine war policy. [9]

Asquith refused and resigned, and the King, at Bonar
Law's suggestion, entrusted the forming of a Government to
Lloyd George.

Churchill's spirits soared as he thought his chance had come, but once again he was doomed to disappointment. Bonar Law flatly refused to support any Government that included Winston. [4]

An emergency meeting of the Conservative Council, headed by Law, resolved by three hundred votes to two that Winston's inclusion in the Government would be an "insult to the navy and the army." "That dangerous and uncertain quality," said the *Morning Post,* "Mr. Winston Churchill—a floating kidney in the body politic—is back again in Westminster." Lloyd George had to delay the appointment until the storm died away. [1]

But he could at least do Churchill one signal service. The following February he published the report of the Dardanelles Commission, appointed by Asquith months before to go into the origin and conduct of the Gallipoli campaigns. The Commission admitted that Winston's proposal for a naval attack on the Straits was the right one and condemned Asquith's handling of the issue and Kitchener's yes-and-no attitude about the supply of troops. Winston's stock began to rise. [9]

Meanwhile, the Russian revolution of February 1917 coincided with a sudden crisis in relations between the United States and Germany. America had almost declared war in 1915 when the *Lusitania* was sunk with a loss of one hundred and fourteen lives. Now Germany announced a policy of unrestricted submarine warfare, hoping to starve England out of the war before America could make her opposition felt. Two months later, on April 15, Woodrow Wilson declared war, a decision rapturously greeted in England and France. [1]

The Germans never understood the horror and indignation with which their opponents and the neutral world regarded the U-boat against merchant ships. To make a neutral ship a prize of war stirred whole histories of internationnal law. To sink her and leave the crew to perish in open boats was in the

eyes of all seafaring peoples a grisly act never hitherto practiced deliberately except by pirates. But the Germans, newcomers on salt water, cared little for ancient traditions of
seafaring folk. Death was to them the same in whatever form
it came to man. Why was it more horrible to be choked with
salt water than with poison gas, or to starve in an open boat
than to rot wounded but alive in No Man's Land? Where was
the sense in drawing distinctions between the two processes?
Thus the German Naval Staff. But the neutrals took a different view. [3h]

America's millions were to be poured across the Atlantic in
the raw, equipped or unequipped, without even a change of
uniform. All that could be arranged later. They were to be
deprived, these raw troops, even of the tremendous moral
support of *esprit de corps*. For they were to be absorbed in the
French and English armies and to complete their training
alongside the fighting men. The American sacrifice was su-
perb. [30]

The following month Churchill clinched his position in the
House with a speech delivered at a secret session held principally as a result of his demands. He accused General Headquarters in France of dissipating the strength and energies of
the army by using up division after division in a war of attri-
tion and urged an active defense on the Western Front until
the United States had thrown her millions of men into the
scale. [2]

In the meantime Britain must concentrate on the anti-
submarine war and keep its sea communications intact. "I
was listened to for an hour and a quarter," he wrote, "at first
silently but gradually with a growing measure of acceptance
and at length approval. At the end there was quite a demonstration." [4]

Although the Conservatives were still grumbling, Lloyd
George offered Churchill the Ministry of Munitions on July

16, 1917. After twenty months of bitter exile, word spread through the House: "Winnie is back." [34]

Lloyd George was inundated with angry letters from his Cabinet colleagues, and for a time the Government tottered. "I knew something of the feeling against him among his old Conservative friends and that I would run great risks in promoting Churchill to any position in the Ministry; but the insensate fury they displayed surpassed all my apprehension, the distrust and trepidation in concentrated form, with which mediocrity views genius at close quarters. Unfortunately, genius always provides its critics with material for censure—it always has and always will. Churchill is certainly no exception to this rule." [4]

John Churchill commented upon the aftermath to Churchill's return to government: "When my uncle was brought back into top-level politics, instantly our cozy home, which my mother and Aunt Clemmie shared in Cromwell Road as an economy measure, became Uncle's war headquarters. Important statesmen, Lloyd George among them, knocked for admission at all hours; dispatch boxes cluttered the hall and stairs, and we used to open doors to find the most unlikely rooms crammed with secretaries banging at typewriters. Telephones were installed at strategic points. Randolph, Uncle's son, and I had a fine time picking them up and shouting rude messages at bewildered operators.

"When my brother, Pebin, and I were given a box of Meccanno we retreated to the one spot in the house which had escaped the invasion: the dining room. My uncle drifted in, puffing at the inevitable cigar. 'And what are you making, eh?' he demanded. 'A cantilever crane,' I told him. 'Hm.' The cigar was sucked thoughtfully. 'A bascule bridge would be much better, you know.'

"A secretary was sent out to buy box after box of Meccano. Then, apparently forgetting he had a war on his hands, my uncle took off his coat and began preparing for the largest model bascule bridge ever, with Pebin and me as assistants. Protests were made by the womenfolk about the inconvenience of half-finished girders resting across the sideboard, but my uncle refused to be deflected. The final construction was a gigantic piece of engineering some fifteen feet long and eight feet high, with a roadway which could be lifted by means of wheels, pulleys and yards of string. The servants were forbidden to touch it, and my uncle gazed fondly at his creation during meals.

"Eventually it proved to be too much of a nuisance in the dining room, stretching as it did from wall to wall across one end, and was transferred into the hall, an even worse site. Visitors, including members of the Cabinet, had to stoop under the raised center section of the bridge to get in and out of the door.

"That summer our two families went down to Lullenden, an old house in Sussex. A boy I knew visited me and we shared a bedroom. During the long light summer evenings, we used to lie awake talking. We were doing this one evening and twilight had come, when we heard some earnest conversation in the garden under our window. My uncle and Lloyd George were standing close together discussing the war. The chance for a practical joke was too good to miss. Opening the window wide, we started tipping the contents of our chamber pots onto the eminent heads below. We did it slowly enough for it to seem merely a few spots of welcome rain, and thought it screamingly funny. Undoubtedly Britain's Prime Minister and Minister of Munitions had never had *that* done to them before. A maid standing in the bow window farther along the wall saw us. We were quickly caught and punished." [17]

"The growth of the Ministry of Munitions had far outstripped its organization," wrote Churchill. "The whole island was an arsenal. The enormous national factories which Lloyd George had planned were just beginning to function.

91

At the Ministry I worked with the largest and most powerful staff in my experience. Here, in the range of palatial hotels that housed the Ministry, were gathered the finest business brains of the country, who, working as private contractors, served the state for honor alone. However, all decisions centered upon the Minister himself. I found a staff of twelve thousand officials organized in no less than fifty principal departments each claiming direct access to the Chief, and I set to work at once to divide and distribute this dangerous concentration of power." [3h]

Churchill grouped the fifty departments into ten large units—design, guns, finance, projectiles, explosives, and so on—each in the charge of a head directly responsible to the Minister. These ten heads then formed a council like a cabinet. [7]

"The relief was instantaneous. Instead of struggling through the jungle on foot I rode comfortably on an elephant whose trunk could pick up a pin or uproot a tree with equal ease, and from whose back a wide view of the scene lay open." [3h]

Churchill was also entrusted with the task of equipping the whole of the American armies as they arrived in France. His initial contract was one of £100,000,000 to supply medium guns, the transaction being arranged on a "no profit basis" and carried out with the utmost satisfaction on both sides. [2]

British and Americans shared one another's stores—to quote Churchill—"as easily as two friends might share a luncheon basket." [9]

He did the job so well that, afterward, General Pershing presented him with the Distinguished Service Medal. He was the only Englishman to wear this decoration. His assignment brought him into close contact with Bernard Baruch, then chairman of the War Industries Board in Washington, and the two men developed a close friendship that continued after the war. [8]

As the country entered the fourth year of the war, with victory apparently no nearer, war weariness became a growing danger and labor troubles supplied Churchill with another set of problems. A series of strikes broke out among munition workers. Most were settled quickly, but one at Coventry threatened to take a revolutionary character. It was no time for fumbling, for the war just then was looking its blackest with the Germans again advancing on the Marne. With the backing of the Prime Minister, Winston gripped his nettle unhesitatingly. He told the munition workers that they could go back to work or be forthwith conscripted and sent to the front. The strike collapsed. [9]

But it left another black mark against his name in the books of labor. [30]

The Ministry of Munitions had large establishments in France, which gave Winston the opportunity of crossing the Channel whenever he wished. He seized the excuse to visit the Front regularly, frequently appearing at Haig's headquarters, where he studied the flagged maps and talked strategy and tactics to his heart's content. [4]

Thus he obtained firsthand knowledge of the requirements of the army as they arose and saw to it that they were speedily supplied. [2]

Finally the French Government provided him with a delightful headquarters in France—the chateau of Verchouq, within the zone of the armies and only two hours' airplane flight from Hendon. He could spend a morning at the Ministry of Munitions, have lunch at Verchouq, follow the course of a battle in the afternoon and return to Whitehall in time for dinner and the rest of the day's work in the evening. [30]

"I managed to be present at every important battle during the rest of the war," he wrote with pride. He was blissfully happy. The fact that airplanes were uncertain seemed to add to his pleasure. Once on his return to London, a valve burst, the engine spluttered and the plane descended towards the gray water. The pilot made a gesture that there was nothing he could do. Then the engine coughed, the plane rose unsteadily and the pilot headed back to France, where he managed to land without damage. On another occasion the pilot had to make a forced landing on English soil. "He sideslipped artistically between two tall elms, just missing the branches," wrote Winston. [4]

Edward Marsh often flew with him. Together they visited Jack Churchill, now a camp commandant, of whom Winston observed, "Jack is an extraordinary fellow—quite unborable." The Minister who provided the munitions was as pleased as Punch at the men recognizing and cheering him. He especially went up to Arras to visit his old regiment, the Royal Scots Fusiliers, in the line. One irresistible daylight raid put the timetable two hours out. "Winston's disregard of time, when there's anything he wants to do, is sublime—he firmly believes that it waits for him." [7]

One summer day, he himself was handling the plane's control and executing a turn one hundred feet over Croydon Airdrome, when the machine refused to respond to the stick. "We were scarcely ninety feet above the ground. The sunlit airdrome seemed bathed in a baleful yellowish glare. A thought formed in my brain: 'This is very like death.' The plane struck the ground with terrific force. Its left wing crumpled and its propeller and nose plunged into the earth. I felt myself driven forward by a frightful and overwhelming force. There was a sense of unendurable oppression across my chest as my belt took the strain. Suddenly the pressure ceased, the belt parted, and I fell forward quite gently on the dial board in front of me, safe." Two hours later he spoke at a House of Commons dinner. [2]

When someone asked him whether he was not afraid at such moments, he replied: "No, I love life, but I don't fear death."

Winston was at the Front when the great and final offensive against the British opened in March, 1918. This was Ludendorff's last hope of winning the war. Both Russia and Italy had collapsed, and the Germans were free to concentrate most of their force in the West. Although the United States had been in the war for a year it had only two hundred thousand men in the line. Ludendorff knew the Americans would be arriving in strength throughout the summer and decided to stake everything on a final, knockout blow before that time. This offensive lasted forty days and cost Britain three hundred thousand casualties.

During the next days an alarming rumor spread that the French regarded the defeat of the British armies as inevitable and, instead of sending reinforcements, were planning to break contact with them. Lloyd George summoned Winston and asked him to hurry to France and find out what was happening. "Go and see everybody," he said. "Use my authority. See Foch. See Clemenceau. Find out for yourself whether they are making a really big move or not."

Clemenceau greeted him with the message: "Not only shall Mr. Winston Churchill see everything, but I will myself take him tomorrow to the battle and we will visit all the commanders of corps and armies engaged."

The next day the two statesmen set forth accompanied by high officials and staff officers, in a fleet of military cars decorated with satin tricolors. First they visited Foch, who gave them a brilliant exposition of the battle, ending emotionally with the assurance that the enemy effort was nearly exhausted. *"Alors, Général, il faut que je vous embrasse,"* said Clemenceau, and the two Frenchmen clasped each other tightly. Next they went to the headquarters of the British Fourth Army, where they had lunch with Sir Douglas Haig. Clemenceau and Haig withdrew to an adjoining room. When they came out Haig seemed content and the Tiger was smiling. "It is all right," he said, "I have done what you wish. If your men are tired and we have fresh men near at hand, our men shall come at once and help you. And now, I shall claim my reward."

The reward was to see the battle. The army commanders protested, but Clemenceau insisted on being driven as far forward as possible. Shells whistled overhead and even Winston finally protested that Clemenceau ought not to go under fire too often. *"C'est mon grand plaisir,"* replied the old Frenchman.

The British lines held, and the British and French armies did not break contact. [4]

It was a particular satisfaction for Churchill to produce the new tanks, the Big Willies, which had been so derided when he first pressed for their development in the early days of the war. [42]

They had been prematurely and inefficiently used on the Somme in September, 1916, when Haig, after the appalling casualty lists of his offensive, had seized on a handful of Churchill's tanks as an expedient that might break the deadlock. Churchill pleaded with Asquith not to allow this disclosure of the new weapon before it could be used in mass formation with decisive effect; but he pleaded in vain. The soldiers were permitted to play with their new toy. The enemy was rattled considerably, but no real breakthrough was achieved. The next morning people read correspondents' accounts of the monsters. [9]

The "herd" of tanks, ran *The Times* report, "huge, shapeless bulks painted in venomous reptilian colors, resembling nothing else that was ever seen on earth, wandered hither and thither like vast antediluvian brutes which Nature had made and forgotten." Above all they were absurd. At each new antic "one could do nothing but sit down and laugh till one's sides ached." And a British airman sent this message in the excitement: "A tank is walking up the High-street of Flers with the British army cheering behind."

More than twelve months were to elapse before, at the battle of Cambrai, adequate use was made of the new weapon, by which date Churchill was Minister of Munitions. Then, for the first time conditions were suited to tank warfare—"a battle made for them," as Churchill proudly said. On November 20, 1917, three hundred and seventy-eight fighting tanks and ninety-eight auxiliary tanks opened the attack without preliminary bombardment. The enemy was completely surprised. The German lines were penetrated on a six-mile front; ten thousand prisoners and two hundred guns were captured. The British lost only fifteen hundred men! [30]

Had there been troops to follow through, a crucial victory might have been gained. But those reserves were lacking: they had been lost in the Somme and sunk in the slime of Passchendaele. Presently the Germans recovered from their fright and came probing back to find small and unsupported forces holding the area they had abandoned. They retook it and Cambrai became the symbol of a lost victory. [9]

But "moving power" now began to have its ardent supporters: on Lloyd George's order tank production rapidly increased, recruiting for the Tank Corps redoubled, training establishments expanded. Winston's victory was won. [4]

On August 8, 1918, the British opened the Allied counter-offensive before Amiens in one of the decisive battles of the world. Six hundred tanks were employed (three hundred and twenty-four of them weighing over thirty tons apiece), and low-flying airplanes created a "noise barrage" as the tanks emerged from an artificial fog. Four days later, twenty-two thousand prisoners and four hundred guns had been taken. When the news came in Churchill got into his airplane and took a couple of days' holiday on the battlefield. Rawlinson, an old friend of Omdurman and Antwerp, and his Fourth Army had used the tanks as they ought to be used. From the Chateau Verchouq, a month later, Churchill sent the Prime

Minister a memorandum that could have been written by nobody else: "The tank men are killed and wounded in considerable numbers, and the wastage of the personnel is high, whereas the tank in any victorious battle recovers very quickly from his wounds and hardly ever dies beyond the hope of recovery. A few months in the grave is nearly always followed by a reincarnation." [3o]

November 11, 1918. "For four years Germany fought and defied the five continents of the world by land and sea and air," wrote Churchill. "Small states were trampled down in the struggle; a mighty Empire was battered into unrecognizable fragments; and nearly twenty million men perished or shed their blood before the sword was wrested from that terrible hand. Surely, Germans, for history it is enough!

"On the morning of the Armistice at the eleventh hour I stood at the window of my room at the Hotel Metropol waiting for Big Ben to tell that the war was over. Suddenly the first stroke of the chime. The broad street beneath me was deserted. Then the slight figure of a girl gesticulating distractedly darted from the portal of a nearby building. The bells of London began to clash. From all sides streams of people poured out, hundreds, thousands pushing hither and thither screaming with joy, a seething mass of humanity. The tumult grew like a gale. Flags appeared as if by magic. After fifty-two months of gaunt distortion, suddenly and everywhere the burdens were cast down.

"My wife arrived and we decided to go and offer our congratulations to the Prime Minister. No sooner had we entered our car than twenty people mounted upon it, and in the midst of a wildly cheering multitude we were impelled slowly forward through Whitehall." [3h]

PART

2

9

War and Peace

"THE war of the giants," as Churchill called it, was over. The peacemakers flocked to Versailles to wrangle over the bones of Germany, and "the quarrels of the pygmies" had begun. [44]

Now that the terrible conflict was over Winston's instinct was to hold out the hand of friendship to Germany. Germany, he argued, should be brought into the democratic family as soon as possible. He urged Lloyd George to send a dozen food ships to blockaded Hamburg But public opinion was hostile to the idea. Nothing was done until General Plumer, in command in Germany, threatened to resign if food were not sent and got his way. [4]

At the Paris Peace Conference, while Clemenceau and Lloyd George strove to formulate settlements based on reason and reality, their countrymen howled for blood and gold. Wilson, the first President of the United States to embark for foreign soil, had formulated his famous "Fourteen Points" as a foundation upon which peace could be built. He sailed "with his head in the clouds," and there it remained.

"The showdown came at the third meeting," wrote Lincoln Steffens, "as Wilson repetitively voiced his dream of a 'permanent peace.'" Suddenly Clemenceau confronted the President bluntly with the realities of war and peace. "We can make this permanent peace," he roared. "We can remove the causes of war." France, he went on, must abandon her African possessions, Britain must relinquish India, and America the Philippines and Puerto Rico; all nations must have complete access to all markets without hindrance and surrender their spheres of influence. "Are you willing to pay these prices?" he demanded. "For if not," and he brought his fist down on the table, "you don't mean permanent peace. You mean war."

Finally Wilson went home, disillusioned with everyone but himself, to find his attempts at peacemaking and American membership in the League of Nations rejected by Congress. [54]

The territorial provisions of the treaty of Versailles left Germany practically intact. The economic clauses of the treaty were malignant and obviously futile. Germany was condemned to pay reparations on a fabulous scale. Few voices were raised to explain that payment of reparations can only be made by services or goods, and that when they arrive in the demanding countries they dislocate the local industry. When Marshal Foch heard of the signing of the Peace Treaty he observed with singular accuracy: "This is not peace. It is an armistice for twenty years." [3a]

In Britain, the end of hostilities was the signal for a general election. The Representation of the People Act, passed in the spring of 1918, had widely extended the franchise and given votes to women. There was impatience to put this reform into practice. The Coalition Government appealed to the country on its war record and scored a sweeping majority, roughly three to one. Great parliamentarians such as Asquith disappeared. [9]

At Dundee the inexhaustible teetotaler Scrymgeour, who had settled into a career of being defeated at the polls by Winston Churchill, implored Dundee to turn the tippler out. Instead, the city stamped its approval on Churchill by voting him an immense majority. Soon he found himself in the unprecedented position of holding two offices—Secretary for War and Secretary for Air. [8]

"Whew!" wrote Sir Henry Wilson, chief of the Imperial General Staff, in his diary, and inquired acidly on meeting his new chief why the Admiralty had not been thrown in as well.

Grave difficulties had blown up over demobilization. Close to four million men under arms were clamoring to be released all at once. A rational scheme had been drawn up earlier to release the key men wanted in industry first, but these were the very men who had been called up to the forces last. [7]

Veterans of the war, men who had been wounded and gone back to the trenches two or three times, were expected to wait for their papers and watch the key men scurry back home to get the pick of the jobs. By January 1919 there were riots at Glasgow and Belfast. At Calais three or four thousand armed men took possession of the town, and two divisions had to be detached from the Army of Occupation to restore order. And in Whitehall Churchill watched while Grenadiers with fixed bayonets rounded up a body of three thousand demonstrators.

Within two days after Churchill took over at the War Office he had summoned Sir Douglas Haig from France for consultation; a week later he crossed the Channel to obtain sanction for his proposals from Lloyd George, then engaged in the Peace Conference in Paris. The new orders got rid of the hated "key man"; release was determined by length of service, and those retained got double pay to reduce the gap between military and civilian rates. Finally the Army of Occupation on the Continent was provided for by retaining the young men who completed their training but had not previously gone overseas.

With the issue of the new orders discontent vanished, discipline was restored and demobilization proceeded uneventfully. At the end of six months a force of over three million men had been released and reabsorbed in civilian life—no mean feat of organization. [2]

But a more gigantic problem faced Winston as War Minister. At the other side of Europe, the huge, sprawling, year-old Bolshevik Russian Republic had made peace with the Germans. In order to keep a fighting front going in the East, the Allies had rushed soldiers into Russia to bolster the White Russian elements who rejected Bolshevism and were still loyal to the alliance. The question now was whether, since the Germans were beaten, they should be withdrawn. [1]

Churchill was obsessed by the dangers of Bolshevism and the threat that the spread of international communism constituted to the civilized world. With the sense of history that so distinguished him among statesmen, he sensed the appeal the evil thing would have, the menace it would grow into, if left to itself to foster and spread. "Of all the tyrannies in history, the Bolshevist is the worst, the most destructive, the most degrading." Lloyd George disagreed with him and wanted to come to terms with the Russians: "His ducal blood," he said of Churchill, "revolted against the wholesale elimination of Grand Dukes in Russia." [7]

Russia was now the scene of revolution and counterrevolution. Lenin and the Bolsheviks had a precarious hold in the capital, St. Petersburg (now Leningrad), and central provinces. In the outer provinces there were a number of anti-Bolshevik movements, led by Admiral Deniken, General Kolchak and others. And in north Russia, there were twelve thousand British and eleven thousand Allied troops. [2]

In the House of Commons Churchill attacked "the foul baboonery of Bolshevism" and came out openly in favor of sending arms to the White Russian forces. But there was no action he could take without the approval of the Supreme Council in Paris. He also sent a flow of memoranda to every influential quarter. Finally in May, 1919, the Supreme Council came to a decision: the Allies would assist Kolchak with munitions, supplies and food to establish a Government of all Russia; at the same time the Allies must soon withdraw their own troops "to avoid interference in the internal affairs of Russia." At last Winston had the authority to act. He poured ammunition and matériel worth many millions of pounds into Russia and made plans for the evacuation of the British forces. For this he called for a volunteer army of eight thousand men. The British public stirred with alarm. Was he trying to plunge them into another war? He was immediately attacked by almost every Labor leader in England. [4]

The White Russian armies went into action with some success, and Allied soldiers, while doing no fighting themselves, cooperated. Once it seemed that Moscow might fall to General Deniken's Whites, and Lloyd George only barely restrained Winston from hastening to the scene in person. "Winston wants to ride on a white charger through Moscow," he told a friend irritably, for he was angry at Winston's stand. [1]

The task of retreating twelve thousand men two hundred and fifty miles up the river Dvina to Archangel in order to embark and evacuate them was extremely hazardous. Andrew Soutar, special correspondent to *The Times*, attached to the British forces at Archangel, returned to London to report to his paper. Winston sent for him. [2]

"When I entered Winston's room," wrote Soutar, "he greeted me affably, placed a chair in position for me so that I should face him and began: 'Now, tell me all about it.' On his writing pad he had a single sheet of paper and a lead pencil.

"I began to describe the situation. His stolid expression conveyed to me the idea that the names of Russian villages and trails and positions were simply blending into a mournful song that came to him from a vast distance. I said to him: 'Give me your pencil and I'll give you a rough sketch with the names of the places.'

" 'I have them all in my head,' he said. And to my surprise, he named village after village, point after point—villages with unproncunceable names. The area covered thousands of miles! He knew his North Russia perfectly. He got to his feet. 'Come and see Wilson,' he said and put his arm over my shoulder to hurry me across the floor.

"In a small map room we found Sir Henry Wilson, Chief of the General Staff, a tall, angular man with a long, hooked, lean nose and a pair of blue, Irish, military eyes. I explained the situation to him. He was most charming, but insisted repeatedly he couldn't send another man out there. 'I really don't think the situation is so serious,' he began. 'Listen to what he's telling you, Wilson,' Churchill interrupted. 'Send Rawlinson out on a destroyer, tonight, and let him fetch them out!' There it was—quick, decisive, unanswerable." [52]

Rawlinson did go out that night on a destroyer, a wise decision. As a result, the removal of British, American, French, and Italian soldiers with their stores was accomplished almost without loss. [2]

With the withdrawal of the Allied troops, Kolchak's armies disintegrated. On January 3, 1920, Denikin's armies were decimated and the fighting ended, leaving the Union of Soviet Socialist Republics alone to take its uncertain but giant steps toward world supremacy. [1]

The great powers, said Churchill, "would learn to regret the fact that they had not been able to take a more decided and more united action to crush the Bolshevist peril at its heart and center before it had grown too strong." For having "done everything in his power to help the loyal anti-Bolshevist forces" Churchill would have to pay with the prolonged distrust and hostility of the political and industrial forces of labor over the next two decades. [7]

Churchill's Russian intervention had lost few lives but a huge amount of money, and his relations with Lloyd George had cooled. After more or less winding up the responsibilities of the Ministry, he hoped to be made Chancellor of the Exchequer. To his intense disappointment he was now given the Colonial Office. [1]

Throughout his life Winston had never received any credit as a peacemaker, yet in the brief eighteen months he was at the Colonial Office he was largely responsible for bringing about two vitally important and lasting peace settlements. The first was in the Middle East. Despite the bitter opposition of the Arabs, the Peace Conference had given the mandate of Syria to the French, who then threw out the Emir Feisal from Damascus. As a result Palestine and Egypt were smoldering with discontent, and a bloody uprising had been suppressed in Iraq. To preserve order, the British were obliged to keep forty thousand troops stationed there, costing the Government £30,000,000 a year. The Prime Minister asked Winston to see what he could do to restore harmony and save the British taxpayer money. Winston set about the matter in his usual independent fashion. [4]

First he created a Middle East Department and then stunned everybody by announcing that he was calling in Colonel T. E. Lawrence—the mysterious, nomadic "Lawrence of Arabia"—to act as adviser to the Government. In the England of the period, this was regarded as beyond the pale: Lawrence was a renegade from his race, a man who had disappeared into the shifting dunes of an inscrutable land to take up life with a heathen people. During the Peace Conference after the war, he had turned up in Paris on behalf of his Arab brothers garbed in the Arabian burnoose and with a formidable dagger thrust into a wide red belt. Offered the Commander of the Bath and the Distinguished Service Order by the King, he turned the honor aside casually. He had been snubbed socially by everybody except Churchill. [8]

Lawrence fused Churchill's faith in his inner vision of what life could and should be. Men could be larger than life size. Of their meeting in Paris Churchill wrote: "From amid the flowing draperies his noble features, his perfectly chiseled lips and flashing eyes loaded with fire and comprehension shone forth. He looked what he was, one of Nature's greatest princes." [54]

Early in the spring of 1921 Churchill called a conference at Cairo and asked Lawrence to attend. [34]

Scotland Yard detailed Sergeant (later Detective Inspector) W. H. Thompson to watch over Churchill. His job was quietly to keep the impulsive Minister in view. [8]

[Excerpts from W. H. Thompson's Report]: "After several days of conference, at which Churchill seemed, by merely adjusting his glasses, to adjust himself to finding a way out when there was none, there came a few days for sightseeing. We drove to the pyramids so that Churchill could paint them. As he painted and smoked by the hour a group of British Tommies came along, off duty. With his back turned to them, Churchill, now under a green umbrella, looked like an upholstered toad slowly incinerating itself. Loud stage whispers of advice came from the Tommies. They wondered if, instead of painting the pyramids, the man might do better to repair them. At this sally, Churchill turned and grinned broadly. 'Gawd! It's Winston!' cried the Tommies.

"From Cairo we headed for the Holy Land. Our train stopped at Gaza. At the hall where Churchill was to speak before a gathering of tribes a great cheer went up from the howling, squealing mob of Lebanese, Iraqui, Turks and Jews outside. Lawrence, robed, burnoosed, sashed, scimitared and slippered, raised his hand slowly for silence, then deferentially waved Churchill ahead with a low sweep of his arm. They went inside and I stood on the porch above the crowd. After two hours I began to feel the crowd's impatience. They started to attack the mounted police who charged in, sabers drawn. Suddenly I realized what the people were crying: 'Shershill! Shershill!' They wanted to see the great man!

"At this instant Lawrence showed himself, held up his

hand and invoked the blessings of Allah, smiled, turned back to the door, opened it and stood proudly beside it, ushering forth Churchill.

"Churchill just stood there, smiling and nodding like a chubby choir boy with the chores of a long service behind him. The crowd cheered and in a joyous rhythm called his name over and over again. We walked slowly back through Gaza, thousands following and pressing about our little procession, to the train. As we pulled away, Churchill stood up at the end of his carriage, while the crowd salaamed in tireless exercise, and a stampede of magnificent horses raced the train for many miles." [55]

"In a few weeks," wrote Lawrence, "Churchill made straight all the tangle." Years later he inscribed a copy of *The Seven Pillars of Wisdom:* "Winston Churchill, who made a happy ending to this show." [7]

It was a brilliant settlement: Britain repaired the injury done to the Arabs by placing the Emir Feisal on the throne of Iraq, troops were withdrawn from Iraq and order maintained by the air force alone, cutting down the cost from £30,000,-000 to £5,000,000. And third, an adjustment was made between the Arabs and Jews in Palestine. The Arab world subsided. [4]

Winston's next task of peacemaking was in Ireland, now in a state of savage civil war. [9]

Relations between the Irish and the Mother Country had deteriorated badly since the war. The Sinn Feiners wanted to sever all connection with England and establish a republic and were prepared to use any methods to realize their aim. They began to burn down houses and murder English officials. The British Government retaliated by sending a special police force who became known as the "Black and Tans," who were instructed to make severe reprisals. [4]

The British conscience was horrified by the terrible tales that filtered back of the deeds of these ruffians, and Lloyd

George decided to make an earnest bid for a peaceful settlement with the Sinn Fein leaders. De Valera came to England, bringing Michael Collins, Arthur Griffith and other Sinn Fein leaders with him. [9]

"One night Mr. Griffith and Mr. Collins came to my house to meet the Prime Minister," wrote Churchill. "It was a crisis and the negotiations seemed to hang only by a thread. Michael was in his most difficult mood, full of reproaches and defiances. 'You hunted me night and day,' he exclaimed. 'You put a price on my head.' 'Wait a minute,' I said. 'You are not the only one.' And I took from my wall the framed copy of the reward offered for my capture by the Boers. 'At any rate yours was a good price—£5,000. Look at me—£25 dead or alive. How would you like that!' He read the paper, broke into a happy laugh, his irritation vanished. Thereafter we never lost the basis of a common understanding." [3i]

At length a treaty was signed, whereby Southern Ireland accepted the temporary severance of Northern Ireland. The Dail ratified the treaty and set up a constitutional government. [9]

"Tell Winston," said Collins, "we could not have done anything without him." Two days later Collins was killed by the gunfire of Dublin extremists. [8]

De Valera had slipped back to Dublin, denounced the pact and branded the fellow negotiators as traitors; a dissenting minority, headed by De Valera, carried on a rebellion against their own government. Outrages continued throughout 1922 along the Ulster border, and in June Sir Henry Wilson was shot in London by a couple of I.R.A. assassins. But by degrees the Irish Government established its control and at last, after seven hundred years of strife and barbarism, Ireland saw the dawning of peace and progress.[9]

10

The Strikebreaker

SINCE the war the Conservatives had been increasingly restive under Lloyd George's coalition. In October 1922 they mutinied and voted to withdraw. Lloyd George promptly called a general election. [1]

The Conservatives scored a sweeping victory. Lloyd George never held office again. Winston fought the election at Dundee, the great Radical working-class stronghold whose electorate was not at all convinced that Winston was a Liberal. "Wherever Mr. Churchill is there is his party," said *The Times*. Most of all they resented his interference in Russia. Three days before the contest opened, however, he was stricken with appendicitis and rushed off to the hospital for an operation. [4]

Dangerously soon after the surgery he summoned a quartet of stretcher-bearers. "Let us proceed to Dundee," he told them. "I have some electioneering to do." He was transported by stretcher and train to his Scottish constituency and carried in a chair onto a platform at the town hall, made no mention of his peculiar appearance, but addressed the large gathering from his seated position. [8]

"I draw no distinction between Socialists and Communists," he began. "I stand as a Liberal and Free Trader." His remarks were the signal for continuous heckling and uproar. Churchill, a sick man, could not make himself heard beyond the edge of the platform. The meeting was abandoned. [2]

Dundee's electorate not only discarded him by twelve thousand votes; they added insult to infamy by giving his seat to the Prohibitionist Scrymgeour, whom he had beaten five times running. [36]

"In the twinkling of an eye," said Churchill, "I found myself without an office, without a seat, without a party and without an appendix." Returning to London from Dundee he stopped his car for a moment in Parliament Square and looked at the great mass of the Houses of Parliament. "Fancy," he said to a companion, "after a quarter of a century as an M.P. I have no right as a Member to enter the House." [1]

Winston was still weak from his appendix operation, and the doctor agreeably recommended the sunshine and sea air of Cannes. Mr. and Mrs. Churchill left for the South of France accompanied by a maid, valet and secretary, plenty of foolscap and his painting kit. Every afternoon Churchill put up his easel on the beach or along the quiet country lanes and painted to his heart's content. He had exhibited five landscapes in Paris in 1921 under the name of Charles Morin and sold four of them for £30 each.

But whereas painting was a pastime, writing was a business. Although he had produced no book since the biography of his father appeared sixteen years earlier, he still regarded the creation of books as his chief occupation after politics, and as soon as he reached the South of France he settled down to work. He worked every morning dictating to his secretary, often pacing up and down the room chewing a cigar. He could talk a book better than write one and often got through three to four thousand words a day. The first of the four volumes of *The World Crisis* appeared in April 1923 and the second in October of the same year. [4]

It was a sensational best-seller critically acclaimed for its weight of words, revelations and imagery, although Balfour described it gently as "Winston's brilliant autobiography disguised as a history of the universe." [1]

From the royalties (£30,000) and a legacy from a great-grandmother, he bought Chartwell, a handsome manor house in Kent. [10]

"The garden at Chartwell contained a large pond," wrote John Churchill, "choked with weeds, which my uncle grandly insisted on calling a lake. No time was wasted in producing a lake worthy of the name. Earth-moving equipment arrived, complete with an army of stout-armed men in overalls. We were all issued boots and spades and ordered to contribute to the work—no guest, however mighty his status in the world outside, was exempt. The pond was drained, the weeds and mud cleared and a wide dam built to control the outflow of water from a spring near the house.

"The lake, about three hundred yards long, was nearly finished when my uncle conceived yet another scheme. Why not have an upper lake for fish? More earthworks, more railway lines and workmen. The lake had started to fill, when plans were drawn up for an upper-*upper* lake for swimming." [17]

Few swam there, though Winston put up a diving board from which he would launch his happy hulk first into the air, then into the complaining waters, using a flailing trudgen that showered onlookers twenty feet away. [55]

Churchill also worked with a professional bricklayer five or six hours a day until he could lay a brick a minute and constructed with his own hands a large part of two cottages. Dressed in workman's overalls with a comical hat on his head, he liked to discuss affairs of state with his guests while he worked. [4]

"See that wall?" he would ask. "You cannot imagine the amount of fun I had building it. I planned out a couple of books while I was laying the bricks." [30]

At the invitation of the general secretary he joined the

Amalgamated Union of Building Trade Works, paid a fee of five shillings and was rated an "adult apprentice." This drew forth a furious outcry. [4]

The union members were proud to include an important M.P. in their membership. The union's council, however, was not, and the president asked Churchill to resign. Churchill was first hurt, then majestically furious. He reminded the union that they had sought his membership and he'd lay bricks with the best of them in a public exhibit to prove his competence; those who were dragging in his "incidental duties" as King's Minister were laying down a smokescreen over the dignity of organized, skilled labor. [55]

Churchill's eccentricities along the line of dress were becoming a public joke. On several occasions while riding with his mother in London's fashionable Rotten Row, he had been taken for her groom. His hats began to be caricatured in *Punch,* and the Guild of London Tailors recorded an official protest against his "sartorial terrifics." At length his clothing came to have a sort of museum value, greatly sought after by collectors. A man arrested for breaking into a secondhand store explained he had spied a fur-lined overcoat, full of holes, which he had recognized as having belonged to Churchill. The proprietor refused to press the charge, doubled the price of the coat. It had an early sale. [8]

In 1923, after Stanley Baldwin—a shrewd, kind, stolid Englishman who liked the countryside, smoked pipes and was a cousin of Rudyard Kipling's—had succeeded to the premiership, a general election took place. Churchill stood as a Liberal Free Trader at West Leicester, where his chief opponent was a Socialist. Winston's campaign was noisy and excited. His violent attacks on the Labor Party drew packed meetings filled with irate hecklers. He was so bitterly hated by a large section of the working class that a brick was hurled at his car and authorities were sent in to protect him. Winston described the hecklers as "more like Russian wolves than British workmen, howling, foaming and spitting, behaving in a way absolutely foreign to the British working classes." He was defeated by thirteen thousand to nine thousand votes. The Labor Leader, Ramsay MacDonald, became the Prime Minister of England.

A month later, a Conservative seat fell vacant in the Abbey Division of Westminster, the most colorful seat in England; it included Buckingham Palace, the Houses of Parliament, Soho, the Strand, Covent Garden and a slice of theater land. Winston set about trying to get himself adopted as the Conservative candidate. His Tory friends used their influence on his behalf. The by-election was an exciting affair and front page news. A Conservative M.P. lent Winston a luxurious house equipped with priceless Gainsborough pictures as his headquarters. Thirty Conservative M.P.'s and a bevy of beautiful society ladies canvassed for him. [4]

They paraded through ill-lit side lanes of Pimlico with Churchill's pictures. Even more effective than the picture of the candidate was the photograph of his baby daughter, Mary, who smiled "Vote for Daddy!" from all the housefronts. [34]

Churchill wrote: "The chorus girls of Daly's Theatre sat up all night addressing envelopes and dispatching the election address. It was most cheering and refreshing to see so many young and beautiful women of every rank and file ardently working on a purely disinterested cause not unconnected with myself. Incomparably the most exciting, stirring, sensational election I have ever fought. I must confess I thoroughly enjoyed the fight from start to finish." [7]

Despite all the glamor and glitter, he was defeated by forty-three votes. But Winston was far from downcast. He had severed his connection with the Liberals, he had a number of powerful Conservative friends, the goodwill of Stanley Baldwin, the Conservative leader, and every day he was establishing himself more securely as a Conservative champion against the forces of "revolution." In the autumn of 1924, he stood for Epping with Conservative support. This time he was successful. A few days later Stanley Baldwin, then Prime Minister, appointed him Chancellor of the Exchequer, the number two post in the Government.

Churchill's first budget was a masterly parliamentary performance. The crowded Chamber expected a lively "show," and Winston did not disappoint them. In the middle he broke off, filled a glass in front of him with excisable liquor and, lifting it, commented cheerfully: "It is imperative that I should fortify the revenue, and this I shall now, with the permission of the Commons, proceed to do." [4]

The House applauded gaily. Churchill smiled. His eyes sought the Gallery, where his wife, his daughter Sarah, and his son Randolph were sitting. In the ranks of the Labor Opposition a lean figure in an ill-fitting Sunday-go-to-meeting suit arose and a voice creaked "Shame! Shame on you!" It was the Prohibitionist Member from his old constituency of Dundee, Mr. Scrymgeour. [34]

One of Churchill's first acts was to put England back on the gold standard for the first time since before the war. This had been the aim of the Treasury and the Bank of England ever since the war, but as it turned out it was a disastrous move. [1]

The coal mines were the first to feel the consequence of Churchill's policy. British coal owners were forced to lower their prices and therefore decided to lower the miners' wages, which would have made mining one of the worst sweated industries in the country. [4]

For a while, the Government managed to keep the miners' wages up by subsidies to the coal owners, but when it seemed that the miners might be abandoned by the Government the other unions rushed to give them moral support. On May 4, 1926, a general strike began. Five million British workers downed tools. Inspiring them was a new figure in British affairs, Ernest Bevin. "History will write," he declared, "that it was a magnificent generation that was prepared to do this rather than see the miners driven down like slaves." This brought his hearers to their feet. "Down with Churchill!" [1]

Winston flung himself into the fray with unconcealed relish. Since there were no newspapers he persuaded the proprietor of the *Morning Post* to lend him his plant. With the help of several of Lord Beaverbrook's typesetters he published a daily paper called the *British Gazette*. "For King and Country" became his battle-cry. Labor Members attacked Winston in the House of Commons for falsifying the news. [4]

Not for a long time had Winston enjoyed himself so much. He stood among the presses—his presses—and listened to the sweet music of their roar, walked among the compositors and linotype operators bent over their tasks. [1]

"He brought a submarine crew up from Davenport to help with the machines," wrote Colin Coote, "and London University students who were studying printing to try their hands at the linotypes. He asked the Automobile Association for volunteers who raced to the office in cars of every vintage and threw bundles of papers at every news agent's shop they saw. He appointed Admiral Hall chief of personnel and security officer. When hotheads in a huge crowd outside tried to start trouble, Churchill sent for police reinforcements who were billeted in the office. One or two attacks were made on men leaving the building. He sent for the army. Irish guards soon joined the policemen in the canteen.

"On the second night he went down to the machine room to find all the presses at work. On the floor stood large enamel mugs. "What have they got in those?" Churchill asked. "Beer, sir," I replied. "Have they got enough?" he said. "Oh yes, sir, plenty." "Nonsense," said the editor, "there is no such thing as enough beer. Send for some more." A pound note changed hands. That night the circulation rose by nearly two hundred thousand and another one hundred thousand copies were added the next night.

"One of my jobs was taking papers off the machine. Suddenly there was a horrible shattering jar. Power was turned off. An oil can was found in the works. Sabotage? Churchill issued orders that no one was to enter the machine room unless he carried a special pass issued by the Treasury; he was meticulous in presenting his every time he went downstairs. Now to repair the ravaged machine before the next night's run." [21]

Winston lighted a cigar and regarded the dying giant. When in doubt call the navy. He asked his admiral to come down. "Can this be fixed at once by the Royal Navy?" he asked. The admiral of course said yes and phoned the Chatham Dockyard, describing what was on its way to their machine shops. The mangled unit of the machinery was isolated from the body of the main assembly, hoisted by block-and-tackle and set in a truck. Cars loaded with police officers rode before and behind the critical cargo. The same afternoon the machinery came back from the Royal Navy all shined up, wrapped in bunting and with a Union Jack sticking out of her top. The next edition appeared as if nothing had happened. [55]

In a week the circulation of the *British Gazette* jumped from two hundred thousand to more than two million and began running out of paper. Winston appropriated the paper supply of *The Times*, whose illustrious editor, Geoffrey Dawson, complained to the Prime Minister. Stanley Baldwin was reading Winston's daily outpouring in growing consternation. In every issue Winston was slamming the trade unions. "For heaven's sake," Baldwin said to Geoffrey Dawson, "give Winston some tips on how to produce a newspaper. Make it out in a letter to me." Dawson did so. Winston replied with a letter of his own on the principles of newspaper production which Dawson had to confess in some delight was "great."

Churchill knew from reports he was receiving from all over the country that the strike was breaking up. He went to the editor's chair at the *British Gazette* office and wrote: "Every man who does his duty by the country and returns to work will be protected by the state from loss of trade union benefits or pension. His Majesty's Government will take whatever steps are necessary in Parliament or otherwise for this purpose." This was signed by the Prime Minister and appeared in heavy type on the front page of the *British Gazette.* On the following day the strike was called off, having lasted seven days and twelve hours. [21]

That night Churchill took a large party to see *Lady Be Good;* its stars were Fred and Adele Astaire. Churchill's party arrived after the show was well started. Adele Astaire recognized Churchill, stopped the show and came to the apron of the stage. "There he is," she cried and called for three cheers for Winston. Winston rose in that rumpled slump of his, bowed and was thrillingly cheered. Then the pit orchestra struck up the opening bars of "God Save the King." "An eloquent testimony," wrote the *Morning Post,* now appearing under its own name again, "to the delight of the London public at the unconditional withdrawal of the general strike." [55]

Sometime after the general strike, when tempers were rising in the House during a speech by Churchill, he paused suddenly, looked fiercely at the Socialist benches, and shouted: "I warn you! If there is another general strike"— the members, tense and angry, waited for the bombshell— "we will let loose on you another *British Gazette.*" The whole House exploded into laughter. [21]

11

A Writer's Hours

WINSTON seldom spent a weekend away from his country house. Chartwell was close enough to London for guests to motor down for lunch and dinner, and almost every Saturday and Sunday there were relays of people coming and going. Winston's favorite relaxation was good political talk. He liked to sit up late at night, woke early in the morning, often did his work in bed, dictating to his secretary and puffing a cigar. His morning work was interrupted frequently by the shouts and cries of his four children, who ranged in age from eleven to one; and when the din was too great he put aside his work and joined them in the garden. They adored his company. He put up a tree house, showed them how to dam the lake and make miniature falls. Like the children themselves, he got so wet he stood dripping outside the house while maids hurried to put newspapers on the floor. He had never forgotten how he himself had longed for his father's confidence and he spent many hours with his son, talking to him as a grown-up and letting him share his interests. Once when he drove Randolph back to Eton he remarked sadly: "I have talked to you more this holiday than my father talked to me in his whole life."

He loved his pet dogs and cats, and was sentimental even about his chickens and geese. A tutor to Churchill's son staying in the house remembers a Sunday lunch when a goose was brought in and placed in front of Mr. Churchill to carve. He plunged the knife in, then paused and said to his wife with deep emotion: "You carve him, Clemmie. He was a friend of mine." [4]

Churchill was in charge of the Treasury for five crowded years, 1924 to 1929, and brought in five budgets. Like his father he did not take to "those damned dots," and this department of state was less congenial to him than any of the numerous others he had occupied.

There is something endearing about a head of that grim department of finance who could say after dinner one evening, when it was all over, "Everybody said that I was the worst Chancellor of the Exchequer that ever was. And now I'm inclined to agree with them." [7]

The election of 1929 put another feeble Labor Government under Ramsay MacDonald into power, obliging Baldwin, Churchill and company to move to the opposite side of the House. [1]

One of the most merciless attacks Churchill ever made in the House of Commons was directed at MacDonald. "I remember when I was a child being taken to the celebrated Barnum's Circus, which contained an exhibition of freaks and monstrosities, but the exhibit which I most desired to see was described as 'The Boneless Wonder.' My parents judged that the spectacle would be too revolting for my youthful eyes, and I have waited fifty years to see the Boneless Wonder sitting on the Treasury Bench." Winston's speech was greeted with howls of laughter; Ramsay MacDonald never forgave him. [4]

Winston remained in the "Shadow Cabinet," which in Great Britain the minority party maintains in anticipation of its eventual return. But the relations between Baldwin and Churchill were worsening daily. In Churchill's words, Baldwin and his supporters were "decided to be undecided, resolved to be irresolute, adamant for drift, all-powerful for impotence."[1]

"It was on India that our definite breach occurred," Churchill recalled. "The Prime Minister pressed forward with his plan of Indian self-government. A conference was held in London, of which Mr. Gandhi, lately released from commodious internment, was the central figure. I felt sure that we should lose India and that measureless disasters would come upon the Indian peoples. I therefore resigned from the Shadow Cabinet." [3a]

To Churchill, Gandhi was "a seditious Middle Temple lawyer posing as a fakir of a type well known in the East, striding half-naked up the steps of the Vice-Regal Palace to parley on equal terms with the representative of the King-Emperor." [10]

At a big demonstration in Albert Hall, Churchill described the India bill as "a hideous act of self-mutilation, astounding to every nation in the world" and denounced "the casting away of that most truly bright and precious jewel in the crown of the King which more than all our other Dominions and Dependencies constitutes the glory and strength of the British Empire." "Unless you are prepared," he told a meeting of businessmen at the Constitutional Club, "to defend your rights and interests in India you will be stripped of every vestige you possess and expelled with ignominy from its shores." In one final speech of denunciation, Winston reiterated all his histrionic prophecies of impending doom in India. [32]

Leo A. Amery, his Harrow schoolmate, rose. "Here endeth the last chapter of the Book of the Prophet Jeremiah," he announced in solemn tones. The House roared. Members had ceased to take Winston seriously on the subject of India.

In 1931 Ramsay MacDonald joined forces with the Conservatives in forming a National Government in order to deal with the financial crisis produced by the American crash.

Although Ramsay MacDonald assumed the premiership, Stanley Baldwin was the real master. Neither man would have Winston in the Government at any price. [4]

Though he kept his seat in Parliament, Churchill became a lonely figure, slumped on the bench below the gangway on the Government side. "I'd quit politics entirely," he told a friend, "were it not for the faint chance I shall one day be Prime Minister." [44]

An anecdote has it that at the time when Churchill found himself in the depth of political wilderness, George Bernard Shaw sent him two complimentary tickets for the first night of a play of his, adding: "Bring a friend, if you have one." Churchill replied that he was detained that night, but would be glad to come to the second performance, "if there is one." [5]

He wrote trifles for newspapers and magazines, gambled at Monte Carlo, played the stock market, receiving, but all too often disregarding, the tips of his American friend, Bernie Baruch, who urged him to stick to his pen. For his potboilers he got the highest rates; no other writer in England, except Shaw, surpassed his earnings of £30,000 a year. [44]

In 1930, he brought out *My Early Life*, a delightful account of his first twenty-six years, probably the most pleasant thing he ever wrote, followed by two volumes of collected essays. [42]

He also did more and more painting. "Painting a picture," he said, "is like trying to fight a battle. It is, if anything, more exciting. In all battles, two things are usually required of the Commander in Chief: to make a good plan for his army and to keep a strong reserve. Both of these are also obligatory upon the painter." [30]

At the end of 1931 he went with Mrs. Churchill to America on a lecture tour and arrived in New York harbor on December 11. Reporters crowded around him on the sundeck of the ship. "The cooperation of the two great English-speaking nations," he said, "is the only hope to bring the world back to the pathway of peace and prosperity. Wherever the pathway leads, we shall travel more securely if we do it together like good companions."

His first lecture, on "The Destiny of the English-Speaking Peoples," was set for December 14 in the Brooklyn Academy of Arts and Music. Churchill went to spend the preceding evening with Bernard M. Baruch. He got out of the car, crossed Fifth Avenue and was run down by a taxi. "It's my fault!" he managed to say. Accustomed to English left-hand traffic he had walked blindly into the car. Mario Contasino, the hackdriver, was immediately exonerated.

At one o'clock in the morning the Lenox Hill Hospital issued the first bulletin: the patient had a sprained right shoulder, with lacerations on the forehead and nose. A slight attack of pleurisy complicated the injury. The telephone rang incessantly. London calling, London calling. The King inquired. Fleet Street asked questions. After a few hours cables had to be brought into the room in laundry baskets. The faithful Thompson of Scotland Yard, standing guard at the door, searched them methodically for American reporters who might be using them as a ruse to get in. When Contasino learned who had run into his cab, he set up an Italian aria of despair. He finally calmed down when Churchill shook hands with him. The handshake, of course, also appeared in the tabloids. Mr. Churchill gave the Contasino family an inscribed copy of his latest book. [34]

Then from his bed of pain he dashed off a lurid description of the episode, for which he received $2500. [44]

It was enough for him to take a rest trip to the Bahamas. One day in Nassau, nearly run down by a young Negro driving too fast, he leaped out of the way and grabbed the top posts of a board fence, in the clutch of old-fashioned fear. Sweat poured down his cream-colored shirt and left him weak and shaking. "They almost got me that time, Thompson," he said, almost piteously. [55]

"I gradually regained at Nassau enough strength to crawl around," wrote Churchill. "In this condition I undertook a tour of forty lectures throughout the United States, living all day on my back in a railway compartment, and addressing in the evening large audiences. On the whole I consider this was the hardest time I have had in my life." [3a]

Back in England he was being urged by friends to attack the enormous volume of papers in the Blenheim archives and to write a definitive biography of the Duke of Marlborough, a task which was to have a vital influence on his outlook and whole personality. [1]

He liked being involved in a major work. "Writing a long and substantial book," he explained, "is like having a friend and companion at your side to whom you can always turn for comfort and amusement."

The story of Marlborough is the story of a struggle for power, the essence of history. It gave Winston the opportunity to vindicate his ancestor and also the opportunity to study the art of war, which had always fascinated him. But even more important than the battles was the cause for which they were fought: the freedom of England and the independence of Europe, a theme to which he responded with all the fire of his being. [4]

He assembled around him the usual relays of secretaries to take the stream of words as he dictated them, and researchers and archivists to check his manuscripts, and labored at his task through the night and into the small hours of the morning. [1]

Even in those days he maintained that he needed only six hours' sleep at the most. At seven A.M., he used to wake up and study all the newspapers. Breakfast was at eight, with a menu that often included beef. Then came work on *Marl-*

borough until lunch at one-fifteen, with a break around eleven for an inspection of the garden. On the way back indoors he visited the goldfish. [17]

He was crazy about fish. His study was lined with small tanks in which the brilliant creatures darted. Out of doors, when he visited his fishponds, he lured the carp to take maggots from his hand. [54]

Lunch was accompanied by champagne and followed by port, brandy and a cigar until three or four P.M., when he resumed *Marlborough* until five-o'clock tea, which was improved by a whiskey and soda. Further work was done until dinner at eight-fifteen. Dinner lasted, with more champagne, port, brandy and cigars, until ten or eleven P.M., at which hour he retired for more dictating, plus whiskeys and soda, until two or three o'clock in the morning.

"I never ceased to marvel," wrote John Churchill, "at the emphasis he put on being able to switch his mind from one subject to another. He would suddenly stop work on the Marlborough book and go out to lay bricks for a new wall or paint a picture or feed the fish or write a political article. Whatever he was doing absorbed his attention so completely that obviously he had forgotten his previous task.

"During some dinner hours there were long periods of silence and thought, which were bearable when two or three of us were present because we could talk in undertones. One evening I was alone with Sarah, my uncle and Mr. Cat. The table was long and very narrow. My uncle sat at the head, and Sarah and I were opposite each other at the middle. At the far end, facing my uncle, was Mr. Cat, sitting on a cushion which had been placed on a chair.

"For this particular meal Mr. Cat was given a slice of pheasant and some cream, which he ate from a plate on the table without making a mess. Mr. Cat got the hiccoughs. At exactly the same moment my uncle got hiccoughs as well, with the result that the two of them seemed to be gravely bowing to each other. Sarah and I had to stuff our table napkins in our mouths in case we laughed. My uncle noticed and was very displeased. 'What on earth do you think you are doing?' he asked crossly. 'I do not see anything funny at all.'

"One evening when the ladies had left the dining room the curtains moved and Mr. Cat appeared. 'Oh, look,' said my uncle brightly. 'Cat has a mouse.' He toyed with his prey, but my uncle was not in the least put out by the drama being played in front of him. The rest of us felt a bit green. 'How interesting to see him exercise control over his victim,' he commented. After a tense moment or two my uncle declared: 'Now is the time.' Suddenly, the entire mouse disappeared down Mr. Cat's throat, head first; he cleaned his whiskers and silently stepped over to the fire for a nap. A stricken silence followed. 'You see,' observed my uncle proudly, 'a whole army destroyed in one move!' " [17]

Churchill's life of Marlborough proved to be a monumental work, running to four volumes. The result was a notable exercise in self-revelation. As he wrote, much of his surface arrogance seemed to fade, the chips fell from his shoulder. "In Marlborough," said Leo Amery, always an honest friend, "Winston found his true model, the fusion of political and military ideas for which he had all his life been groping." [1]

He visited every battlefield on which Marlborough fought, studying the composition of the armies until he knew the strategy and tactics as well as Marlborough himself. He made one of these expeditions abroad in the summer of 1932. [4]

"As our family, and my old friend and technical adviser Professor Frederick Lindemann, wended our way from one ancient city to another from the Netherlands to the Danube," he wrote, "I asked questions about the Hitler Movement, the prime topic in every German mind. In Munich a gentleman introduced himself: Herr Hanfstaengl, a favorite of the Fuehrer. Speaking excellent English, he gave a most interesting account of Hitler's activities. I asked him to dine. He had probably been told to get in touch with me. After dinner he went to the piano and played and sang all the English tunes that I liked. He said I ought to meet the Fuehrer, that he came every day at five o'clock to the hotel and would be glad to see me. I knew nothing of Hitler's doctrine or record at this time. However, in the course of conversation with Hanfstaengl, I happened to say, 'Why is your chief so violent about the Jews; how can any man help how he is born?' He must have repeated this to Hitler, because the day after he came round with a serious air and said that the appointment he had made with me to meet Hitler could not take place as the Fuehrer would not be coming to the hotel that afternoon. Thus Hitler lost his only chance of meeting me." [3a]

12

The Gathering Storm

SHORTLY after Churchill returned from Munich, Germany flatly demanded the right to rearm. "The timely redress of inequality," *The Times* called it. Winston warned Members of the House of Commons not to delude themselves: "Equal status is not what Germany is seeking. All these bands of sturdy Teutonic youths, marching through the streets and roads of Germany, with the light of desire in their eyes to suffer for the Fatherland, are not looking for status. They are looking for weapons, and, when they have the weapons, believe me they will then ask for the return of their lost territories and lost colonies."

Two months after Winston's speech, in January 1933, Hitler came to power. But the British Government took notice neither of Churchill nor Hitler. In March "the MacDonald Plan" urged further disarmament upon the French. Winston attacked it with all his force. "Thank God for the French army," he declared, to the disgust of a large section of the House. The French Government agreed with Winston Churchill and refused to reduce the size of their army. Hitler's answer was to leave the League of Nations. This, said the pacifists, was the logical consequence of France's refusal to cooperate. [4]

The England of the mid-thirties, of which Baldwin was the embodiment, wanted to turn its back on Nazi Germany, hoping that if one didn't look at it, it would go away. Oxford undergraduates held a debate whose motion was: "In the next war this House will not fight for King and Country." The motion was carried. Since Oxford had not won the annual boat race against Cambridge in years, Churchill wondered what was the matter with these young men "who can't row and won't fight." [1]

At one of his infrequent appearances at a party caucus, he delivered a furious tirade against knuckling down to Hitler. "Is it for this," he concluded, "you propose to fling away the ancient heritage bequeathed to us by the architects of our magnitude and renown?" Harold Nicolson followed him out of the room, congratulated him and, as a writing man, asked if he had improvised the final phrase on his feet. "Improvised be damned," Churchill snapped, "I thought of it this morning in my bath and I wish now I hadn't wasted it on this crowd." [44]

The Cliveden Set, which included Geoffrey Dawson of *The Times* and other writers and politicians of all shades of opinion, met at Cliveden, the country home of Lord and Lady Astor; they were all agreed on one thing: the appeasement of Germany. The battles between Winston and Lady Astor were long and furious. "If I were your wife," Lady Astor roared at him, "I would put poison in your coffee." To which Churchill replied with dignity, "And if I were your husband I would drink it." [1]

Winston was convinced that the next war would be largely decided in the air, and uppermost in his mind was the swiftly growing German air force. [4]

"May there not be methods of using explosive energy," he had written in 1925, "incomparably more intense than anything heretofore discovered—a bomb no bigger than an orange with a secret power to blast a township at a stroke and explosives guided automatically in flying machines by wireless without a human pilot in ceaseless procession upon a hostile city? Certainly every one of these new avenues to destruction is being studied on both sides of the Rhine." [3a]

"This cursed hellish invention of war from the air," he now told the House of Commons, "has revolutionized our position. We are not the same kind of country we used to be when we were an island, only twenty-five years ago." He pressed for "an air force at least as strong as that of any Power that can get at us." [26]

The chief disadvantage of being out of office at this time was that Churchill had no official information to support his contentions. And so he set about creating an intelligence service of his own. Close friends at the War Office and the Foreign Office now became frequent visitors to Chartwell. He renewed acquaintanceships in Ministerial circles in France and began to establish new lines in Berlin. Refugees from Nazi Germany and, as time went on, from Austria and Czechoslovakia made their way to Winston's home. Soon his intelligence service was supplying information which made his speeches to the House of Commons important events. [4]

James Drawbell has recorded this scene in his autobiography: "His other activity was writing articles about German rearmament figures which were often hotly refuted in the House of Commons. 'You aren't making much money out of these articles,' I said to him one day at lunch at Chartwell. 'Is it really worth your while?' He glanced at me over the cigar he was lighting. 'I have no complaint. Let me show you something.' He got up and shuffled across to the door in his carpet slippers, returned carrying an ordinary office ledger. This he placed in front of me on the table and opened it. 'You see,' he said, 'it comes to quite a bit in the long run.'

"The ledger contained the record of the resale of his British articles to other newspapers and magazines throughout the world. Particularly the European newspapers, and the price paid for each one. I glanced down the columns, roughly totted up the amount. It hardly seemed proper that Mr.

Churchill should hawk his articles around Europe for *these* amounts. 'It's still not an awful lot,' I said. 'It's almost as if you didn't care how much—or how little—you make so long as you're in these newspapers.'

"He was smiling, the cigar going well. My eyes went back to the ledger. Then something clicked in my brain. In every capital and important city of Europe, in every main newspaper office—these listening posts of secret information— Churchill had established a vital contact with editors and leading journalists. Mr. Churchill took the ledger from me. He said nothing. The smile had gone from his face. 'You know,' I said, 'all this could add up to a pretty useful private Intelligence Service.' He closed the book, looked at me over the rims of his spectacles, his eyes thoughtful and brooding. 'Yes,' he said, 'couldn't it?' " [20]

Although Germany had been forbidden a military air force under the Versailles Treaty, Churchill learned that her large civil aviation force and her national glider clubs had been so organized that they could be expanded instantaneously for war. He warned the House that Britain was only the fifth air power in Europe. [4]

When making a speech he marched up and down the platform like a caged tiger. He looked as if he were about to explode: a square-hewn, heavily breathing man with red spots on his prominent cheekbones, the smooth round face cut up to right and left by a deep furrow, thin lips tightly closed, the eyes more darkly gleaming than in his boyhood pictures, the firm chin resting on a little cushion of fat. [34]

"Germany's illegal air force is rapidly approaching equality with our own," he thundered. "By the end of 1936, that is, two years from now, the German military air force will be nearly fifty per cent stronger, and in 1937 nearly double."

It soon became apparent that Mr. Churchill's private intelligence was far better than the Government's. In March 1935, the German Chancellor stated openly that the German air force had achieved parity with the British. And in May of the same year Stanley Baldwin was forced to make an astonishing retraction to the House. "I was completely wrong." [4]

"The Government majority appeared captivated by Mr. Baldwin's candor," wrote Churchill." There was even a strange wave of enthusiasm for a Minister who did not hesitate to say that he was wrong.

"I felt a sensation of despair. To be entirely convinced and vindicated in a matter of life and death to one's country, and not to be able to make Parliament and the nation heed the warning, or bow to the proof by taking action, was an experience most painful." [3a]

For now the Admiralty added its own folly: an Anglo-German Naval Agreement which was not worth the paper it was written on. [7]

The main feature of the agreement was that the German navy should not exceed one-third of the British. This allowed Germany to set her yards to work at maximum activity for at least ten years with no practical limitation or restraint of any kind. The Admiralty also proceeded to concede to Germany the right to build U-boats, explicitly denied to her in the Peace Treaty, up to sixty to one hundred per cent of the British submarine strength. They immediately laid down the *Bismarck* and *Tirpitz,* the strongest vessels afloat in the world, and had fifty-seven U-boats actually constructed when the war began. [3a]

The Naval Agreement encouraged Mussolini's aggression against Abyssinia and his open defiance of the League. The Labor party, under the leadership of Ernest Bevin, threw over its pacifism to implement the League with force if necessary and bring Mussolini to heel. Profoundly convinced that he must keep the peace at any price, Baldwin took the opportunity to catch the Labor party off balance and force an election on the pledge that he would resist aggression and uphold the League without any large increase in armaments. He won a thumping majority from a bemused country. "Thus an administration more disastrous than any in our history," Churchill sums up, "saw all its errors and shortcomings acclaimed by the nation." [7]

"It had been widely bruited," he wrote, "that I should join the Government as First Lord of the Admiralty. But Mr. Baldwin lost no time in announcing that there was no intention to include me in the Government. There was much mocking in the press about my exclusion. But now one can see how lucky I was. Over me beat the invisible wings. And I had agreeable consolations. I set out with my paintbox for more genial climes without waiting for the meeting of Parliament. Cruising around the eastern coasts of Spain, we landed at Tangier, where I learned that Mr. Lloyd George was at Marrakesh, where the weather was lovely. We all motored thither." [3a]

The Pasha of Marrakesh invited Winston and Lloyd George to a feast served in Arab style, the diners squatting on low divans before great brass dishes and pots in which roast mutton, pigeons, fowls, cous-cous in endless procession were set before them. There were neither plates, knives nor forks, the thumb and first two fingers of the eater's right hand being expected to do the work of tearing portions from chicken carcass and mutton joint, digging out tidbits from the stews and conveying them to the mouth. Winston was at first distinctly embarrassed and awkward at this unfamiliar game. Then, flinging himself into the spirit of the occasion with a sudden schoolboy outburst, he cried: "To hell with civilization!" and plunged his hand up to the wrist in the dish before him. [9]

"I lingered painting in delightful Morocco and did not return till the sudden death of King George V on January 20," he wrote. [3a]

Churchill perceived that a new force had come into being in England. The conquest of Abyssinia had profoundly

134

shocked the British people, and Baldwin's prestige had sunk to its lowest level. Labor and Liberal leaders who had regarded Churchill as an archenemy were now marching behind his banner. He was also supported by a small splinter group of Conservative M.P.'s, but the bulk of the Parliamentary Conservative Party was staunchly behind their leader, Stanley Baldwin. And Baldwin was still determined not to take any risk which might lead to war.

Although Baldwin had excluded Churchill from office, he now offered him a sop: he invited him to sit on the newly constituted Committee of Air Defense Research. Winston asked that Professor Frederick A. Lindemann be placed on the technical subcommittee so that they might work together. For the next five years he mastered every aspect of scientific air defense—including radio-location. [4]

We owe "window," the dropping of strips of tinfoil to simulate a bomber and confuse enemy radar, to Churchill. It was Lindemann's idea in 1937, but it was Churchill, as with many inventions, who pressed it on the Air Defense Research Committee. In each case he was able to grasp the principles, appreciate the possibilities and put behind the scientists all the weight of his authority, spurring them to achieve the "impossible." [21]

By 1939 twenty radar stations were in operation between Portsmouth and Scapa Flow, and it was possible to detect aircraft from fifty to one hundred and twenty miles away flying above ten thousand feet. [4]

"What surprised the Germans," wrote Churchill, "was the extent to which we had turned our discoveries to practical effect and woven all into our general air-defense system. In this we led the world." It was this that tipped the scale against superior numbers in the Battle of Britain. [7]

In March 1936, Hitler electrified Europe by marching into the Rhineland in direct contravention of all the treaties. France was paralyzed with fear. Winston tried to galvanize the world through collective action of the League of Nations. "If Germany fortifies the Rhineland, which she is bound to do," he pointed out, "it will enable the main German forces to swing round through Belgium and Holland." Of all the statesmen in the Western world Winston Churchill alone had perceived the danger. [4]

Baldwin finally gave in to public pressure and agreed to appoint a Minister to coordinate the country's defenses. Everyone expected him to choose Winston. He chose instead a minor politician, Sir Thomas Inskip. "There has been no similar appointment," said one statesman, "since the Roman Emperor Caligula made his horse a consul." One aged lobby correspondent fell off his chair in a dead faint.

At the end of the year England took time off from Hitler for its two-week plunge into the Abdication crisis. Edward VIII, the King of a few months, was determined to marry a middle-aged American woman who had been twice through the divorce courts. Baldwin had always distrusted the heir to the Throne, and many senior politicians shook their heads over inside reports of the Prince's indiscretions. The Prince of Wales fell off horses the way Winston crashed airplanes. Both men meant one thing to the established order of English society: trouble. [1]

Baldwin gave the Sovereign two clear choices: he could either renounce Mrs. Simpson and keep the throne, or wed Mrs. Simpson and abdicate. There was to be no morganatic marriage. Winston had known Edward VIII since his childhood, and as Home Secretary had read out the proclamation creating him Prince of Wales. The King sent for him on his own initiative to ask for advice and help. [4]

When Winston rose in the Commons to plead that Baldwin take no irrevocable decision without consulting the House, he was howled down with such venom that he sank to his seat staggered and abashed. *The Times* with some pleasure reported that it was the worst rebuff in modern political history. [1]

The King chose abdication, and Churchill helped him write an address of farewell. Edward composed the first draft, but Churchill stuck in any number of majestic phrases and smoothed it all up. When the King broadcast the famous speech which began, "At long last I am able to say a few words of my own," Churchill heard it on his radio at Chartwell and modestly commented on the impressive literacy of the King. Then he went up to his workroom, where he resumed his invention of majestic phrases for Marlborough. [8]

Now Baldwin gave way to Neville Chamberlain as Prime Minister. Watching as Baldwin passed in the smoking room, Churchill growled: "Well, the light is at last out of that old turnip." [44]

Thus Baldwin's pipe was replaced by the umbrella as the national symbol. For fifty years or more Neville Chamberlain had stood in the shadow of his great father, Sir Joseph, and his brilliant half-brother Sir Austen. Now with unpretentious casualness he stepped into the foreground. With his black hair surrounded by a band of silver, bushy eyebrows arched over dark eyes, prominent nose jutting from the thin face, his thin lips, upright carriage, invariable black suit with black tie, he looked like a raven. [34]

Chamberlain had been a competent and energetic Lord Mayor of Birmingham before turning to national statesmanship. A matter-of-fact businessman, he could not conceive that any responsible person should be anything else. He would talk turkey with Hitler and Mussolini; he could make bargains with them as one businessman to another, and the world would be able to get on peacefully with its own business. He had no use for the League of Nations or Collective Security. Needless to say, he did not invite Winston to join his new Cabinet. [9]

Anthony Eden, his Foreign Secretary, was the first Minister to be sacrificed to the cause of appeasement. [2]

Eden, the most resolute and courageous figure in the administration, was not a happy man in his office. He feared the Hitler peril and was alarmed by the weakness of Britain's armaments. He tried to convey his misgivings to the Prime Minister, who refused to listen to him and advised him to "go home and take an aspirin." [3a]

Eden was unpopular in Berlin, and in November 1937, Chamberlain quietly arranged for Lord Halifax, who was a master of foxhounds, to go to Germany to visit a hunting exhibition. "But *incidentally*," twittered one of the Cliveden friends, "he will visit Hitler." Two months later Eden resigned on a technicality, and Churchill, seeing almost the last wise head to go, was reduced to despair. [1]

"I must confess that my heart sank," he wrote, "and for a while the dark waves of despair overwhelmed me. In my long life I have had many ups and downs. But now, on this night of February 20, 1938, and on this occasion only, sleep deserted me. One strong young figure standing up against long dismal tides of drift and surrender seemed to embody the life-hope of the British nation. Now he was gone and I saw before me the vision of death." [3a]

For the vacancy at the Foreign Office, Chamberlain chose Lord Halifax, ex-Viceroy of India, Master of Foxhounds. Halifax had barely settled down at his desk before Hitler struck. German troops and Nazi blackshirts advanced into Austria. Austrian democrats in their thousands were plundered, imprisoned, killed. Austrian independence was ended, the state absorbed into the Reich. [2]

A few days later in the House of Commons, Churchill stood addressing the Speaker, his shoulders hunched, his head thrust forward, his hands in his waistcoat pockets. His words rang through the House with terrible finalty. "For five years I have watched this famous island descending incontinently, fecklessly, the stairway which leads to a dark gulf. It is a fine broad stairway at the beginning, but after a bit the carpet ends. A little farther on there are only flagstones, and a little farther on still these break beneath your feet. If mortal catastrophe should overtake the British nation, historians a thousand years hence will never understand how it was that a victorious nation suffered themselves to cast away all that they had gained by measureless sacrifice. Now the victors are vanquished and those who threw down their arms are striding on to world mastery."

When Mr. Churchill sat down there was deep silence for a moment. Then the House broke into a hubbub of noise; Members rattled their papers and shuffled their way to the lobby. Asked what he thought of the speech, a prominent Conservative replied lightly: "Oh, the usual Churchillian filibuster; he likes to rattle the sabre and he does it jolly well." [4]

Three months after snatching Austria, Hitler prepared to seize Czechoslovakia and began to move troops to the Sudetenland frontier. If Czechoslovakia resisted him and war followed, France was pledged to come to her aid and Britain would have to come to the aid of France. Chamberlain worked desperately to avoid this. He sent word to Hitler that he would come to Germany to talk things over. Hitler's first terms were the cession of the Sudetenland. [9]

Chamberlain flew back to London and sought the acquiescence of the Czechs in the dismemberment of their state. Pressed by Britain and France, the Czechs gave their reluctant, heartbroken assent. On his return to Germany for a second meeting, at Godesburg, Chamberlain was informed that he was too late—Hitler had put up the price. Vaster demands were advanced. This was more than Chamberlain was prepared to stomach. The Czechs ordered mobilization; an exodus from London began. Air-raid wardens distributed gas masks, shelters were improvised in the parks, the fleet was mobilized. Hitler announced his ultimatum: Five days in which his requirements must be met. Churchill protested against submission to Hitler's demands: "The idea that safety can be purchased by throwing a small state to the wolves is a delusion." [2]

Chamberlain broadcast his willingness to visit Germany again. Hitler, delighted to get his triumph cheaply, invited Chamberlain to Munich. The Godesberg terms were presented in a slightly modified form, but Chamberlain, together with the French leader, Daladier, grasped eagerly at the pretext and signed on the dotted line. He then flew back exultantly to London, waving in triumph a scrap of paper bearing Hitler's autograph and announcing that he had brought peace. "Peace with Honor!" he called it. [9]

For many days the people had been preparing for war. They had foreseen financial ruin and sudden death. Suddenly, in the twinkling of an eye, the clouds dispersed: there was to be no war. And this miracle had been performed by one man only. The aged Prime Minister of England had saved the world. [19]

In the House the Tories greeted Chamberlain deliriously. Doggedly, Winston rose to his feet amid howls and catcalls. "I will begin by saying what everybody would like to ignore but which must nevertheless be stated, namely, that we have sustained a total and unmitigated defeat."

"Nonsense," cried Lady Astor. [1]

"I do not grudge our loyal, brave people," he went on, "who were ready to do their duty no matter what the cost, who never flinched under the strain of last week—I do not grudge them the natural, spontaneous outburst of joy and relief when they learned that the hard ordeal would no longer be required of them at the moment; but they should know the truth. They should know that we have maintained a defeat without a war."

Churchill was forced to pause until the clamor had died down. "And this is only the beginning," he persisted, "the first sip, the first foretaste of the bitter cup which will be proffered to us unless, by a supreme recovery of moral health and martial vigor, we arise again and take our stand for freedom as in the olden times." [2]

Six months after Munich—in March, 1939—the Germans occupied Czechoslovakia. When the news arrived, Chamberlain said he felt as if he had been cheated at cards, which was not much consolation to the Czechs. The cry for the return of Churchill to the Cabinet now came from almost every section of the country. A new England was arising from the death of Czechoslovakia. But Chamberlain was not aware of it. The Germans hated Churchill. To appoint Winston to the Cabinet would be little short of a declaration of war. "If there is any possibility of easing the tension and getting back to normal relations with the dictators, I wouldn't risk it by what would certainly be regarded by them as a challenge." [1]

In the second week of August, the French invited Churchill to visit the "impregnable Maginot Line." On returning home he looked through the windows of Chartwell at the beautiful and peaceful gardens, then said slowly and sorrowfully, "Before the harvest is gathered in—we shall be at war." [25]

At five-thirty on September 1, 1939, the German tanks rolled across the Polish frontier, shot the legs off the Polish cavalry horses and stormed for Warsaw. [1]

That evening Clementine joined ambassadors and peers in the Distinguished Strangers' Gallery of the House. All eyes were on Winston, sitting in his accustomed seat, his face clearly lined with grief. The debate was brief. He said nothing. Clementine watched him until he stood up and walked out slowly and silently. [25]

On September 3 Britain and France declared war. That same day, under the awful pressure of the crisis, Chamberlain turned back to the man who had predicted it from the beginning: he invited Churchill into his War Cabinet as First Lord of the Admiralty.

13

A Walk with Destiny

WHEN the Nazis poured into Poland in September 1939 and their purpose became clear even to Chamberlain, there was no choice but to put Winston into his old post at the Admiralty. Out to the fleet went a happy cable: "Winston is back!" [10]

The effect on Churchill was equally electric. The unlit lamp now blazed. Preceded by two bottles of Scotch and one of seltzer, he took up the same offices that he had occupied in World War I. They overlooked the Horse Guards Parade where he had himself pushed around the first experimental tanks which he had sponsored in the hope of breaking the stalemate on the Western Front. He called for his old octagonal desk which he liked because "eight or ten men could sit around it facing each other." Back came the same map on which he had plotted the position of the King's ships twenty-five years before. [44]

In that small room beat the pulse of the world. The wireless tower on the Admiralty roof was in constant communication with all British warships on the seven seas. Sea battles in the South Atlantic and the Eastern Mediterranean were directed from Churchill's desk. [34]

Clerks grown old in the Admiralty marveled how the man of sixty-five could pick up with the fire of the man of forty. In and out of his office stumped the First Sea Lord, Sir Dudley

Pound, on his stiff leg. In and out flew the reports and the preemptory orders, sometimes a bit too preemptory. One morning, working on into the dawn in the old port-and-starboard-light tradition, he sent an officer to rouse little Sir Tom Phillips, who was later to go down with the *Prince of Wales.* "Will the Vice Chief of Naval Staff come at once to see the First Lord on a matter of importance." Sir Tom growled, "Go back and tell the First Lord that the Vice Chief of Naval Staff says he can bloody well dispose of the matter himself." [44]

At the outbreak of the war—September 3, 1939—a great exodus of Government offices, commercial concerns and private citizens had begun. Schemes of evacuation of schoolchildren and mothers with little ones were at once put in hand. Nearly a million and a half were moved in the first three days. These feverish preparations were carried through with grim faces. The nation knew it was total war.

Yet for all their seriousness, the people were uplifted in heart. This terrible thing that had scared them for years had come and they had not run away, but faced it. The long shame of appeasement was over. Churchill put their mood into words when, on the announcement of war, he said: "Outside, the storms of war may blow and the lands be lashed with the fury of its gales, but in our own hearts this Sunday morning there is peace. It is a war, viewed in its inherent quality, to establish on impregnable rocks the rights of the individual, and it is a war to establish and revive the stature of man." [9]

From across the Atlantic came a significant signal. President Roosevelt wrote, "It is because you and I occupied similar positions in the World War that I want you to know how glad I am that you are back again in the Admiralty." [7]

"I responded with alacrity," wrote Churchill, "using the signature of 'Naval Person' and thus began that long and memorable correspondence—covering perhaps a thousand communications on each side and lasting till Roosevelt's death five years later." [3a]

Churchill now began to make conscientious tours of the arsenals, the shipyards, the graving docks, the fitting basins, going to the Clyde, the Tyne, and the Tees. [44]

"I spent two days at Scapa," he wrote, "inspecting the harbor and the entrances with their booms and nets. The rest of the fleet was hiding in Lock Ewe and the Admiral took me to them in the *Nelson*. I had last visited Sir John Jellicoe in this very bay. Most of the captains and admirals of those days were dead or passed into retirement. The responsible senior officers now presented to me as I visited the various ships had been young lieutenants or even midshipmen in those far-off days. Only the ships had been laid down in my tenure. It seemed that I was all that had survived in the same position I had held so long ago.

> *"I feel like one*
> *Who treads alone*
> *Some banquet hall deserted,*
> *Whose lights are fled,*
> *Whose garlands dead,*
> *And all but he departed!"* [3a]

About the huge anchorage there were mockups of battle wagons so true to the illusion of the real thing that they could not be taken for fakes even when one was right on them. Churchill pointed to the fake battleship on the far end of the northern string and told one of the warrant officers that it would be spotted by German pilots as a dummy. "But she's not even been spotted by our own reconnaissance, sir," he was told. "Then they need spectacles!" "How so, sir?" "No gulls about her!" he snapped. "You'll always find gulls about a living ship. Drop garbage for the dummy too. Feed the gulls and fool the Germans!" And they did. [55]

On the very day that war was declared, a German U-boat had torpedoed and sunk without warning the S.S. *Athena*—a passenger liner—off the north coast of Ireland. As three hundred of the passengers were Americans, Goebbels promptly declared that Churchill had done it! During the first fortnight of the war, German submarines sank one hundred and eleven thousand tons of British shipping. Churchill at once put in hand a system of convoys, and the U-boats were remorselessly hunted down. He was able to announce that by the end of 1939 the Germans had lost half the number with which they entered the war. [9]

Then came the Battle of the River Platte when the cruisers *Exeter* and *Ajax* ran down the *Graf Spee* and forced her to scuttle in South American waters. "In a cold dark winter," said Churchill, "it has warmed the cockles of our hearts." [42]

The incident was not over; some three hundred and thirty of the British seamen taken by the *Graf Spee* from vessels she sank in her raiding career were imprisoned in a supply ship, the *Altmark*, which tried to wiggle back to Germany through Norwegian territorial waters. [9]

This same ship had been known for a long time in the British press as a "hellship." Churchill said two words: "Find her." Every ship, plane and submarine was ordered to assist in the hunt. A Lancaster plane found her a day later, hugging Norway. [55]

On Winston's express orders, H.M.S. *Cossack* thrust past the Norse naval craft guarding the entrance to a narrow fjord, grappled with and boarded the *Altmark*, and British seamen, prisoned in the depths of an empty oiltank, heard a shout, "The navy is here!" There were yells of delight as the men greeted their rescuers and were brought off home in triumph. Hitler was furious. [9]

There was, meanwhile, much public speculation as to the relations between Neville Chamberlain and the First Lord of the Admiralty. Doubts were set at rest. "You know," said

Churchill, "I have not always agreed with Mr. Chamberlain. But he is a man of very tough fiber and I can tell you he is going to fight as obstinately for victory as he did for peace." In council he was careful to avoid being drawn into controversy with his chief and quick to defend his leader even against family critics in his home. [2]

During the winter of that year Mr. and Mrs. Neville Chamberlain came to dine with the Churchills in their crammed apartment above Admiralty House. [25]

"We were a party of four," wrote Churchill. "Although we had been colleagues under Mr. Baldwin for five years, my wife and I had never met the Chamberlains in such circumstances before. During dinner the war went on and things happened. With the soup an officer came up from the Ward Room below to report that a U-boat had been sunk. With the sweet he came again and reported a second U-boat had been sunk; and just before the ladies left the dining room he came a third time reporting that a third U-boat had been sunk. Nothing like this had ever happened before in a single day. As the ladies left us, Mrs. Chamberlain, with a naive and charming glance, said to me, 'Did you arrange all this on purpose?' I assured her that if she would come again we would produce a similar result." [3a]

But between Chamberlain and Churchill there could be no sympathy. [7]

Duff Cooper noted in his diary, "Winston told me Chamberlain doesn't take him into his confidence." Chamberlain himself, however, was thoroughly happy with the conduct of the war. He was already over seventy and suffering from gout, but still eager to absorb more and more responsibility. In the spring of 1940 he announced complacently that "Hitler has missed the bus!" The assertion became one of the unluckiest remarks any Prime Minister ever made. The Germans struck, swallowed Denmark overnight, invaded Norway and compelled an Anglo-French expeditionary force to withdraw almost as soon as it had landed. Hitler had missed the bus, indeed! A furious house packed itself in like sardines to debate the conduct of the war. [1]

All their wrath turned on Chamberlain for his bad advice and guidance. Mr. Leo Amery, a staunch Conservative, attacked the Prime Minister in an impassioned speech ending with Oliver Cromwell's words to the Rump of the Long Parliament: "You have sat here too long for any good you have been doing. Depart I say, and let us have done with you! In the name of God, GO!" [4]

Chamberlain, his acrid mouth downturned contemptuously at the corners, appealed to his friends in the House—"and I have friends in the House"—to stand by him. Lloyd George replied savagely. "The Prime Minister has appealed for sacrifice," he said. "I say solemnly that the Prime Minister should give an example of sacrifice because there is nothing which can contribute more to victory in this war than that he should sacrifice the seals of office." A vote of censure was put down against the Government. [1]

When Churchill intervened to say that he, as First Lord, took complete responsibility for everything that was done by the Admiralty, Lloyd George waved him aside. "I hope," he said, "that my Right Honorable friend will not allow himself to be converted into an air-raid shelter to keep the splinters from hitting his colleagues." At the end of the debate the vote was taken. The Government emerged with a majority of not more than eighty-one in a total of four hundred and eighty-one. [2]

Scores of Tories had abstained and many actually voted against their leader. It was a thundering demonstration of no confidence. Chamberlain walked out of the House a dumbfounded but far from broken man. [1]

Calling in Churchill and Lord Halifax, he told them that the new Prime Minister had to be either Churchill or Halifax. For once the voluble Churchill was silent. For a long minute he stared fixedly into space until Halifax modestly declined the task. [56]

And so, after forty years in Parliament, Churchill was at last in power. [10]

"As I went to bed at about 3 A.M.," he wrote, "I was conscious of a profound sense of relief. At last I had the authority to give directions over the whole scene. I felt as if I were walking with Destiny, and that all my past life had been but a preparation for this hour and for this trial. I slept soundly and had no need for cheering dreams. Facts are better than dreams." [3a]

Winston had at last found his destiny. The world looked to him, and all the pent-up energy of the immense machine that throbbed in his heart and mind was brought into play. The tremendous task that had fallen upon him equaled his stature as a man, and he grasped the supreme power of the state with eager hands. [4]

No one who ever heard them will ever forget those great speeches in which he divined and gave expression to the resolve of the whole nation, those vivid phrases, struck out white-hot from the anvil of his mind. [39]

"On May 13," recalled Sir Edward Spears, "I went to the House to listen to the new Prime Minister make his first speech, a pronouncement memorable for all time. He was quite calm, his jaw set. His first sentences, simple, matter-of-fact, were an explanation of the reasons which had led him to recall the House. Then suddenly he was transformed into an inspired leader dedicating a nation to measureless sacrifice. Looking up and above the crowded benches at the high, narrow, cathedral-like windows which let in broad slits of light, he said slowly: 'I have nothing to offer but blood, toil, tears and sweat.'

"The House had been attentive; a great hush now came over it. Then followed deep murmured approval as if the House were saying Amen. Ten minutes earlier it had been a strong-willed, earnest, worried assembly, smarting from many deep slashes; now it was a cohesive force whose heart throbbed in unison with that of its leader. They cheered his words almost before he had uttered them. '*You ask, what is our policy?*' he went on, as if he were baring the heart of the nation before heaven. '*It is to wage war, by sea, land and air, with all our might and with all the strength that God can give us; to wage war against a monstrous tyranny, never surpassed in the dark, lamentable catalogue of human crime, that is our policy.*'

"The House roared its approval. '*You ask, what is our aim? I can answer in one word: it is victory, victory at all costs, victory in spite of terror, victory, however long and hard the road may be . . .*' He pledged himself, the Commons and the people, to follow the path from which there was no turning; and the Commons, voicing the very mind of the people, pledged its troth to him for better or for worse until victory was achieved." [53]

14

"Sail On, O Ship of State!"

CHURCHILL at once set about shaping a small, efficient machine that could make decisions swiftly. [4]

"I feel entitled to claim the aid of all," he declared, "and I say 'Come, then, let us go forward together with our united strength.'" He was a symbol of indomitable strength, an incomparable orator who could rally his beleaguered England. "Their will was resolute and inconquerable," he said later, "and it fell to me to express it. It was the nation and the race dwelling all round the globe that had the lion's heart. I had the luck to be called on to give the roar." [10]

He organized a War Cabinet comprised of only four members (later in the war it grew to seven) besides himself: two Labor leaders, Clement Attlee and Arthur Greenwood, and two Conservatives, Mr. Chamberlain and Lord Halifax. This Cabinet met almost daily and took all the supreme decisions of the war; sixty or seventy other Ministers of all parties formed the membership of the Coalition Government, but, as Winston pointed out, it was only the members of the War Cabinet "who had the right to have their heads cut off on Tower Hill if we did not win." Churchill, the overriding figure in the Cabinet, was also leader of the House of Commons and Minister of Defense as well. The Chiefs of Staff reported directly to him. Thus, by permission of the War Cabinet, he became virtually a dictator. [4]

But even before he could put together his new Coalition Government, all of France was falling. [10]

In an exterminating air attack upon the heart of Rotterdam, the Germans fired the city. Rotterdam surrendered. Queen Wilhelmina escaped to London, her Cabinet following by a few hours. Four days later the Dutch army ceased firing, a paralyzing blow to the British and Belgians. German mechanized divisions, roaring down the valley of the Somme clear to the Channel at Abbeville, split the British and Belgian forces in Flanders and separated them from the main French armies. Brussels fell, then Namur. On May 26 King Leopold III ordered the Belgium forces to capitulate. [55]

Most of the British Expeditionary Force, with some French detachments, were bottled up in a steadily diminishing pocket, separated from the main French army to the south. [1]

Churchill wired the British commanders, "MARCH TO THE NORTH CHANNEL PORT. FIGHT ANYTHING THAT GETS IN THE WAY." [8]

The encircling Germans began to close in on Calais. The order was given to evacuate the town. Churchill protested—It would add to the peril of Dunkirk—and the order was countermanded. "The British Brigadier," wrote Churchill in tribute to the gallantry shown, "given an hour to surrender, spurned the offer, and four days of intense street fighting passed before silence reigned over Calais." [2]

Now the only port left open in northern France was Dunkirk, a dirty little harbor which small vessels could use at high water. But the Germans had been at pains to bomb and wreck it. Britain's troops were strung out as far as Arras, and now the whole weight of the German Army—tanks, artillery, bombers—was flung savagely upon them. [9]

At 6:30 A.M., May 26, 1940, came the news from Dunkirk of the quick necessity for evacuation. Churchill sprang out of bed and grabbed for his telephones without putting in his false teeth. His voice came through in almost unrecognizable form, but there was no mistaking the rolling phrases and impassioned commands to action. Standing in his nightshirt, he put the Admiralty on a crisis footing, then turned to the nation as a whole. In less than an hour word had spread: "Winnie needs boats." First the navy headed full tilt for the scene with ships of all sizes and kinds, from minesweepers to big warships. But these were only the beginning. [8]

"By the night of the twenty-seventh," Churchill wrote, "a great tide of small vessels began to flow towards the sea, first to our Channel ports and thence to the beaches of Dunkirk and the beloved army: lifeboats from liners in the London docks, tugs from the Thames, yachts, fishing craft, lighters, barges and pleasure boats. Everyone who had a boat of any kind, steam or sail, put out for Dunkirk. I missed the head of my Admiralty Map Room and one or two other familiar faces. They had got hold of a Dutch *schuit* which in four days brought off eight hundred soldiers. Altogether there came to the rescue of the army eight hundred and sixty vessels." [3c]

A benediction was upon them, for that week the restless Channel spread calm and waveless. Under clear skies, through the long sunlight of summer days and brief nights lit by stars and the bright sickle of a waning moon, the little ships plied tirelessly to and fro, standing in to the Dunkirk beaches where weary men had waded far out into the shallow sea to clamber aboard the rescuing craft, and then swung about to bear their living cargo back to the homeland. [9]

Wrote Churchill: "British airmen maintained successive patrols over the scene and fought the enemy at long odds. Hour after hour they bit into the German fighter and bomber squadrons, taking a heavy toll; German aircraft were shot down in scores, which presently added up into hundreds. The whole Metropolitan Air Force, our last sacred reserve, was used. Sometimes the fighter pilots made four sorties a day.

"There was never any question of leaving the French behind. Here was my order to General Spears (Paris): 'We wish French troops to share in evacuation to fullest extent. We must share this loss together as best we can.' " [3c]

Instead of the twenty thousand, which a week earlier had seemed to be the most one could hope to rescue, more than eighty-five per cent of the whole British Expeditionary Force —three hundred and thirty-eight thousand men—had been snatched from death or captivity. [9]

The cheerful London *Daily Mirror* expressed the whole thing in a headline of two words: BLOODY MARVELLOUS [1]

The men were back, but not their weapons. All their equipment, their guns, their tanks, all the paraphernalia of the army, had to be abandoned. Britain had an armless army to defend her shores. Some batteries on the coast had no more than a dozen shells for their guns. [2]

Churchill made no attempt to disguise the rescue as a victory. Instead, he painted England's position in dark colors. Europe was gone, Russia had joined the Fascists, and America proclaimed her unshakable neutrality. [8]

In the Cabinet Room at 10 Downing Street, he marshaled his thoughts. It was Sunday evening, June 2, 1940. Two days from now he must render his report on Dunkirk to the nation. On the far side of the room Mary Shearburn, his secretary, was poised at a typewriter. To sit closer, within earshot, would never do. The Old Man liked freedom to pace.

Thoughtfully, Churchill began, *"We must be very careful not to assign to this deliverance the attributes of victory . . ."* Swiftly Miss Shearburn's fingers flew over the keyboard, typing each paragraph in the triple spacing that was the Prime Minister's whim. As he dictated, Churchill marched from the fireplace to the velvet-draped French windows and back. Sometimes he growled, "Gimme!"—ratcheting the paper from the typewriter to scan a phrase.

It was past midnight now; the room was colder. Miss Shearburn was tired, and Churchill's voice had grown faint. Head bowed, he was struggling with tears. Loving him because his feelings were naked to the bone, Miss Shearburn yet invoked a silent curse on his mumbling.

But now sobs shook the foundation of his voice: *"We shall not flag or fail. We shall go on to the end. We shall fight in France, we shall fight in the seas and oceans . . . we shall defend our island whatever the cost may be. We shall fight on the beaches, we shall fight in the fields and in the streets, we shall fight in the hills . . ."*

Racked by grief for his stricken land, Churchill could not go on. A full minute passed. Then, almost trumpeted, came the next sentence: *"We shall NEVER surrender."*

It was the turning point. "All the tears," Mary Shearburn recalls in wonder, "had gone from his voice." Churchill was marching again. *"Even if, which I do not for a moment believe, this island or a large part of it were subjugated and starving, then our empire beyond the seas . . . would carry on the struggle . . ."*

On and on Churchill marched, faster and faster, his voice a drumbeat, charged with faith, thundering to a finale.

". . . until, in God's good time, the New World, with all its power and might, steps forth to the rescue and liberation of the Old." [18]

Churchill's noble eloquence warmed the United States to his cause: Roosevelt sent over five thousand rifles to replace the Dunkirk losses. "The President and I believed Mr. Churchill meant what he said," explained Secretary of State Cordell Hull. [10]

From America also came a moving world broadcast from Dorothy Thompson: "The master of the dyke against world chaos is you, Churchill. Around you is a gallant company of ghosts. Elizabeth is there and Shakespeare, the man who made the English renaissance—the world's renaissance. Drake is there, and Raleigh and Wellington; Burke is there and Walpole and Pitt; Byron is there and Wordsworth and Shelley. All the makers of a world of freedom and law are there. And when you speak, Churchill, brave men's hearts everywhere go out to you. Through our hearts and our prayers, we in America say: 'God give you strength, God bless you. May you live to cultivate your garden in a free world, liberated from terror and persecution, from war and fear.'"

A recording was made and friends persuaded Churchill to listen to it. At the end, while emotion still hung in the air, the Prime Minister's eyes, no longer clouded, glistened as he looked round at the other faces: "Do people really feel like that?" he asked, wonderingly. "Do they feel like that about me?" [20]

Churchill had turned England into an armed camp. Trucks roared down to the seacoast night and day as Britain built gun emplacements, machine gun nests and tank traps at a feverish pace. A Home Guard armed with everything from rifles to pitchforks grew to a million men. True to his speeches he laid plans to "fight in every street of London and its suburbs. It would *devour* an invading army, assuming one ever got that far. We hope, however, to drown the bulk of them in the salt sea." [10]

Time after time Churchill flew to Paris to bolster the politicians, but was met with abuse, appeals, hysteria, and hopelessness. He could not believe such men as Pétain and Weygand, who had fought so well in the First World War, were so paralyzed by fright in the Second. He sent General Sir Edward L. Spears to France to try to keep the country in the field. Spears loved France almost as much as he loved England. [1]

Mussolini, who decided that France was doomed, chose this moment to declare war. He wanted to be in at the kill and get his pickings of the carcass. Churchill addressed a last-minute appeal to him not to plunge Italy, whose traditional friendship with Britain was so strong, into this struggle, but he got only an insolent defiance in reply. [9]

"About eleven o'clock the morning of June 11," wrote

155

Churchill, "there was a telephone message from Reynaud, who had also cabled to President Roosevelt. The French tragedy had moved and slid downward. For several days I had pressed for a meeting of the Supreme Council. I had difficulty obtaining a rendezvous, but we must know what the French were going to do. We could no longer meet in Paris, Reynaud told me; he could receive us at Briare, near Orléans." [3c]

In the large dining room of Weygand's house, where the conference was to be held, the Frenchmen sat with set white faces, looking for all the world like prisoners hauled up from some deep dungeon to hear an inevitable situation. De Gaulle alone among his compatriots had a look of confidence and self-possession. Reynaud asked Weygand to report on the military situation. The Commander in Chief's news was bad. The overwhelming superiority of the Germans in aircraft and tanks and manpower had compelled a withdrawal. There was not a single battalion in reserve. "There is nothing to prevent the enemy reaching Paris. I am helpless. *C'est dislocation*"— the breakup. Churchill, hunched over the table, his face flushed, was watching Weygand intently. His expression was not benevolent. [53]

"Weygand requested that every British fighter air squadron should immediately be thrown into the battle," Churchill wrote later. " 'Here,' said Weygand, 'is the decisive moment. It is wrong to keep any squadrons back in England.' In accordance with the Cabinet decision, I replied: 'This is not the moment. That will come when Hitler hurls his Luftwaffe against Great Britain. If we can keep command of the air and the seas we will win it all back for you.' I knew twenty-five squadrons must be maintained at all costs for the defense of Britain and the Channel, and nothing would make us give up these." [3c]

The Prime Minister had looked at de Gaulle several times, searching for something he had failed to find in the other French faces. "That he returned several times to study de Gaulle," wrote Sir Edward Spears, "made me think he had detected in him the thing he was looking for. I could see that Churchill was gathering his immense reserves of moral strength in an attempt to carry the French with him out of the slough of despond into which they had fallen."

If the French army could hold out till the spring of 1941, said Churchill, the British would have from twenty to twenty-five divisions to employ anywhere. Britain was not only willing to suffer as France was suffering, she would gladly draw upon herself the full weight of Nazi ferocity. He hoped the Germans would turn on England: it would give the R.A.F. the opportunity of smashing the German air force. He also wanted the French to fight in Paris, describing how a great city, if stubbornly defended, could absorb immense armies. The French froze. But Churchill, if he had noticed the perceptible movement which had led all the French to sit back tensely in their chairs, did not heed it. There was nothing Great Britain would not do for France except give up the struggle. Even should the Germans occupy all France they would not win the war. Britain would fight on until Hitlerism was destroyed.

Pétain's face might have been a mask of white plaster. "To make Paris into a city of ruins will not affect the issue," he said, looking at his hands spread on the table. Weygand said something about the Germans' having a hundred divisions to spare to invade Britain. "What would you do then?" Drown as many as possible on the way over, answered Churchill, and knock the others on the head as they crawled ashore. Finally the conference petered out as Darlan told Churchill positively that whatever happened the French fleet would not fall into German hands. [53]

"Before leaving," wrote Churchill, "I made one particular request to M. Reynaud. Over four hundred German pilots, the bulk of whom had been shot down by the R.A.F., were prisoners in France. They should be handed over to our custody. M. Reynaud willingly gave this promise, but soon he had no power to keep it. These German pilots all became available for the Battle of Britain, and we had to shoot them down a second time." [3c]

Then the Nazis struck hard. France tottered. Before it fell, Churchill offered the people of France a common citizenship with England: [30]

"The two Governments," ran the proposed declaration, "declare that France and Great Britain shall no longer be two nations, but one Franco-British Union. Every citizen of France will enjoy immediately the citizenship of Great Britain; every British subject will become a citizen of France. The Union will concentrate its whole energy against the power of the enemy no matter where the battle may be. And thus we shall conquer." [53]

The British War Cabinet endorsed the proposal. De Gaulle, in London, telephoned the terms to Bordeaux. [2]

Reynaud took up the receiver. The next moment his eyebrows went up. He repeated each word as he wrote it down. Finally he stopped and said into the telephone: "Does he agree to this? Did Churchill give you this personally?" [53]

Churchill's voice was heard on the line. "Hello, Reynaud, you must hold out. Our proposal may have great consequences." [2]

"At five o'clock the French Council of Ministers met," wrote Reynaud later. "Weygand, who had learned from the listening-in posts of the proposal, had been campaigning against it. So I had hardly finished giving reasons why the proposed Union should be accepted enthusiastically by France when they broke out into denunciations of it, declaring that they would never agree to France's becoming a British Dominion (sic). Not one voice was raised in support of me in the council even among those who till then had backed me strongly in my desire to continue the war." [21]

Three days later, Paris was evacuated. Two days after this, Verdun fell. With savage irony, the same day the Russians moved into Lithuania, Latvia and Estonia. Pétain followed Paul Reynaud as head of the French Government. His first day as Premier he asked the Germans for an armistice. And five days after asking for it, he got it. [55]

On June 18, after the fall of France, came Churchill's thundering call to sacrifice that few who heard it on that day have forgotten: "The Battle of France is over. I expect that the Battle of Britain is about to begin. Upon this battle depends the survival of Christian civilization. The whole fury and might of the enemy must very soon be turned on us. Hitler knows that he will have to break us in this Island or lose the war. If we can stand up to him, all Europe may be free and the life of the world may move forward into broad, sunlit uplands. But if we fail, then the whole world, including the United States, including all that we have known and cared for, will sink into the abyss of a new Dark Age. Let us therefore brace ourselves to our duties and so bear ourselves that, if the British Empire and its Commonwealth last for a thousand years, men will still say: 'This was their finest hour.'" [10]

To General de Gaulle, who had been brought to England to coalesce the Frenchmen willing to fight for freedom and give them hope, Churchill now lent the full support of his Government. [30]

This young officer de Gaulle, tall and somewhat uncertain of his position though not of his destiny, spoke to France over the B.B.C. and said, *"Moi, Général de Gaulle, soldat et chef français, j'ai conscience de parler au nom de la France."* [1]

The German armistice terms required France to place the vessels of the French fleet under German and Italian control. The British Cabinet met to make the most unpalatable heart-rending decision of the war. The *Dunkerque* and the *Strasbourg* and the two great battleships nearing completion must be immobilized or destroyed. Vice Admiral Somerville, with a strong naval force, sailed for Oran. He carried Churchill's instructions: "You are charged with the most disagreeable task a British admiral has faced: we rely on you to carry it out relentlessly."

The French admiral was presented with an ultimatum: he must sail his ships away or sink them—failing that, force would be used. The French refused to submit. [2]

A ten-minute bombardment followed; one battle cruiser was damaged and beached, the other battleship and aircraft carrier and two destroyers sunk or burned. It convinced the world that the man who ordered the Oran bombardment really meant business. [9]

Already American assistance was coming in growing volume, arms for soldiers, destroyers for the navy, traded for the use of British bases. But it was not enough. Britain's dollars had run out. Her holdings in American stock were disposed of, great businesses were sold for dollars, and gold bullion shipped by warship across the Atlantic. Now the national pockets were empty.

Churchill sat down at his desk to importune the President in a begging letter of four thousand words, the longest he ever wrote—and the most successful. "If we go down Hitler has a very good chance of conquering the world." Roosevelt, though deeply moved, was still tied by the restraints of neutrality, but legal ingenuity devised the means within the limits of the Constitution. Arms could not be given to the British, but, under the terms of a half-forgotten statute, they could "for the public good" be leased. So the magnificent solution was announced. Britain was to be supplied with everything she required. There would be no reckoning in terms of dollars. The defense of Britain was the best defense of the United States. It was the beginning of Lend-Lease, the most unsordid act, as Churchill called it, in the history of any nation. America became the arsenal of democracy.

Not long afterward, Wendell Willkie arrived in London

with a letter of introduction from the President, who, in his own handwriting, had written out a verse from Longfellow:

> *Sail on, O Ship of State!*
> *Sail on, O Union, strong and great!*
> *Humanity with all its fears,*
> *With all the hopes of future years,*
> *Is hanging breathless on thy fate!* [2]

15

"Their Finest Hour"

A S Prime Minister, Churchill had the right to the use of Chequers, the permanent residence of England's impermanent Prime Ministers, where he could get as much done under less distracting and noisy conditions as in his own Chartwell. Chequers offered no overhead. Chartwell was expensive, and Churchill's extra income from writing had evaporated since the war. Winston liked everything that had a kingly ring to it, some florid medievalism in him, an affinity for the flamboyant, provided it wore the respect of centuries.

Chequers has a Great Hall, and often Churchill would turn on the radio, find music with a beat to it, then begin marching up and down the Hall in ecstatic disregard of the household and guests, shouting imaginary orders, making sharp parade-ground turns when he came to the Hall's limits, then marching back. He often did this in a brilliantly colored dressing gown—he had several such gowns, all garish and expensive. His favorite tunes included "Keep Right On to the End of the Road," "Run Rabbit Run," and "Home Sweet Home." For the last, not fashioned for marching, he would make unusual concessions in his footwork so as not to break rhythm. During his marching his mind concentrated on his problems, one by one, and he always had a complete answer for the Cabinet Members who came down each weekend to go over with him the latest emergency.

His greatest pleasure was to have private showings of films in his house; the noisier and busier the story and the more compelling its plot, the more it relaxed his mind. He could sit still for two hours looking at a film, know in detail what he'd looked at, but come away with a brand-new war plan in his mind, take it to one of his secretaries and set it down in detail. [55]

Eric Ambler, the English author and a subaltern attached to the gun crew at Chequers, was once invited on one of Churchill's birthdays into the house with his battery captain and two other subalterns. Having been ushered into a large, darkened room in which there appeared to be a seated audience of some size, Ambler was shown to a chair on the left of a swaddled figure that he took to be an uncommonly cold-blooded woman wrapped all around in an eiderdown quilt. Then he noticed that, through a tiny aperture resembling the vent in a wigwam, the figure was smoking a cigar. His neighbor was Churchill.

No sooner had the film—*A Hundred Men and a Girl* with Deanna Durbin—started than a low rumble, with gestures, issued from the figure in the eiderdown. Alarmed, with visions of a gastric emergency, Ambler leaned forward. As he did so, the cigar came more plainly into view, held in one hand and stabbing at the air like punctuation. It finally dawned upon Ambler that Churchill was rehearsing a speech, but enjoying the movie at the same time, for he broke into chuckles at exactly the right spots. "The total effect was 'Mumble mumble mumble, demumble *mumble* demumble— Ha!—demumble mumble? Er, mumble demumble—Cor!—.' " [8]

After such film showings, he would chat briefly with his guests, then separate himself from them and go to work till 3 or 4 A.M., sometimes clear through the night. He was awake at 8 A.M., never needing to be called. He barked for the newspapers and read them while he ate breakfast—ham, bacon (two or three times a week a good-sized sole), small mountains of toast under a cover, a pot of tea and a jug of milk with jam or jelly. It was very dangerous to interrupt him during this period. Phones were cut off and important people were, to their irritation, kept waiting till he had rung to have his breakfast service taken away. Then he shaved and bathed, but did not dress yet. Official bulletins were brought in; he moved about from chair to chair, reading them. He lighted his first cigar, which presently went out. He would chew on it for an hour before realizing it was dead. He did not inhale, but blew the smoke about in meditative balloons, often peering into them as if he might have dropped something of value into their center and were seeking to locate it.

Often he'd return to bed, leaning against a wall of pillows that he kept plopping into more accommodating shapes. On the bedtable before him were rubber pads for his elbows. After his reading and before his appointed callers began to come in, his staff of secretaries came by, one by one. This continued until about one o'clock.

One morning he needed some special information from the Admiralty. "Good morning, Captain," he said when a super-conscientious naval officer was on the phone, "This is Winston Churchill. I want you to look up for me—" "I'll call you back first thing this afternoon, Mr. Churchill." "No, I'll wait," said Winston, and left the telephone, laying it down on the bed. He grinned mischievously. While the Prime Minister went on working, the captain began to dig; he was soon back with what Churchill wanted. Three minutes. Churchill thanked him, hung up, then grinned again. "They can always find it faster if they have to find it themselves," he said. [55]

The fact that the Prime Minister worked in bed in the morning, slept in the afternoon, and went off to the country for long weekends certainly enabled him to remain fresh. But it imposed a heavy strain on the Chiefs of Staff. His usual hour for meeting them was 9:30 P.M. and he often kept them up until one or two in the morning and poured out floods of memoranda upon all problems great and small; much time had to be spent in answering them. Everybody appreciated Churchill's great qualities. But there were few who did not sometimes doubt whether these were adequate compensation for the immense additional effort they imposed upon the Service Staffs.

Somebody said that Churchill was exactly like the horse in Job:

> He paweth in the valley, and rejoiceth in his strength: he goeth on to meet the armed men.
> He mocketh at fear, and is not affrighted; neither turneth he back from the sword.
> The quiver rattleth against him, the glittering spear and the shield.
> He swalloweth the ground with fierceness and rage: neither believeth he that it is the sound of the trumpet.
> He saith among the trumpets, Ha, ha; and he smelleth the battle affar off, the thunder of the captains, and the shouting.

Hitler, now in dominant victory as the autocratic arbiter of an area stretching from the North Cape to the Brenner and from the English Channel to the River Bug, was disposed to be magnanimous. In peace terms offered by the Fuehrer in his Reichstag speech of July 19, 1940, all that he demanded of Britain was the jettisoning of Churchill, the recognition of his own status as conqueror and arbiter of Europe and the return of Germany's colonial possessions. Had Britain concurred, America might well have withdrawn into isolationism; collaboration governments might have been established in the capitals of Europe and in London, and the *Pax Germanica* have lasted for an indefinite period. There stood between Adolf Hitler and the realization of his grandiose ambitions only the defiance of Mr. Winston Churchill, backed by the obstinate and traditional refusal of the British people to recognize, let alone acknowledge, defeat. [57]

As England girded for its test, there was glory in the air. Spirits were enormously high. Churchill prepared a slogan— *You Can Always Take One of Them With You*—for use when invasion came. The King himself set up a shooting range in Buckingham Palace and practiced assiduously with pistols and tommy guns. "This was a time," said Churchill, "when it was equally good to live or die." [10]

He even carried his own pistol, and he would often pop it into view and say with roguish delight: "You see, they will never take me alive. I will always get one or two before they can shoot me down." [55]

At this point, Churchill took an astute gamble. While the invasion threat was at its height, he nonetheless sent half of England's tanks—two armored regiments—to reinforce General Sir Archibald Wavell in Egypt. Wavell later smashed the Italian army several times the size of his own, capturing thirty-eight thousand Italian prisoners who turned out to be unenthusiastic about the Axis cause, with the loss of only one hundred and thirty-three British lives. As his defenses mounted, Churchill was almost eager for the invasion. "One could not help liking the picture which presented itself with growing definition," he later wrote. [10]

Coastal defenses were strengthened, pillboxes erected beside roads, rivers and canals, signposts and place-names were removed or obliterated to deny help to invaders. [9]

Meanwhile on both sides of the Channel the opposing forces stood ready. Over there, four thousand ships of the Nazi invasion fleet lay huddled in the ports from Rotterdam to Le Havre. Von Rundstedt, head of the German invading forces, waited on the Grand Admiral; the Grand Admiral waited on Goering. Hitler hesitated. The day was fixed—it was postponed. The R.A.F. played havoc with the invasion fleet and, with the R.A.F. so destructively active in the air, the

Germans had no stomach for the Channel crossing. Goering announced that air raids on London would herald the invasion. [2]

During this time, the operations room of No. 11 Group, Fighter Command, was Churchill's favorite port of call. It was the nerve center from which he could follow the course of the battle for control of the air over Britain. The sequel to a visit in mid-August must be told. There had been heavy fighting throughout the afternoon; at one moment every squadron in the group was engaged. There was nothing left in reserve, and the map table showed new waves of attackers crossing the coast.

"As the evening closed in," wrote Lord Ismay in his *Memoirs*, "the fighting died down, and we left by car. Churchill's first words were, 'Don't speak to me. I have never been so moved.' After about five minutes he leaned forward and said, 'Never in the field of human conflict was so much owed by so many to so few.' The words burned into my brain, and Churchill, as everyone knows, used them in a speech that was heard throughout the world." [33]

On August 8, and for the first week, the Luftwaffe attacked shipping and South Coast ports and harbors. On August 15, the next stage of the attack began with assaults on airfields in south and southeast England. It proved costly. In ten days some seven hundred German planes had been shot to pieces. [9]

Churchill watched the turning-point battle of September 15 from the underground headquarters of Fighter Group 11. Fascinated by the blinking lights that traced the movements of the planes, he reflected that the battle, "like Waterloo, is on a Sunday." That night, at Chequers, he got the resounding news that the R.A.F. had shot down one hundred and eighty-three planes while losing less than forty. Two days later, Hitler called off Operation Sea Lion—the invasion he had been mounting along Channel ports—and began an indiscriminate bombardment of London. [10]

German papers were suggesting that it might not be necessary to invade England, as she might collapse under the severe air-raid punishment inflicted on her. Britain's answer was given on the very same day by Churchill in Parliament: "This wicked man is the respository and embodiment of many forms of soul-destroying hatred; this monstrous product of former wrongs and shames has now resolved to try to break our famous island spirit by a process of indiscriminate slaughter and destruction. What he has done is to kindle a fire in British hearts here and all over the world which will glow long after all traces of the conflagrations he has caused in London have been removed." [9]

The drone of enemy planes overhead, the screaming and crashing of bombs and the answering thunder and flashing of antiaircraft defenses were an irresistible smell of danger to him. Londoners were taking it and Winston was determined to take it too. [25]

It was with the greatest difficulty that he was persuaded not to sleep at 10 Downing Street, a natural target for German bombers, but to move to the shelter in a Government building by Story's Gate which came to be known as the "Annex." Often, amid the steady crash of exploding bombs, he insisted on going up on the roof to see the sights. On one of these occasions an air-raid warden approached him timidly and said: "If—if you'll kindly excuse me, sir, would you mind moving?" "Why?" growled Winston. "Well, sir, you are sitting on the smoke vent, sir, and the building's full of smoke." [4]

Once, while standing at the doorway of 10 Downing Street admiring some particularly colorful bursts of shrapnel, Churchill was seized and flung inside by his faithful bodyguard, Inspector Thompson, just before a gigantic explosion outside. "Don't do that!" Churchill roared, but he was chastened when he learned that an employee standing outside had been severely injured. [10]

Often, when they entertained guests for dinner there on blitz nights, Winston and Clementine would see their visitors to their cars, frequently stepping out into the street with them as the searchlights swept the sky, guns boomed and bombs dropped. [25]

"We were dining in the garden room of Number 10," wrote Churchill, "when the usual night raid began. The steel shutters had been closed. Several loud explosions occurred around us. Suddenly I had a providential impulse. The spacious kitchen at Number 10 Downing Street looks out through a large plate-glass window twenty-five feet high. I became acutely conscious of this big window behind which Mrs. Landemare, the cook, and Nellie, the kitchen maid, never turning a hair, were at work. I got up abruptly, went into the kitchen, told the butler to put the dinner on the hot plate in the dining room, and ordered the cook and other servants into the shelter.

"I had been seated again at table only about three minutes when a very loud crash, close at hand, and a violent shock showed that the house had been struck. We went into the kitchen to view the scene. The devastation was complete. The bomb had fallen fifty yards away, and the blast had smitten the large, tidy kitchen, with all its bright saucepans and crockery, into a heap of black dust and rubble. The big plate-glass window had been hurled in fragments and splinters across the room and would, of course, have cut its occupants to pieces.

"As the raid seemed to grow in intensity, we put our tin hats on and went out to view the scene from the top of the Annex building. Before doing so, I could not resist taking Mrs. Landemare and the others from the shelter to see their kitchen. They were upset at the sight—principally on account of the general untidiness!" [3c]

When Churchill heard that the Germans had just missed hitting the home of Stanley Baldwin, whose failure to arm Britain in the 1930's had drawn his most caustic diatribes, he growled, "Very ungrateful of them." But he was extremely solicitous for the safety of the late Archbishop of Canterbury, who had a makeshift bomb shelter in the crypt of Lambeth Palace. "That will never do," said Churchill, insisting on a deeper and stronger shelter. "And if by chance you should suffer a direct hit, I am afraid, my dear Archbishop, we shall have to regard it as a divine summons." [44]

Eventually, the Annex adjoining 10 Downing Street was strengthened, and the Churchills moved back. "Here during the rest of the war my wife and I lived comfortably. My wife even hung up our few pictures in the sitting room. From the roof near the cupola of the Annex there was a splendid view of London on clear nights. They made a place for me with light overhead cover from splinters, and one could walk in the moonlight and watch the fireworks." [25]

One night during a heavy bombing, Mrs. Churchill said to Inspector Thompson, "Inspector, I have asked Mr. Churchill to come downstairs to bed in the shelter. He has promised to come down—will you see that he does?" "I will do my best, madam," Thompson replied, knowing full well how difficult this would be.

"To my surprise," wrote Thompson, "about 2:30 A.M. Winston came along the corridor and announced he was going downstairs to bed. He had a mischievous grin on his face. I went to my own room, and shortly after, my bell rang. I went to his room. He was standing beside his bed in his dressing gown. Smiling, he said, 'Pick up my clothes, Thompson. I have kept my promise. I have been down here to bed; now I am going upstairs to sleep.'" [55]

It was from the Annex, with the bombs crashing down outside as he spoke, that Winston made one of his memorable broadcasts on October 21, spoken in French: "Good night then: sleep to gather strength for the morning. For the morning will come. Brightly will it shine on the brave and true, kindly upon all who suffer for the cause, glorious upon the tomb of heroes. Then will shine the dawn. Vive la France!" [25]

The great speeches followed one upon the other, like the tolling of a mighty bell. All over the world, wherever English was understood, men of different faiths and parties stopped to listen to the erstwhile outcast. It was not only the elegance that held them. In this one beleaguered figure they recognized the will and purpose, perhaps even the conscience, not just of England but of the whole Western liberal world. [44]

Soon after taking over the rooms provided for him at Number Ten Annex, Churchill issued an order to the whole British Government against whistling in the corridors. "One morning we were on our way from the Annex to Downing Street," wrote Inspector Thompson. "A boy passed, whistling loudly and not too well. He half saluted Winston by a lift of eager brows as youngster passed statesman. 'Stop that whistling,' Churchill thundered. 'Whatever for?' the boy properly challenged. 'It's a horrible noise.' 'Then shut your ears!' the boy hurled back upon the astonished Prime Minister. The boy returned to his enjoyment full blast. I saw a slow smile break over Winston's face. He repeated the boy's words aloud to himself and chuckled. Then he looked up at me. 'Shut your ears,' he said. 'Shut your ears!' " [55]

After every raid Churchill plodded about the ruins next day, a portly picture of strength and solace. One morning, on a visit to a poor district in Peckham, he found himself surrounded by a crowd of people, many of whom had just lost their homes. They were "cheering and manifesting every sign of lively affection, wanting to touch and stroke my clothes. One would have thought I had brought them some fine substantial benefit which would improve their lot. I was completely undermined, and wept. Ismay, who was with me, records that he heard an old woman say, 'You see, he really cares. He's crying.' " [10]

"They were tears not of sorrow," wrote Churchill, "but of wonder and admiration. 'Give it 'em back!' they cried, and 'Let *them* have it, too.' I undertook forthwith to see that their wishes were carried out." [3c]

Often Clementine tramped with him through mud and slush to visit gun sites, or joined him as he drove in a jeep through the shattered streets giving his V-sign acknowledgment to the cheering people. When he stubbornly went out at night while bombs were falling, she insisted on going too. "I was at Downing Street the morning after one of their blitz-area visits," said General Sir Frederick Pile, "when Clementine brought in a little posy of flowers for Winston. She said, 'These have just come from one of the women we saw yesterday in the East End to thank you for your visit.' He slumped down on the table, buried his face in his hands, and wept."

"We went to one of the rest centers," wrote Lord Ismay, "where they were taking people who had been bombed out, and there was an old woman who was the picture of misery, pouring her soul into her handkerchief. Suddenly she looked up, saw Winston, and her whole face lit up. She waved her handkerchief and cried: 'Hooray! Hooray! Hooray!' and the way she looked at him was the nearest thing to blasphemy that I have ever witnessed. It affected both him and Clementine. Tears were pouring down his face. He was fortunate that he could release emotion. If tears had been so difficult for him as they are for some men, he would have been in agony." [25]

In *Their Finest Hour*, Churchill wrote: "These pages cannot describe the problems of London government, when often night after night ten or twenty thousand people were made homeless, and when nothing but the ceaseless vigil of the citizens as fire guards on the roofs prevented uncontrollable conflagrations; when hospitals filled with mutilated men and women were themselves struck by the enemy's bombs; when hundreds of thousands of weary people crowded together in unsafe and insanitary shelters; when communications by road and rail were ceaselessly broken down; when drains were smashed and light, power, and gas paralyzed; and when, nevertheless, the whole fighting, toiling life of London had to go forward.

"Till now the hostile attack had been confined almost exclusively to high-explosive bombs; but with the full moon of October, when the heaviest attack of the month fell upon us, about four hundred and eighty German aircraft dropped three hundred and eighty-six tons of high-explosive and, in addition, seventy thousand incendiary bombs. Hitherto we had encouraged the Londoners to take cover. Now 'to the basements' must be replaced by 'to the roofs.' An organization of fire-watchers and fire services on a gigantic scale and covering the whole of London was rapidly brought into being. At first fire-watchers were volunteers; but the numbers required were so great and the feeling that every man should take his turn upon the roster so strong, that fire-watching soon became compulsory. Women pressed forward to take their share. Large-scale systems of training were developed to teach the fire-watchers how to deal with the various kinds of incendiaries which were used against us. Many became adept and thousands of fires were extinguished before they took hold. The experience of remaining on the roof night after night under fire, with no protection but a tin hat, soon became habitual. At this time anyone would have been proud to be a Londoner.

"One evening when I was on my way to King's Cross," Churchill continued, "the sirens sounded, the streets began to empty, except for long queues of very tired, pale people, waiting for the last bus that would run. An autumn mist and drizzle shrouded the scene. The air was cold and raw. Night and the enemy were approaching. I felt, with a spasm of mental pain, a deep sense of the strain and suffering that was being borne throughout the world's largest capital city. How long would it go on? How much more would they have to bear? What effects would their exhaustion have upon our productive war-making power? What would happen if the drains got into the water supply? Early in October the main sewage outfall was destroyed and we had to let all our sewage flow into the Thames, which stank, first of sewage and afterwards of the floods of chemicals we poured into it. I feared the long nights for millions in the crowded street-shelters would produce epidemics. But it appeared that man is a gregarious animal and the mischievous microbes he exhales go out and devour each other and man walks off unharmed. The fact remains that during this rough winter the health of the Londoners was actually above the average. The power of enduring suffering in the ordinary people when their spirit is roused seems to have no bounds.

"Then a new and damaging form of attack was used against us. Large numbers of delayed-action bombs were plentifully cast upon us. These bombs had to be dug out, exploded or rendered harmless, a task of utmost peril. Special companies were formed in every city, town and district. Volunteers pressed forward for the deadly game. Some survived, others ran twenty, thirty or even forty courses before they met their fate. The unexploded-bomb detachments presented themselves wherever I went on my tours. Somehow their faces seemed different from those of ordinary men: gaunt, haggard, their faces had a bluish look with bright gleaming eyes and exceptional compression of the lips. One squad I remember which may be taken as symbolic of many others. It consisted of three people—the Earl of Suffolk, his lady private secretary, and his rather aged chauffeur. They called themselves 'the Holy Trinity.' Their prowess and continued existence got around among all who knew. Thirty-four unexploded bombs did they tackle with urbane efficiency. But

the thirty-fifth claimed its forfeit. Up went the Earl of Suffolk in his Holy Trinity. But we may be sure that, as for Great-heart, 'all the trumpets sounded for them on the other side.'"
[3c]

Each night the city learned to know the unpleasant music of the approach of the German bombers, the halting drone of enemy propellers, the swish and thud of bombs, the glare of fires, and the swift rush of automobiles through the empty streets. Each morning, as it picked its way to work across the broken glass, it counted the destruction; but each day it found that London was still there. Its great pulse beat steadily and it accepted Mr. Churchill's cheerful calculation that "it would take ten years at the present rate for half the houses of London to be demolished. After that, of course, progress would be much slower." [26]

The night bombings ranged far and wide over the rest of the country as well: Merseyside and Tyneside, Cardiff and Swansea, Bristol and Plymouth, Birmingham and the Midlands took their share of destruction. [9]

"Our train wasn't allowed to enter Bristol that night, because of the raid going on, the worst the city had ever suffered," recalled Lord Ismay. "When we finally arrived at Bristol station we were guided to our hotel by the city's chief constable: the first thing both Winston and Clementine wanted, after spending the night in the train, was a bath." But bombs had interrupted the hotel's hot water supply. Undaunted, the hotel manager was determined to give service to his distinguished guests. "I'll see what I can do," he announced and disappeared. There followed an amazing sight. The entire hotel staff joined with all the guests to form a human plumbing system. Kettle after kettle, jug after jug of hot water was relayed by hand upstairs from the basement to the second floor. Every link in the human plumbing chain was laughing and so were the recipients of the water at the other end. Always the considerate husband, Winston shared half the bath water with Clementine. [25]

Then, on November 15, a savage and concentrated attack was launched on Coventry. [9]

The raid started early in the dark hours of the fourteenth, and by dawn nearly five hundred German aircraft had dropped six hundred tons of high explosives and thousands of incendiaries. The center of Coventry was shattered. [3c]

While examining the resulting havoc, Churchill was unable to speak. He walked, silent, between the bare walls of the cathedral, shaking his head, looking about at the blind windows, listening to the wind in the frames. He picked up a relic of the smashed cathedral and brought it with him.

"We came back to London," recalled Inspector Thompson. "We were very tired. It showed in increasing irritability of the Prime Minister. He would turn on any handy person and let off steam. Because I was *always* handy, I got a good deal of these scaldings. General Sir Hastings Ismay, secretary to the War Cabinet, was present during one of these outbursts. He smiled with a sudden flash of intimate understanding: 'I get it just the same, Thompson. If it lightens the load, it's worth it.'" [55]

By the spring of 1941, the blitz was growing more intermittent. From time to time there would be a violent raid on London or some big provincial city, but the raid-free nights became more common. When, in June, Hitler turned against Russia, the skies above Britain cleared, and Londoners fell asleep with a sense of something strange, missing the thunderous uproar which had for so long been their nightly lullaby. [9]

16

Hands Across
the Atlantic

ONE gray winter morning a fortnight after Christmas,
1940, a frail, exhausted man arrived at Bournemouth:
Harry Hopkins, Roosevelt's closest confidant, had come to
Britain at the President's request.

Hopkins was fascinated by Churchill. To him Churchill
"always seemed to be at his command post on the precarious
beachhead and the guns were continually blazing in his
conversation; wherever he was, there was the battlefront—
and he was involved not only in the battles of the current war
but of the whole past from Cannae to Gallipoli."

"The President is determined that we shall win the war
together," Hopkins told the Prime Minister. "He has sent me
here to tell you that at all costs he will carry you through, no
matter what happens to him." [6]

"What is the answer that I shall give in your name," Churchill broadcast to the nation, "to this great man, President
Roosevelt, the thrice-chosen head of a nation of one hundred
and thirty million? Here is the answer which I shall give:
GIVE US THE TOOLS AND WE WILL FINISH THE JOB!" [9]

Churchill went on working day after day, night after night,
because work was wonderful. His sense of responsibility in
the long and bitter agonies of the war was massive and

unremitting. Yet he got his own fun out of his own misery. At a War Cabinet meeting a proposal was advanced for giving a few weeks' holiday leave, on some sort of roster, to senior civil servants who had been carrying grievous and continuous burdens. "Well," said Winston, "I suppose, since you insist, that I must agree. But I confess that I do not understand how anybody, privileged before history to play a part in this mighty struggle, can bear to be separated from his duty for even five minutes." [39]

"The Hole in the Ground"—a labyrinth of passages under Great George Street in London—was the nerve center of British war direction. Along the walls of the corridors that linked the Cabinet War Room with one hundred and fifty other rooms leading one to another, thick brown pipes lay like shiny snakes. Messages were folded in circular canisters and blown along them by compressed air, much as salesmen in old-fashioned department stores received change. In the main corridor was a small door with two words painted on it: *Prime Minister*. Here, in a room so narrow it resembled a prison cell, its walls covered by maps, Churchill made all his famous wartime broadcasts. He sat in a swivel chair at a desk at the far end, under whitewashed oak beams. He also had a dining room, which he rarely used, and a small bedroom for Mrs. Churchill.

But the room from which Churchill directed the war was the Cabinet War Room. About forty feet square, it had double doors which were always locked when a meeting was in progress. Tubular metal chairs with green leather upholstery faced a huge hollow table covered in black baize. In front of Mr. Churchill's place stood a piece of cardboard on which someone had laboriously printed Queen Victoria's remark: *"Please understand there is no pessimism in the house and we are not interested in the possibilities of defeat: they do not exist."*

Churchill dominated every meeting of the War Cabinet.

Around ten-thirty in the evening, the Ministers would be called to discuss some supply or manpower problem—they were always desperately short of everything: men, factories, ships, steel, guns, tanks. By the time the atmosphere in the War Room was blue with smoke and sharp with acrimony, the "Old Boss" would trundle in, wearing his siren suit, with dragon-decorated slippers and a cigar. At once each Minister would passionately press his claim to priority. The Old Boss would pass by, unruffled, to take his seat, and then ask General Ismay what was on the agenda. As Ismay replied, Churchill would toss the butt of his cigar in the fire bucket behind him. He never took aim, but he rarely missed— marines on guard outside the room made considerable sums selling these butts as souvenirs. Then Churchill would quell the clamor with a wisecrack: "Same old story," he grunted once, "too many little pigs and not enough teats on the old sow."

A few steps down the corridor was the smallest room in "The Hole," little larger than a telephone booth, fitted with a lock taken from a lavatory door, marked "Vacant" and "Engaged"; it contained a seat facing the wall, with a clock to one side: two black hands recorded Greenwich time and two red ones the corresponding time in Washington. From this tiny hutch, unnumbered feet below ground, Mr. Churchill had a direct line to President Roosevelt in the White House. In his slippers with pompons, wearing his magnificent mandarin dressing gown embroidered in red and gold dragons, the belt pulled tightly round him, his cigar clamped like some miniature torpedo between his teeth, he would stump along the corridor towards the telephone, his complexion as cherubic and pink as if he had just risen from eight hours' sleep.

"Put the President on," he would say in an imperious way, waiting, head down, glowering under his brows, impatient of a second's delay. Roosevelt was not at all eager to come to the telephone until he knew for certain that the Prime Minister was actually at the other end. And Churchill was also reluctant to be closed in the airless telephone room, waiting while the President was being wheeled to the telephone in the White House. So General Leslie Hollis and his opposite number in Washington would pretend that their principals were actually on the line when they were not. "The President is just coming, sir," the American would say. "He is picking up the telephone at this very moment." And Hollis would claim Churchill was stubbing out his cigar and reaching for the instrument. Eventually they would make contact, Hollis would leave the smallest room, and the indicator on the door would turn from "Vacant" to "Engaged." The blue smoke would curl up underneath and above the door, so that the whole place seemed on fire. When Churchill came out, it appeared as though he were stepping from the heart of a furnace. [31]

He was dogmatic, domineering, provoking, infuriating, but he was an inspiration. At some of the more lively meetings, there would be exhortations and harangues, explosive expostulations. Disregarding the agenda, Churchill would discourse till time had run out and no decision would be reached. Or, encountering persistent opposition to a pet project, the vials of his wrath opened, he would denounce defeatist generals with cold feet. Did none of them want to fight the "Narzees"? [2]

Nothing was too small for the Prime Minister's attention. At one of the worst periods of the war he sent out (a) a persistent correspondence on whether candy would have to be rationed, (b) orders that tree-felling operations should keep in consideration the beauty of the English countryside, and (c) that girls in the A.T.S. (Auxiliary Territorial Service) should be treated kindly and as ladies. [1]

After he read in *The Times* that senior officers in a certain army command were expected to take part in long cross-country runs the Secretary of State for War was taken to task. "Who is the general of this division," asked Churchill, "and does he run the seven miles himself? If so he may be more useful for football than war. In my experience officers with high athletic qualifications are not usually successful in the higher ranks." He waged gleeful war on official jargon. One morning he tossed a report across his desk to the Chief Government Whip. "Typical Foreign Office jargon," he said with an angry snort. "It contains every cliché but 'Please adjust your dress before leaving.'"

To the young staff officers in the War Office who frequently came to contact the Prime Minister, Churchill seemed a galvanic figure. He inspired a sense of awe. One Saturday an officer on the Military Operations staff went to Downing Street to bring the maps up to date, a task which fell to him once a week, and he chose Saturday as Churchill was usually at Chequers. On this morning he was lying full length on the floor, marking alterations to the British front line. His tunic was unbuttoned, and beside him on the floor he had placed his cap and Sam Browne belt.

Suddenly he heard the door open, and into the Map Room came the Prime Minister and the American General Simpson. Ignoring the silent figure on the floor, they talked for a few minutes, and then left the room. A second later the door opened once more. To his astonishment the recumbent artist, still busily drawing his chalk lines, heard the clink of coins landing in his upturned cap. He looked round just in time to see Mr. Churchill stealthily retreating, a beaming smile on his face.

In the beginning of April, Churchill, as Chancellor of Bristol University, conferred Degrees on John Winant, the United States Ambassador, and Robert Menzies, the Prime Minister of Australia. In a great speech that morning, the Prime Minister referred to "this turning point in the history of the world," and paid tribute to the fortitude of the British people. But the days which now followed were to test even his buoyant optimism. [6]

General Sir Archibald Wavell sent troops he could not spare from Africa to Greece to help England's gallant ally. Marshal Erwin Rommel, who had moved from Africa with German soldiers to stiffen the Italians, took advantage of the situation, attacked and drove the British back to the Egyptian border, leaving behind the British outpost of Tobruk, which was besieged but held out. The Germans then struck at Greece and Yugoslavia and knocked them both out of the war. [1]

In Parliament, early in May 1941, the Prime Minister said, "It is a year almost to a day since men of all parties joined hands together to fight this business to the end. When I look back on the perils which have been overcome, upon the great mountain waves through which the gallant ship has driven, when I remember all that has gone wrong, and remember also all that has gone right, I feel sure we have no need to fear the tempest. Let it roar, and let it rage. We shall come through."

Those were the last words he spoke in the old Chamber. [39]

On May 10, the enemy returned to London with incendiary bombs. More than two thousand fires were lit and, by the smashing of nearly one hundred and fifty water mains, coupled with the low tide in the Thames, there was no way to put them out. It was the most destructive attack of the whole night blitz. It was historic also. It destroyed the House of Commons. [3b]

"The next morning," wrote Guy Eden, "I stood with Winston Churchill amid the still-smoking ruins. His eyes traveled sadly along the space where the floor of the Chamber had been, to the site of the Table from which he had delivered many a speech, up to the galleries from which thousands had listened to him. His jaw muscles worked tensely. The end of the walking stick he carried was ground silently and savagely

One of the earliest pictures of Winston taken in childhood, with his American mother

1895. After leaving Harrow School and the Royal Military Academy, Sandhurst, Churchill was commissioned in the 4th Queen's Own Hussars. Three years later he distinguished himself at Omdurman in the Sudan

1908. Winston Churchill and Miss Clementine Hozier announce their engagement

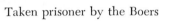

Taken prisoner by the Boers

Wide World

Cult

1911. The Home Secretary
at the Sidney Street skirmish

1915. Churchill resigned as First Lord of the Admiralty and joined
the British Army in France. Here he is seen with a group of officers
at the French 33rd Corps Headquarters

1924. Churchill campaigns for Parliament as a Conservative

1930–1939. Although a Member of Parliament, Churchill held no office in the Government. At his country home in Westerham, Kent, he devoted much of his time to writing and took up some new hobbies

1940. A weeping Churchill,
standing in the ruins of the House
of Commons, vows to rebuild
the chamber "exactly as it was"

1943. At Algiers, Churchill discusses Allied strategy with the Chiefs of Staff

1945. Churchill crosses the Rhine and sets foot on German soil, followed by General Simpson, General Sir Alan Brooke and General Montgomery

At Yalta in the Crimea, the "Big Three" meet to make final plans for victory

On the afternoon of V-E Day, Churchill appears on the balcony of Buckingham Palace to share with King George VI and his family the ovation of the cheering crowds gathered below

1946. No longer Prime Minister, Churchill resumes his peacetime hobbies. Here he relaxes and paints in Miami

1951. Churchill relaxes in his garden with his wife, his daughter Diana (left),
son Randolph (right), and some of his grandchildren. Later in the year he again
became Prime Minister

1953. Churchill attends the three-power conference in Bermuda with President Eisenhower and Joseph Laniel, the French Prime Minister

1954. Now Sir Winston, Churchill is installed as a Knight of the Most Noble Order of the Garter by Her Majesty Queen Elizabeth II

into the powdering cinders. At last he moved, and in the dim light I could see that tears were running unchecked down his cheeks. Turning abruptly to an official, he controlled his voice with an effort and said quietly: 'This Chamber must be rebuilt—just as it was. Meanwhile, we shall not miss a single day's debate.' "

Brushing the sleeve of his coat across his eyes, with the gesture of the schoolboy hiding his tears from public gaze, Churchill strode off, back to his War Room, with its map-covered walls, back to his planning and scheming for victory. [21]

In the sheer determination to get things done, he often overshot himself, only to be pulled up by a saving humility. Thus, when reports came in that the Germans were mistreating British prisoners, he wrathfully ordered the manacling of German prisoners in reprisal. The British press was horrified and, journeying up to Scotland one day in his private railroad carriage, he asked his parliamentary private secretary, Brigadier Harvie Watt, what he thought of it all. Watt said he did not like it. The Prime Minister raged and Watt subsided. Churchill then buried himself in his papers and no more was said for an hour. Presently, he called softly, "Harvie . . ." "Yes, sir . . ." "I am troubled by the points you raise." [44]

Meanwhile, the gunshot marriage of Hitler and Stalin had not been wearing well; during the spring a general, surreptitious eastward movement of German troops had been observed. Churchill had little doubt that Russia, not Britain, was to be the victim of 1941. [37]

On Sunday, June 22, while the Prime Minister was at Chequers, he received a message which transformed the whole aspect of the war. The German invasion of Russia had begun. [6]

Churchill immediately set forth British policy: "If Hitler invaded Hell I would make at least a favorable reference to the Devil in the House of Commons." [10]

183

"No one has been a more consistent opponent of communism than I have been for the last twenty-five years. I will not unsay a word I have spoken about it. All this fades away before the spectacle that is now unfolding. Any man or state who fights against Nazidom will have our aid. Any man or state who marches with Hitler is our foe. I see ten thousand villages of Russia and I see advancing upon all this in hideous onslaught the Nazi war machine, with its clanking, heel-clicking, dandified Prussian officers, the crafty expert agents from the cowing and tying-down of a dozen countries. I see also the dull, drilled, docile, brutish masses of the Hun soldiery plodding on like a swarm of crawling locusts." [3b]

Churchill promised to provide everything that Britain could spare. Supplies were sent north across the sea by way of Archangel: fighter planes, the first demand of every British commander; rubber, consigned from precious reserves; lead, wool cloth. [2]

In return, he got little from Moscow but surly and insistent demands for the immediate opening of a Second Front, which could only be a fiasco. During that first year, when through her necessities Russia was a liability and Britain was sending so much that she herself wanted so sorely, no word of recognition was ever vouchsafed and, for his pains, Churchill received many rebuffs and only rarely a kind word. [37]

At the same time he was well aware that the whole outlook of the conflict had been altered by this one fateful stroke. It seemed almost unbelievable, but of her own volition Germany had committed herself—in defiance of all the lessons of history—to a major war on two fronts. [6]

"One afternoon in late July," recalled Churchill, "Harry Hopkins came into the garden of Downing Street and we sat together in the sunshine. Presently he said that the President would like very much to have a meeting with me in some lonely bay or other. Placentia Bay, in Newfoundland, was chosen, the date of August 9 fixed, and our latest battleship, the *Prince of Wales,* placed under order. I had the keenest desire to meet Mr. Roosevelt, with whom I had now corresponded with increasing intimacy for nearly two years. A conference between us would cause our enemies concern, make Japan ponder and cheer our friends. The utmost secrecy was necessary because of the large numbers of U-boats then in the North Atlantic. To insure secrecy the President, who was ostensibly on a holiday cruise, transshipped at sea to the cruiser *Augusta* and left his yacht behind him as a blind. Meanwhile Harry Hopkins, though far from well, obtained Roosevelt's authority to fly to Moscow in order to obtain directly from Stalin the fullest knowledge of the Soviet position and needs. He was to join the *Prince of Wales* at Scapa Flow."

> *Former Naval Person to President Roosevelt:* 4.5 Aug 41
> Harry returned dead-beat from Russia. We shall get him in fine trim on the voyage. We are just off. It is twenty-seven years ago today that Huns began their last war. We must make a good job of it this time. Twice ought to be enough. Look forward so much to our meeting. Kindest regards. [3b]

On the second day at sea a drastic alteration of course was necessary. A U-boat disguised as a ketch had been sighted ahead on the intended route. By now the *Prince of Wales* had left her escorts, who were unable to keep pace with her in the heavy seas, and she was driving on alone at top speed. [6]

The crew could never be sure when Churchill was apt to burst in on them. Wearing an impish grin, and smoking a cigar, he would clamber down a companionway and make pointed inquiries of a work party. If the group was called to attention, he said, "No, no. Carry on. I want to walk about without interfering. Allow the men to be at ease, so that I can have personal contact with them." In the Warrant Officer's

Mess he found the darts in poor condition and presented his hosts with a costly new set he bought from a canteen. [8]

The Map Room in the *Prince of Wales,* a replica in miniature of that at the Admiralty, had been fitted up on the Prime Minister's instructions. An enormous map of the Atlantic Ocean occupied one wall. The opposite wall bore large maps of the Russian front. The position of every ship and every known U-boat was plotted hour by hour upon the map. U-boats were represented by sinister little coffin-shaped ebony pins. Sometimes Captain Pim, an officer from the Admiralty, would rise with a message in his hand and remove a U-boat pin.

"We were due to anchor off Newfoundland the following morning," wrote H. V. Morton, official correspondent for the trip. "We met after dinner for the nightly film in a mood of great cheerfulness. The film was *Lady Hamilton,* the story of Lord Nelson and Emma Hamilton—Churchill had already seen it four times. The lights went out. As in Nelson's day, England was again at war, fighting for her life. Churchill seemed to retreat into himself, absorbed in the story of a man who gave everything he had so that England might live in freedom and peace. As the last scene came and Nelson lay dying in the cockpit of the *Victory,* and they bent above him and told him that the day was his, the man watching so intently took a handkerchief from his pocket and wiped his eyes without shame.

"The lights went up. Mr. Churchill stood facing us. 'I thought this would interest you gentlemen,' he said, 'many of whom have been recently engaged with the enemy in matters of equal historical importance. Good night!' He bowed and went out.

"The great day had come at last. Rounding a promontory and entering the mouth of Placentia Bay, we saw the American warships waiting at anchor for us. As we approached the cruiser *Augusta* with the President aboard we saw upon her forward gun deck a group of men in uniform, and in the center a tall man who wore a light brown suit.

"Mr. Roosevelt was watching our approach, scrutinizing us for the first sight of Mr. Churchill. As we drew abreast, I saw him remove his hat and stand in salute as the *Prince of Wales* went by. At that moment Mr. Churchill, standing to attention on the quarterdeck, raised his hand to the peak of his cap. The bosun's pipes shrilled, the band of the Royal Marines crashed into 'The Star-Spangled Banner.' Like an echo across the strip of water came the notes of 'God Save the King.' So we passed to our anchorage where, with a great noise, our anchor chains descended into the Newfoundland fathoms." [43]

As Churchill mounted to the deck of the *Augusta,* his expression was grave. Then walking slowly up to President Roosevelt, he took him strongly by the hand and presented a letter from King George. His face broke into a triumphant grin as the memorable Roosevelt smile—head thrown back and tilted at a cocky angle—greeted the visitor from war-ravaged England. [8]

"That afternoon," recalled Morton, "we saw approaching, in motor boats, a pyramid of fifteen hundred cardboard cartons. Each carton contained an orange, two apples, two hundred cigarettes, and half a pound of cheese—a box for every sailor on the *Prince of Wales,* and inside each one a card with the words: 'The President of the United States of America sends his compliments and best wishes.'"

While the pyramid was being distributed, Mr. Churchill came on deck. Official photographers, nervously maneuvering for pictures of the Americans and their gifts, wondered if the Prime Minister might object to such scenes upon the quarterdeck. But Churchill walked up and was soon in sole charge of the operation. "Come over here!" he called to the American sailors and grouped them with a number of British sailors. Stepping back, he critically examined the group.

"Wait a moment, don't take it yet!" Waving his cigar at the sailors, he shouted, "More tooth!" The men burst out laughing and the shutters clicked. Churchill, twinkling mischievously, took his place among them and was photographed. [43]

Churchill has written a poignant description of the scene that summer morning in the quiet sunlit bay, when the President came aboard the *Prince of Wales* with all his staff for Sunday service: "The close-packed ranks of British and American sailors completely intermingled, sharing the same books and joining fervently in the prayers and hymns familiar to both. I chose the hymns myself—'For Those in Peril on the Sea' and 'Onward Christian Soldiers.' We ended with 'O God, Our Help in Ages Past.' Every word seemed to stir the heart. It was a great hour to live." [7]

"That afternoon," wrote Morton, "Churchill decided he would spend a little time ashore. A whaler was brought round to the gangway, towed by a motor launch. Churchill appeared on deck, dressed again in his siren suit, in company with Mr. Averell Harriman, Sir Alexander Cadogan, and Commander Thompson. We watched them depart and an hour later saw them returning. Mr. Churchill was sitting in the whaler holding a bunch of pink wild flowers he had collected on the beaches and the hills.

"In the evening the Prime Minister dined with the President. Just as he was leaving he asked me if I did not think the church parade had been a wonderful sight. Then he added, 'I have an idea that something really big may be happening—something really big . . .' He turned away and descended the gangway to the launch." [43]

"President Roosevelt told me at one of our first conversations," Churchill wrote, "that he thought it would be well if we could draw up a joint declaration laying down certain broad principles which should guide our policies along the same road. I gave him the next day a tentative outline of such a declaration. Considering all the tales of my reactionary, Old

World outlook, and the pain this is said to have caused the President, I am glad it should be on record that the substance and spirit of what came to be called the 'Atlantic Charter' was in its first draft a British production cast in my own words." [3b]

The Charter demanded the right of self-government for all nations, equal economic opportunities, progress and social security, freedom from fear and war, the disarmament of aggressor nations and the establishment of a permanent international system of security. [9]

It was never inscribed on parchment and signed, sealed and taped; it was merely mimeographed and released. Nevertheless, its effect was cosmic and historic. Point Three stated: "They respect the right of all peoples to choose the form of Government under which they will live." (That clause was by Churchill himself.) That one small word "all" came to be the cornerstone of the structure of the United Nations. [51]

At five o'clock on the afternoon of August 12 the *Prince of Wales* sailed for home. [6]

"So far," wrote Morton, "we had taken good care to avoid convoys. But all the time Mr. Churchill was longing to see one. Now the chart showed a magnificent convoy of seventy-two ships ahead of us. Mr. Churchill pointed out that only a slight deflection from our course would take us into them. A wireless warning to the corvettes was sent out. That evening I ran out on the quarterdeck and saw an amazing sight. We were racing through the middle of the convoy covering many square miles of the Atlantic: tramps, tankers, liners and whalers, salty old tubs and cargo boats of every age and size on each side of us, the nearest only two hundred yards away. It was like meeting a town at sea with all the chimneys smoking.

"Colored flags and a pennant flying from our foremast read: 'Good Voyage, Churchill.' As each ship read the message we could hear the sound of cheering, we could see skippers laughing inside wheelhouses, trying to wave with one hand and touch off the siren with the other. Upon our bridge Winston Churchill—waving his hat in the air, making a V with the forefingers of his right hand—was cheering as madly as any of the men who were cheering him.

"Having passed through them, we turned and saw our white wake streaking backward. Then to our surprise the *Prince of Wales* with her destroyers began to describe a circle and we raced back behind the convoy. Why? The Prime Minister insisted on seeing it all over again!" [43]

"It would be an exaggeration," wrote Robert Sherwood later, "to say that Roosevelt and Churchill became chums at this conference or at any subsequent time"; but it was at Placentia that they established "an easy intimacy, a joking informality, and a moratorium on pomposity and cant." Coming events were to show that intimacy and mutual understanding between the two leaders of the English-speaking world was perhaps the most important outcome of all that happened in Placentia Bay. [6]

December 7, 1941. I turned on my wireless set [Churchill wrote] *shortly after the nine o'clock news had started. Some sentences were spoken regarding an attack by the Japanese on American shipping at Hawaii. Then the butler, Sawyers, came into the room saying: "The Japanese have attacked the Americans." I got up from the table and walked to the office. I asked for a call to the President. Mr. Roosevelt came through. "Mr. President, what's this about Japan?" "It's quite true," he replied. "They have attacked us at Pearl Harbor. We are all in the same boat now."*

To have the United States at our side was to me the greatest joy. Now England would live. Our history would not come to an end. Saturated and satiated with emotion and sensation, I went to bed and slept the sleep of the saved and thankful. [3b]

Churchill boarded ship at once and proceeded with his entire entourage of admirals, field marshals and generals straight to a White House Christmas. Two fears sped him on his way. One was of a panicky diversion of American power to the Pacific; the other, that America's concentration on her now-declared war would prevent a further meshing of Anglo-American decisions. If his fears had any basis in fact, the meeting in Washington quickly dispelled them. [44]

On the afternoon of December 22, the *Duke of York* arrived at the mouth of Chesapeake Bay. While the rest of the party boarded a special train, Churchill, impatient to reach Washington, went on ahead in a U.S. navy plane. [6]

His trip cloaked in wartime censorship, Churchill dropped out of the sky with breathtaking suddenness, giving Washington new vigor. The day after his arrival, he sat beside Franklin Roosevelt behind the broad desk of the oval office in the Executive Offices, waiting with poker-faced calm while two hundred–odd U.S. and foreign newsmen gathered for a press conference. Those who crowded up front saw a pudgy man with cheeks like apple dumplings, blue eyes beneath crooked restless eyebrows, the merest foam-flecking of sandy gray hair on his bald pink pate, a long black cigar clenched at a belligerent angle above his bulldog jaw. From the sleeves of his blue sack coat extended long cuffs, half hiding the small hands folded placidly across his middle.

Franklin Roosevelt introduced his guest. There were shouts from the rear by newsmen who couldn't see. Churchill stood up, grinned, climbed on his chair, waved his hand. The applause and cheers rattled the windows. He had won his first U.S. audience.

With Churchill had come his Minister of Supply, Lord Beaverbrook, and eighty-two other civilian and military aides. As the conversations progressed, President Roosevelt talked to Russia's Ambassador Maxim Litvinoff, to China's Dr. Hu Shih and Dr. T. V. Soong, Dutch Minister Alexander Loudon, representatives of the Latin American republics and occupied European nations. Prime Minister W. L. Mackenzie King arrived from Canada.

At the same time British Foreign Secretary Anthony Eden was in Moscow and the two conferences kept in close touch. This was no mere U.S.–British meeting of minds. It was, as far as possible, to embrace the foes of the Axis all over the world. [56]

Since Churchill knew of Roosevelt's habits of going to bed early, he made a pretense of retiring himself at a fairly reasonable hour; but Roosevelt knew that his tireless guest and Hopkins would go on talking and he did not want to miss any of it so he stayed up much later than usual. Churchill was one of the few people to whom Roosevelt cared to listen, and vice versa. [51]

However, Churchill did complain to his British associates that Roosevelt seemed to him an unusually talkative man. "He tries to monopolize the conversation." Roosevelt had an identical view of Churchill. At one conference, the President remarked to James Byrnes that it would be wonderful if Churchill could refrain from making long speeches—they "hold up the business." [8]

As in England, Churchill's working day began at breakfast-time. Often he would continue to dictate a stream of directives and memoranda as he lay in his bath. [6]

Once he sent for Brigadier Leslie Hollis to read him some secret reports that had just arrived. Suddenly Mr. Churchill gripped his nose between thumb and forefinger and disappeared like a pink, plump porpoise under the surface of the bath water. Hollis stopped reading for a few seconds until the Prime Minister surfaced again, wiping water from his eyes and hair. Accusingly, he looked over the rim of the bath at Hollis. "Why did you stop reading?" he asked in an aggrieved tone. "Don't you know that water is a conductor of sound?"

Hollis had brought his civilian secretary, Mr. Jones, with

him. One day he gave him some documents to take to Mr. Churchill's secretary. As Jones stood in the corridor where Mr. Churchill had his rooms, the great door of one of the bedrooms began to open and President Roosevelt emerged in his wheelchair. He asked Jones whether Mr. Churchill was ready to receive him and he nodded towards another door. Jones knocked on this door and the gruff voice of the Prime Minister grumbled something within. "Please open it for me," said Roosevelt, and Jones did so. To his horror, Churchill was revealed wrapping a towel around himself and looking with some surprise at the entry of the American President. [31]

Roosevelt started to apologize and made as if to leave, but Churchill protested it was quite all right. "The Prime Minister of Great Britain," he said, "has nothing to conceal from the President of the United States." [51]

On Christmas Eve Winston Churchill stood bareheaded while Franklin Roosevelt, on the South portico of the White House, went through the annual ceremony of turning on the outdoor Christmas tree's lights before some two thousand spectators inside the grounds, more thousands outside. Then he joined the President in broadcasting Christmas greetings to the nation. "I spend this anniversary far from my country, far from my family, and yet I cannot truthfully say that I feel far from home."

Congressmen who had gone home for the Christmas holiday scurried back to Washington for a joint session of Congress on December 26. A thousand men and women crowded into the small galleries; another five thousand stood in the damp weather outside the Capitol. An ovation greeted Churchill from isolationist and interventionist Congressmen alike. He shoved his thick, horn-rimmed glasses over his nose, blinked, balanced himself like an old sailor. With a sly grin, he made his joke: "I cannot help thinking that if my father had been American and my mother British, instead of the other way around, I might have got here on my own." [56]

By far the greatest ovation greeted his challenge to the Japanese: "What kind of a people do they think we are? Is it possible they do not realize that we shall never cease to persevere against them until they have been taught a lesson they and the world will never forget?" [51]

Two days later he addressed the Canadian House of Commons. He described his last visit to France just before the country was overrun. "When I warned them that Britain would fight on alone their generals told their Prime Minister that in three weeks England would have her neck wrung like a chicken. Some chicken! Some neck!" [6]

During the fourteen days that Churchill was in the White House, he and Roosevelt and Hopkins had lunch and dinner together every day but one. It was at the lunches that most of the major problems were thrashed out, so that when the President and Prime Minister went into the full dress meetings they were often already in agreement. There were at least eight major White House meetings and twelve meetings of the two sets of Chiefs of Staff. [51]

The entire military and economic resources of Britain and America were to be pooled; agreement had also been reached for the creation of a combined Chiefs of Staff Organization to assume the main responsibility for the conduct of all operations. Most important was the decision that the first aim of the Allies must be the defeat of the Axis in Europe; settlement of America's score in the Pacific would come later. [6]

"I think you should make every effort," wrote Hopkins to Roosevelt at the time, "to get religious freedom in this document." [51]

About this, Churchill wrote in *The Grand Alliance:* "The President exerted his most fervent efforts to persuade the Soviet ambassador to accept the phrase. The President had a long talk with him about his soul and the dangers of hell-fire. The accounts which Mr. Roosevelt gave us on several occasions of what he said to the Russian were impressive. Indeed,

I promised Mr. Roosevelt to recommend him for the position of Archbishop of Canterbury if he should lose the next Presidential election. Litvinov reported the issue in evident fear and trembling to Stalin, who accepted it as a matter of course." [3b]

Thus the words "religious freedom" appeared in the final Declaration. On New Year's Day, 1942, the representatives of twenty-six countries gathered in the White House and signed the document which gave birth to the United Nations. [51]

The strain of public appearances, speeches and constant meetings now began to tell on Churchill. When Edward Stettinius, one of the President's special assistants, suggested a few days' rest at the house he owned on the coast of Florida, Churchill gratefully accepted. [6]

During his "rest," Churchill worked about fourteen hours a day, interspersing his stints with frequent swims. When the group arrived, Inspector Thompson started in to one of the local shops for a bathing suit and asked the Prime Minister if he would like one too. "I don't think I need one," Churchill said. "It is entirely private here. Nobody knows I am staying in this place, and I have only to step out of the back door into the sea."

The Inspector suggested he could be seen "through glasses." Churchill's reply was, "If they are that much interested it is their own fault what they see."

Shortly afterward he came out on his beach wrapped in a huge white bath towel, and Thompson felt relieved. Approaching the water, however, Churchill yanked the towel free and tossed it to an attendant standing nearby. Then, naked, he dove into the sea, swam out a way and began to turn over and over "like a porpoise," agitating the water so violently that a fifteen-foot shark swam up to see what was going on. The shark's impression was apparently unfavorable, for it got out pretty fast. "My bulk must have frightened him away," said Churchill. [8]

When Churchill left for home, on January 14, Hopkins sent with the Prime Minister's party some presents for his friend "Clemmie" and a note in which he said: "You would have been quite proud of your husband this trip. First because he was ever so good natured. I didn't see him take anybody's head off and he eats and drinks with his customary vigor, and still dislikes the same people. If he had half as good a time here as the President did having him about the White House he surely will carry pleasant memories of the past three weeks." [51]

PART
3

PART

3

17

Operation Torch

IT was not a happy homecoming. [6]

The House was restless and angry at the way the war was going. Singapore was falling, together with Malaya and Burma. [42]

Worse was to come. In the desert, where all had promised so well and British forces under Auchinleck had reached the Libyan frontier, Rommel suddenly launched a successful violent counterattack. From the newspapers came blunt criticism of the conduct of affairs on the home front and Mr. Churchill's wisdom in combining the role of Prime Minister and Minister of Defense. "The whole people want Mr. Churchill as Prime Minister to lead them through the war to victory," said *The Times*. "But a considerable proportion feel that they need a different Government." [6]

"I resolved to yield nothing to any quarter," wrote Churchill, "to take the prime and direct personal responsibility upon myself and to demand a Vote of Confidence. The British people can face peril with fortitude but they bitterly resent being deceived or finding that those responsible for their affairs are themselves dwelling in a fool's paradise. On January 27 the debate began.

" 'We have had a great deal of bad news lately from the Far East,' I said, 'and I think it highly probable, for reasons which I shall presently explain, that we shall have a great deal more. No one will pretend for a moment that disasters like these occur without there having been faults and shortcomings. It is because things have gone badly and worse is to come that I demand a Vote of Confidence. No one need be mealy-mouthed to debate and no one should be chicken-hearted in voting. Everyone in these rough times must do what he thinks is his duty.'

"I gave them some account of the Desert battle and presently came to the larger issue of our nakedness in the Far West. I had to burden the House for nearly two hours. 'I stand by my original program, blood, toil, tears and sweat, which is all I have ever offered, to which I added, five months later, "many shortcomings, mistakes, and disappointments." But it is because I see the light gleaming behind the cloud and broadening on our path that I make so bold now as to demand a declaration of confidence from the House of Commons as an additional weapon in the armory of the United Nations.'

"The debate ran on for three days. The result was a vote of confidence of four hundred and sixty-four to one. Congratulations poured in from all over the Allied world. 'It is fun,' cabled the President, 'to be in the same decade with you.' " [3d]

During the debate the Prime Minister had also been reproached for the "perfectly intolerable" working hours which he imposed on his subordinates. "The hour when most men, exhausted by the day's labor, were seeking recreation or sleep," writes Sir Alan Brooke's biographer, Arthur Bryant, the Prime Minister "awoke to full and volcano-like activity ten times greater than that of any ordinary being." He would then gather his jaded advisers around him and bombard them with plans and projects, facts and figures. [6]

Enjoying, despite his sixty-seven years, a wonderful unflagging—and at times almost impish—pugnacity and zest, he subjected them, often without realizing it, to a continuous, harrowing and exhausting, if stimulating, martyrdom. He was instinctively testing their plans by making them oppose him and argue them out in the teeth of his powers of debate and invective. Provided they stood up to him, he became the spokesman of the very arguments he had so fiercely criticized. "How often," wrote Brooke, Churchill's Chief of the Imperial General Staff, "have I seen Winston eyeing me carefully, trying to read my innermost thoughts, searching for any doubts that might rest under the surface."

When the American Chief of Staff, General George Marshall, stayed with the Prime Minister for the first time, and dinner was followed by a review of the war which went on till 2 A.M. and then by a film which lasted till 2:45 A.M., "his face," Brooke wrote, "was a study. He was evidently not used to being kept out of his bed till the small hours of the morning and was not enjoying it much. I wonder how he would have liked to work permanently with Winston, and be kept out of bed three or four nights a week. He certainly had a much easier life of it with Roosevelt; he informed me that he frequently did not see him for a month or six weeks. I was fortunate if I did not see Winston for six hours."

Winston never had the slightest doubt that he had inherited all the military genius of his great ancestor, Marlborough. His military plans and ideas varied from the most brilliant conceptions at the one end to the wildest and most dangerous ideas at the other. To wean him away from these wilder plans required superhuman efforts and was never entirely successful insofar as he tended to return to these again and again. [15]

When Malaya was overrun from the north, the British troops fell back on Singapore. The traders, drinking their "pegs" on the broad verandas of the Singapore Yacht Club, could not believe the Japanese would ever dare to attack them; but when they found the enemy at their door, their hands flew up and Singapore surrendered on February 15. [9]

Churchill was dumbfounded. He had thought Singapore

was impregnable. He could not eat or sleep. It was as if, through carelessness, he had caused the death of one of his own children. [55]

The surrender of the Dutch East Indies quickly followed, and by March 7 they, too, were in enemy hands. Rangoon fell the next day and the Japanese then drove northward through Burma. Their navy poured into the Indian Ocean and sank freighters passing down the east coast of India and bombarded the ports of Madras Province. On May 6 the last American resistance in the Philippines ended and Japan was left in unchallenged supremacy from the Aleutians to the Timor Sea and from the frontier of Assam to the Gilberts in the mid-Pacific. It seemed as if her dream of a vast Asiatic Empire was about to be realized. [9]

With the loss of Burma came the Japanese threat on the country's independence. [6]
Indian mainland. India's leaders began to agitate for their

Winston, no enthusiast for Indian self-government, accepted it as the national policy and sent Sir Stafford Cripps to India with proposals that would give India full Dominion status and autonomy after the war. The Indian Congress party turned it down. [9]

Roosevelt pressed Churchill to grant India her independence at once, naively suggesting that she model her provisional government along the lines of America's original states. [4]

"I was thankful that events had already made such an act of madness impossible," wrote Churchill. "The President's mind was back in the American War of Independence, and he thought of the Indian problem in terms of the thirteen colonies fighting George III at the end of the eighteenth century. I, on the other hand, was responsible for preserving the peace and safety of the Indian continent, sheltering nearly a fifth of the population of the globe. This was no time for a constitutional experiment with a 'period of trial and error' to determine the 'future relationship' of India to the British Empire. Nor was the issue one upon which the satisfying of public opinion in the United States could be a determining factor. We could not desert the Indian peoples by abandoning our responsibility and leaving them to anarchy or subjugation and so have betrayed not only the Indian peoples but our own soldiers and the gallant Indian Army fighting by their side to a welter of chattering politics and bloody ruin.

" 'Anything like a serious difference between you and me,' I replied to the President, 'would break my heart, and would surely deeply injure both our countries at the height of this terrible struggle.'

"On April 12 Cripps left Delhi by air for England. Nehru held to his resolve that the Japanese must be resisted. He was alone. The majority of the Congress leaders reverted to the total pacifism of Gandhi who wrote: 'Free India would be better able to cope with invasion. Unadulterated noncooperation would then have full sway.' " [3d]

There was never any question of the British resigning India to the Japanese. Reinforcements were pushed out to India. They had to travel round the Cape of Good Hope, and north past Madagascar, which was held by a Vichy collaborator. There was acute danger he would allow the Japanese to take control, as Vichy officials had done in French Indochina. An expedition was sent out which wrested the whole of Madagascar from Vichy and placed it under control of the Free French. The highroad to India was now securely protected. [9]

The only source of good news during this time was the Russian Front. The Red army, continuing its amazing counterattacks, drove the snowbound, frostbitten Germans out of many of their positions. [51]

"Hitler forget about the winter," said Churchill in a mocking broadcast. "There is a winter, you know, in Russia. For a good many months the temperature is apt to fall very low. There is snow, there is frost, and all that. Hitler forgot about this Russian winter. He must have been very loosely educated. We all heard about it at school; but he forgot it. I have never made such a bad mistake as that." [10]

On May 30 the first thousand-bomber raid was made on Cologne, followed by another the next night on Bremen. [9]

Winston sent his congratulations to the Bomber Command. It was the biggest air raid in history up to that time. Two nights later they did it again, plastering Essen and the Ruhr with more than one thousand planes in the air. [55]

In the Pacific, too, the tide slowly began to turn. Japanese naval craft ran into a strong American force in the Coral Sea and were heavily defeated. Another big battle took place off Midway Island, where some twenty of the enemy ships were sunk by the Americans, who established themselves in the Solomons and began steadily to clean up the Japanese bases there and to prise the enemy out of one stronghold after another in difficult jungle warfare. [9]

Meanwhile, although the Germans had been checked in front of Moscow, the opinion of the Combined Chiefs of Staff was that Russia would go down if German forces were not drawn off to the West. Hence Russian pleas for a Western Front were given a sympathetic ear, especially by American strategists. Technicians were instructed to draw up two alternative plans: one, for a last-resort cross-Channel leap; the other, far more to Churchill's liking, for a full-scale show in the Mediterranean, where England had a going concern in the Army of the Nile. [44]

The Allies, argued Churchill, should not make any substantial landing in France in 1942 unless they were going to stay there. An unsuccessful operation would not help the Russians, would expose the French population to Nazi vengeance, and would gravely delay the main operation in 1943. He shrank from the conception of a frontal attack and dramatized the possible cost of invasion, describing the Channel as a "river of blood"—recalling the carnage of Passchendaele and the Somme in the First World War. He urged the North African operation instead of the the trans-Channel assault in 1942. [51]

Meanwhile he set down his own ideas for the invasion of Europe in the year 1943. The way to burst into France was not to match twelve divisions against twenty-five, but to employ an army prodigious in strength that would submerge resistance. He issued his celebrated directive that was the genesis of the floating harbors for the Normandy beaches. Addressed to the Chief of Combined Operations and dated May 30, 1942, it concluded: "Piers for use on beaches: They must float up and down with the tide. The anchor problem must be mastered. Let me have the best solution worked out. Don't argue the matter. The difficulties will argue for themselves." The researches resulted in the "Mulberry," the floating landing stage, fabricated at home and ferried across the Channel for use on the Normandy coast. [2]

"On June 13," wrote Alan Brooke, "the P.M. called me up and told me he was thinking of starting for Washington on Thursday next and would like me to come with him. He considered Roosevelt was getting a little off the rails and some good talks as regards Western Front were required." [15]

Scarcely had Churchill arrived in Washington than Roosevelt handed him a slip of paper saying that Tobruk had fallen. "I am the unhappiest Englishman on American soil since the defeat of Burgoyne," Churchill stated to the press. And well he might have been. At home Parliament turned wrathful. One of his Tories called for a vote of no confidence in the Government. The Socialist Cripps waited catlike for the revolt to bring Churchill down. Without delay, Roosevelt diverted American equipment to retrieve the desert fiasco. [44]

Discussions in the White House continued through lunch and dinner and far into the night. Churchill poured out his matchless prose in opposition to the trans-Channel operation in 1942 and in favor of the North African operation as a means of relieving the crisis in the Mediterranean. He was vigorously opposed by Marshall and Hopkins. For better or worse, Churchill's arguments always made an appeal to Roosevelt, who was also interested in saving lives. One can only guess at the extent of the conflicts that went on in Roosevelt's mind and heart when he had to decide whether to follow the advice of his own most trusted advisers (including Hopkins) or Churchill's warnings that the Channel would be a "river of blood."

On his last day in Washington, June 25, "the Prime Minister and the President," noted Hopkins, "had not agreed upon any joint statement which the two of them would make upon Churchill's arrival in London." [51]

As he stepped aboard a British Overseas Aircraft Clipper, Churchill called for a whiskey and proposed a toast: "Here's to England, home and beauty—and a damn good row."

Back home, he settled Parliament with a brilliant two-day defense of his conduct of the war. But something else was settled in the privacy of No. 10. Following close on his heels to England came the American Chiefs of Staff, attended by Harry Hopkins. In two days and a night of talk it was decided to pull the lever on operation "Torch," involving an American landing on the shores of Europe, but in North Africa, to be coordinated with a British drive westward from Cairo. [44]

General Dwight D. Eisenhower, now Commanding General of the European theater, roughed out the plans to be cabled to Washington for endorsement. The President was delighted with the decision. [2]

"I cannot help feeling," Roosevelt wrote to the Prime Minister, "that the past week represented a turning point in the whole war and that now we are on our way shoulder to shoulder." [15]

Meanwhile, with the worsening of the situation in North

Africa, the Prime Minister's impatience mounted. The riddle of the desert must be solved. The missions across the Atlantic had given Churchill the taste for intervening personally as the man on the spot. Colleagues might protest that at sixty-seven he was too old for capering round in the air. He was not to be deterred. He took off on August 1 in an American bomber, from which the racks had been removed, flying at night over enemy territory to Cairo, where a full conference of advisers was assembled. Having probed army opinion, Churchill was confirmed in his view that Auchinleck must be replaced. General Montgomery, at work with Eisenhower in England on the invasion of North Africa, was ordered off to Egypt. By the time "Monty" arrived, the Prime Minister had flown east to Moscow. [2]

The landing in North Africa meant that there could now be no Second Front in Europe in 1942. And someone—Churchill—had to break the unpleasant news to Stalin. [6]

Averell Harriman flew with him, and they arrived late in the afternoon of August 12. [51]

The meeting of Churchill and Stalin resembled the head-on collision of two competitive bison. [8]

When Churchill made it clear that the Western Second Front would be replaced by operations in North Africa, Stalin began to turn on the heat, and through the interpreter he passed a lot of abusive questions, such as: "Are you going to let us do all the work while you look on? Are you never going to start fighting? You will find it is not too bad if you once start!" [15]

Churchill had kept his temper in hand, but at these taunts he broke forth. His fist crashed on the table, and words poured from him in a torrent. Only on account of the bravery of the Russian soldiers did he pardon the unpardonable things that had been said. For a year Britain had fought alone against the Hitlerites. Now, with Russia joined with Britain and the United States, victory was certain, but . . .

The words flowed on as he gathered speed. The official note-taker, spellbound, put down his pen to listen. Churchill paused to chide him and then started off anew. Stalin threw back his head and roared with laughter: "I do not know what you are saying," he broke in, "but, by God, I like your sentiment." Thereafter tension declined, and cordiality grew. [2]

The evening's banquet was held in Catherine the Great's magnificent state rooms in the Kremlin. There were about a hundred present, including most of the members of the Politburo and many of the leading Russian generals. The British and American guests were received by Stalin, dressed, as usual, in a short lilac-colored cotton tunic and with his trousers stuffed into his boots. He sat at the center of the table with P.M. on his right and Harriman on his left. [15]

"The dinner passed off in a very friendly atmosphere," Churchill recalled. "Wavell made an excellent speech in Russian. I proposed Stalin's health, and Alexander Cadogan proposed death and damnation to the Nazis. Stalin and I were photographed together, also with Harriman. I left about 1:30 A.M., as I was fatigued. When I said good-bye to Stalin he said that any differences that existed were only of method. After a cordial handshake I took my departure and got some way down the crowded room, but he hurried after me and accompanied me an immense distance through corridors and staircases to the front door, where we again shook hands.

"We were to leave at dawn on the sixteenth. On the evening before, I went at seven o'clock to say good-bye to Stalin. I asked particularly whether he would be able to hold the Caucasus mountain passes and also prevent the Germans reaching the Caspian, taking the oilfields round Baku, and then driving southward through Turkey or Persia. He spread out the map. 'We shall stop them,' he said with confidence. 'They will not cross the mountains.'

"Our hour's conversation drew to its close, and I got up to say good-bye. Stalin seemed suddenly embarrassed, and said in a more cordial tone than he had yet used with me. 'You are leaving at daybreak. Why should we not go to my house and have some drinks?' I said I was in principle always in favor of such a policy. So he led the way through many passages and rooms into a roadway still within the Kremlin and to the apartment where he lived: four rooms, moderate size, simple, dignified. A very aged housekeeper appeared and later a handsome red-haired girl who kissed her father dutifully. She started laying the table while Stalin uncorked various bottles. Then he said, 'Why should we not have Molotov? He is worrying about the communiqué. We could settle it here. There is one thing about Molotov—he can drink.' I then realized there was to be a dinner. Molotov arrived. We sat down, with two interpreters. Molotov assumed his most affable manner and Stalin chaffed him, unmercifully. More and more food arrived. Presently we talked about the convoys to Russia. Stalin made a rude remark about the almost total destruction of the Arctic convoy in June. 'Mr. Stalin asks,' said the interpreter, with some hesitation, 'has the British navy no sense of glory?' 'You must take it from me that what was done was right,' I answered. 'I really do know a lot about the navy and sea war.' 'Meaning,' said Stalin, 'that I know nothing.' 'Russia is a land animal,' I said; 'the British are sea animals.' He fell silent and recovered his good humor.

"About one, Mr. Cadogan arrived with the draft and we set to work to put it in final form. A suckling pig was brought to the table. He invited Cadogan to join him, and when my friend excused himself, our host fell upon the victim singlehanded. We actually sat at this table from eight-thirty till two-thirty the next morning, which, with my previous interview, made a total of more than seven hours." [3d]

As Churchill's bomber lifted from the Moscow airport, his companions, eyeing him closely, could tell that here was a happier man. Men who worked with Churchill believe that his refusal to go into Europe while pressing for the Mediterranean was the wisest decision of his career. [44]

However, Colonel Ian Jacob, one of Churchill's military advisers, though he admired the brilliant way the Prime Minister played his cards, doubted whether much had been achieved. "I would say that to make friends with Stalin," he wrote in his diary, "would be equivalent to making friends with a python." [15]

Churchill returned to Cairo in a lighter mood. In Alexander's car he drove out from Cairo beyond the pyramids to Montgomery's headquarters, his first view of the celebrated Montgomery caravan drawn up amid the sand dunes. He celebrated the occasion by bathing in the Mediterranean, to the entertainment of the troops on the beaches, who watched with delight unconcealed as his figure, unclothed and untanned, was seen advancing into the sea. That night, despite Montgomery's nondrinking and nonsmoking, the guest was suitably provided with brandy and cigars. [2]

Said Montgomery to Churchill: "I don't drink and I don't smoke and I am one hundred per cent fit." Churchill answered, "I drink and I smoke and I am two hundred per cent fit." [30]

Only a week had passed since the changes in the Eighth Army command, but already there was a difference in the atmosphere. "Electrifying" was the word Churchill used to describe the transformation in the morale of the army. He cabled home: "Everything has been done and it is now my duty to return home, as I have no part to play in the battle which must be left to those in whom we place our trust." Never was he less inclined to separate himself from the scene of action. Alan Brooke had the greatest difficulty in heading him off for home. Churchill hated to concede he must miss the coming show. [2]

On October 23, Montgomery struck at Rommel, struck hard, irresistibly. At El Alamein, German tank formations were smashed and their line of communication and supply blasted. After ten days of titanic struggle, Rommel's lines were hopelessly broken, and British troops were pouring forward through the gaps. Three days later, the total of prisoners had mounted to forty thousand and an equal number of the enemy killed or wounded. The Germans left their Italian allies to their fate, stole their transport, and hurried off westward at fast as they could, with the British army hotly pursuing them.

Then, on November 8, "Torch," history's greatest amphibious operation to date, took place far away to the west. A vast fleet of American and British transports, secretly assembled in the Atlantic, suddenly swooped down on Algeria and Morocco, and the armies aboard them poured into French North Africa.

With this invasion, the initiative passed from the Axis to the Allied nations. The North African campaign rolled forward. In a month from the El Alamein battle, the Eighth Army had chased Rommel out of Egypt and right across Cyrenaica.

"This is not the end," Churchill warned. "It is not even the beginning of the end. But it is, perhaps, the end of the beginning!" [9]

18

Meeting in Teheran

IN mid-November, Stalin suddenly struck, not from the Stalingrad Front, but well to the northwest and to the south of the city, in a vast pincer attack. Hitler refused to allow his troops there to withdraw, and presently the whole doomed army—more than three hundred thousand strong—was encircled and trapped. He brutally ordered it to fight and die. Cornered in the snow and bitter frost of a Russian winter, the troops tried to obey him. The Red army closed in for the kill. Finally, in January 1943, the German Commander, Von Paulus, surrendered with fifteen other generals and the remnants of his fine army, now reduced to twelve thousand men. [9]

The time had come for high-level talks on strategy. Churchill and the President desired that Stalin take part. When it was suggested that the meeting be held in Africa in January, 1943, Stalin declined: developments on the Eastern Front made it impossible for him to leave Russia. After much canvassing of the possibilities, the little suburb of Anfa, near Casablanca, was chosen as the rendezvous, even though there were risks: the place was within range of enemy bombers and there were fanatics among the people. [2]

The site, just outside the city, consisted of the Anfa Hotel, with a number of villas surrounding it, on a knoll overlooking the sea. The view out over the Atlantic, or overland to Casablanca, was truly magnificent. The dazzling blue of the water, the white of the buildings in Casablanca and the red soil dotted with green palms and bougainvillea and begonia, made a beautiful picture in the sunlight. [15]

Roosevelt was in a lighthearted mood. He had made the crossing by air—his first flight since becoming President—and to Harry Hopkins he appeared to be a sixteen-year-old schoolboy on a holiday. [2]

The staff talks were spread over eight days. The chief issue was again whether the Allied effort in 1943 should be concentrated on Germany or Japan. Once it was decided to throw the main weight of the Anglo-American forces against the mainland of Europe it was agreed to press on with preparations for the cross-Channel operations; plans were approved for an early assault on Sicily, stepping-stone to the Italian mainland; and Alexander was chosen as Eisenhower's Deputy Commander in Chief in the Mediterranean theater. The talks then ranged over future operations in the Pacific and Burma theaters, the Russian convoy program, reinforcement of Chennault's forces in China and the air offensive against the Ruhr.

On most evenings Churchill and Roosevelt dined together, and there was often the atmosphere of a family party, for Elliott Roosevelt and Franklin Roosevelt, Jr., had joined their father; Randolph Churchill had flown across from the Tunisian Front; and Harry Hopkins's son, Robert, a sergeant in the American army, had been given leave for the occasion. An important item on the Conference agenda was the question of French leadership in North Africa. General Giraud was already in Anfa. [6]

"I was anxious for de Gaulle to come," wrote Churchill. "I asked the President to telegraph inviting him. The General was very haughty and refused several times. I then got Eden to put very great pressure on him. At last he arrived. But he would not call upon Giraud.

"I had a stormy interview with de Gaulle, making it clear that if he continued to be an obstacle we would not hesitate to break with him finally. He stalked out of the villa and down the little garden with his head high in the air. Eventually he was prevailed upon to have a talk with Giraud. In the afternoon he went to see the President and to my relief they got on unexpectedly well. The President was attracted by 'the spiritual look in his eyes.' " [3d]

At the press conference held at the conclusion of the talks the two French generals were persuaded to shake hands in public. The occasion was enlivened by some of Mr. Churchill's best French. The phrase "pulling his punches" was translated as "minimisant ses punches."

It was during this conference that the President spontaneously used the much criticized phrase about "unconditional surrender" in defining Allied aims. (It had not appeared in the draft of the official communiqué.) Writing to Hopkins's biographer after the war, Churchill said, "I would not myself have used these words, but I immediately stood by the President and have frequently defended the decision. It is false to suggest that it prolonged the war. Negotiation with Hitler was impossible. He was a maniac with supreme power to play his hand out to the end, which he did; and so did we." [6]

"The conference over," Churchill continued, "the President prepared to depart. But I said to him, 'You cannot go all this way to North Africa without seeing Marrakesh. Let us spend two days there. I must be with you when you see the sunset on the snows of the Atlas Mountains.' So it was decided that we should all go to Marrakesh with its fortune-tellers, snake-charmers and the most elaborately organized brothels in the African Continent.

"The President was carried up the tower in a chair and sat enjoying a wonderful sunset on the snows of the Atlas. We had a jolly dinner and sang songs. I sang and the President joined in the choruses. He was to depart just after dawn for his long flight to Washington. He came round on the way to the airplane to say another good-bye. I was in bed but would not hear of letting him go to the airfield alone, so I jumped up and put on my zip and slippers and drove with him to the airfield and saw him comfortably settled down, greatly admiring the courage under all his physical disabilities. I then returned to the Villa where I painted from the tower the only picture I ever attempted during the war." [3d]

Back in London, Churchill was ill with pneumonia for nearly a month. [55]

During his recuperation, he turned up at Buckingham Palace, a wan and tired figure bent over his cane, loudly bemoaning his infirmities. The King's private secretary, Sir Alan Lascelles, rushed to take his arm. Before he could grasp it, the Prime Minister suddenly whirled around, gave the V sign, uttered a Bronx cheer, and scampered off to his audience with the King. [44]

Meanwhile, the American and British armies were gradually closing in on the Germans from all sides, causing the army to retreat toward Tunis. Finally, on May 12, the campaign in North Africa came to an end. [55]

"Nearly a quarter of a million prisoners were taken," Churchill wrote. "Africa was clear of our foes. One continent was redeemed. In London there was, for the first time in the war, a real lifting of spirits. I asked that the bells of all the churches should be rung. I was sorry not to hear their chimes, but I was already at the White House on the other side of the Atlantic." [3d]

Goodwill between Whitehall and Washington was now at a low ebb. Churchill's advisers muttered that the Americans were not living up to the Casablanca agreements; Admiral King was diverting to the Far East naval craft essential for the assault on Europe. The Americans, on the alert against British imperialism, looked askance on moves in the Mediter-

ranean. Long-range exchanges by cable intensified differences. Churchill concluded it was imperative for the Joint
Staffs to meet face to face and hammer out an agreement.

In Washington, the Americans demanded the closing
down of operations in the Mediterranean once Sicily had
been taken. Admiral King resisted any suggestion that would
direct forces from the Pacific theater of war; "Vinegar Joe"
Stilwell added to the tension by his antagonism toward the
"Limeys" and all their doings. The British were driven to
despair. [2]

On the weekend of May 15, Roosevelt announced that he
was taking everyone out to Shangri-La, his camp in the
Catoctin Hills, in Maryland, to relax and get some mountain
air. [6]

On the drive the President's car passed through the old
town of Frederick. Churchill saw the roadside signs advertis-
ing Barbara Frietchie candy and asked about them. Roosevelt
explained that Barbara Frietchie was a semilegendary character of our Civil War about whom John Greenleaf Whittier
had once written a poem. All the President could remember
of it was:

> Shoot, if you must, this old gray head,
> But spare your country's flag, she said.

Whereupon Churchill proceeded to recite the entire poem,
stating afterwards that he had not thought of it in at least
thirty years. A little further on he saw a road sign pointing to
Gettysburg and asked how far away that was. It was,
roughly, forty miles. He said, "Why, this may have been the
very road by which Longstreet moved up," and then went on
to review the whole battle. [51]

After twelve days of conferences an agreed program was
arrived at. The utmost that could be wrung from the Americans on the Mediterranean strategy was the issuing of in-

structions to prepare for the possibility of extending the Italian campaign. Churchill voiced his protest. For an hour he harangued the Joint Chiefs, pressing the need to go ahead with the invasion of Italy. His arguments made no impression on the Americans. [2]

To Churchill, who saw so clearly that the collapse of Italy could undermine the whole foundation of the Reich and that the means for achieving this were now at hand, it was an agonizing impasse. But he felt that all was not yet lost. If he could take General Marshall with him to Algiers and hold further talks with the Allied commanders on the spot, Marshall's own doubts might well be dispelled. Roosevelt offered no objection. On the morning of May 26, in pouring rain, Churchill and Marshall took off from the Potomac River. [6]

As soon as Churchill landed in Algiers he was trundling along with Eisenhower. He made no secret about his purpose: to secure the decision he wanted for knocking Italy out of the war. Three times that evening, with three different approaches, he stated his case. Eisenhower was relieved that General Marshall was at his side to sustain the United States point of view. On the second evening there was a reiteration of the arguments used on the first. To back his arguments he offered British shipping to carry the war into Italy. The British people would be proud to halve their rations if need be to release ships to use against the Italians. At times he would become intensely oratorical, using humor and pathos, drawing on every source for his quotations from Greek classics to Donald Duck. Finally Eisenhower declared that if Sicily were polished off easily, then he would cross the Strait of Messina and establish a bridgehead on the Italian mainland. Churchill was satisfied. [2]

"On July 1 we flew to Tunis," wrote Lord Alanbrooke. "From there we motored to Carthage, where a large party of men from the desert armies had been assembled in the old Roman amphitheater, a most wonderful setting for the P.M.'s address—the acoustics so perfect that no loudspeakers were necessary. That night we had a very amusing dinner at Eisenhower's camp. Churchill, delighted at having had the chance of speaking from the Carthage amphitheater, was in remarkable form. 'Yes, I was speaking from where the cries of Christian virgins rent the air while roaring lions devoured them—and yet—I am no lion, and certainly not a virgin!'" [15]

On July 12, Sicily was invaded. The Italian forces had no will to fight. In the towns of Sicily the Allied armies were greeted as liberators, rather than conquerors. German resistance was stiffer, and British troops on the east had to overcome strong opposition. [2]

To the surprise of London, Eisenhower then proposed that carrying the war to the mainland by an attack on the toe and heel of Italy be accompanied by a landing in Salerno Bay, nearly two miles up the coast, and seizure of the port of Naples. The Prime Minister was delighted. "Why," he asked, "crawl up the leg like a harvest bug from the ankle upwards? Let us rather strike at the knee." [15]

On July 19, Mussolini hurried north to meet his Nazi master. He came back to Rome and his fall. On the evening of Sunday, July 25, people in Britain heard with grim satisfaction that he had been cast out by his Fascist associates. In the House, two days later, Churchill pronounced, with relish, his downfall. [2]

In August, Churchill was at Quebec for a conference which settled, among other matters, that Lord Louis Mountbatten should command the army to reconquer Burma and Malaya, Churchill describing him as "the complete triphibian." A solution of a sort was also found for the quarrels of the French factions in North Africa: De Gaulle had a movement, Giraud had an army; by the new solution de Gaulle became head of a "Committee of Liberation," and Giraud Commander in Chief of its forces. In effect de Gaulle had won. [37]

Churchill accompanied Roosevelt back to the White House after the conference and remained in Washington off and on for three weeks. [51]

Roosevelt, never averse to criticizing British imperialism and probably with tongue in cheek, suggested to Churchill that much good might come from a meeting between the Prime Minister and Mrs. Helen Ogden Mills Reid, who, he said, was particularly interested in Indian affairs. Mrs. Reid, vice-president of the New York *Herald Tribune,* considered the people of India had been brutally oppressed by the British. She came to lunch at the White House. The question of India was brought up. At once Churchill said firmly, "Before we proceed further let us get one thing clear. Are we talking about the brown Indians in India, who have multiplied alarmingly under the benevolent British Rule? Or are we speaking of the red Indians in America, who, I understand, are almost extinct?" This brilliant opening so disconcerted Mrs. Reid that she never began her peroration at all, and the topic was instantly dropped. [6]

"Mr. Churchill," wrote Inspector Thompson, "was invited to Hyde Park. We stayed several days. I hated Hyde Park. There is no peace there. The Roosevelts always become superactive in the country. The President wanted to fish. Or he wanted to visit his own museum. Or Mrs. Roosevelt wanted everyone on a picnic. When the Roosevelts want something, they get it. They are worse than Winston himself. Day and night I was on the alert, chasing over the damn acreage with a creel on my hip or an abominable hot dog in midair or a whole hamper of sandwiches on my head, and mustard on my trousers; festooned with cameras, aswarm with Roosevelt grandchildren, myself not infrequently challenged by unfamiliar American police (this was the worst!), and a bad bed at night right under a revolving floodlight. By

God, I will take Chequers in the blitz to a Roosevelt weekend-with-the-children." [55]

On September 6, Churchill went to Cambridge, Massachusetts, to receive an honorary degree from Harvard University, a ceremony long planned. Roosevelt, a member of the Class of 1904, took a great deal of interest in it. He telephoned President James Conant, expressing the hope that there would be plenty of pageantry and color in the ceremony. Conant conceived the idea that the Prime Minister should be outfitted with the scarlet academic robe of Oxford, from which he had received the LL.D. degree, rather than the austere American cap and gown. There were none of these robes in Cambridge or in Boston, but Conant finally located one at Princeton and borrowed it for the occasion. [51]

That night on the special train taking them back to Washington, Churchill stayed up very late, awaiting the last diplomatic pouch. He read over the cables. Then he rose with his wife, put her hand between his two and said, "Clemmie, it's been a wonderful day." [44]

Another effort was made in mid-October by the President and the Prime Minister to get Premier Stalin to agree to a meeting at some place that would be convenient to all three. Stalin insisted that the only place outside of Russia to which he could agree was Teheran, the capital of Iran. [35]

The principals at the Teheran meeting monopolized the stage: the astute Roosevelt, the subtle Stalin and the Old Incomparable who stood for Britain. [2]

Within a quarter of an hour of Roosevelt's arrival, Stalin called on him. Stalin's affability at this first meeting with the President confirmed Roosevelt's impression that henceforth all would be well if the handling of the Russian leader was left to him. Long before he had remarked naively to William Bullitt, former U.S. ambassador in Moscow, "I have a hunch that Stalin doesn't want anything but security for his country, and if I give him everything I possibly can, and ask nothing from him in return, *noblesse oblige,* he won't try to annex anything and will work for a world of democracy and peace."

Furthering this hunch, Roosevelt now made it plain to Stalin that on a number of matters he and Churchill did not see eye to eye. And when on the following morning the Prime Minister invited the President to lunch with him he declined point-blank, on the ground that Stalin might think he and Churchill were "hatching their own schemes." Churchill, much upset by this rebuff, retorted: "I insist on one thing— that I be host at dinner tomorrow evening. I think I have claims to precedence: I come first in seniority and alphabetically; I represent the longest-established of the three Governments; and tomorrow happens to be my birthday." [6]

Churchill led his thirty-four guests into the dining room, upon whose long, decorated table rested a birthday cake with sixty-nine candles and beside it, several presents. President Roosevelt had bought him a blue and white porcelain bowl whose accompanying card read, "For Winston Spencer Churchill, on his 69th birthday at Teheran, Iran, November 30, 1943, with my affection and may we be together for many years." [8]

Roosevelt, not making as much progress with Stalin as he would have liked, tried to ingratiate himself with the Russian dictator by making fun of Churchill. "I began almost as soon as we got into the conference room," he told Frances Perkins. "I said, lifting my hand to cover a whisper (which of course had to be interpreted), 'Winston is cranky this morning, he got up on the wrong side of the bed.' A vague smile passed over Stalin's eyes, and I decided I was on the right track. I began to tease Churchill about his Britishness, about John Bull, about his cigars, about his habits. It began to register with Stalin. Winston got red and scowled, and the more he did so, the more Stalin smiled. Finally Stalin broke out in a deep, hearty guffaw, and for the first time in three days I saw light. I kept it up until Stalin was laughing with me, and it was then that I called him 'Uncle Joe.' He laughed and came over and shook my hand." [4]

Churchill was sorely tried by the diplomatic excursions of his friend the President. He looked to Roosevelt for sympathy, understanding and common purpose, and he was troubled by any crack in the fabric of their friendship. [2]

The chief issue at Teheran, which still sings around the very word "Teheran," was "Overlord," the invasion of Western Europe by Great Britain and America—the killers' thrust against Germany straight through France. [27]

Churchill suggested two parallel operations, France and the Balkans. "It was quite obvious to everybody in the room," said Roosevelt, "what he really meant. That he was above all else anxious to knife up into Central Europe in order to keep the Red army out of Austria and Roumania, even Hungary, if possible. Stalin knew it; I knew it, everybody knew it." Stalin, equally aware of his own motives, argued for a western invasion and against a splitting into two of the Allied forces, an arrangement that also suited Roosevelt. "It's a pleasure working with Stalin," he reported to his son, "there's nothing devious. He outlines a subject he wants discussed and sticks to it."

Elliott Roosevelt asked his father whether Churchill might not have a case for a Balkan invasion, but his father argued, "Trouble is, the Prime Minister is thinking too much of the *post*-war, and where England will be. He's scared of letting the Russians get too strong. Maybe the Russians *will* get strong in Europe. Whether that's bad depends on a whole lot of factors." [31]

As the prime movers of continental power, Roosevelt and Stalin held the aces. The United States could by 1944 supply at least sixty divisions for crossing the Channel; the Russians claimed they had three hundred divisions on the Eastern line; the Englishmen could promise only twenty in the West. Stalin twigged Churchill, saying that "American horsepower" and "Russian manpower" would decide the war. In principle Churchill was always for the cross-Channel leap in 1944; but he wanted to be certain that enough forces would be committed to prevent disaster on the first try. "We must not fail," he said in effect. "We must be sure."

In the end the decision rested with the United States, which at last could promise sufficient equipment and manpower. And the great Normandy landing was agreed to. [44]

19

Overlord

ONE night at Teheran Stalin gave a dinner. The subject of Germany was brought up. Stalin said emphatically that the only way to prevent her resurgence as an aggressive nation was to round up and shoot fifty thousand officers and technicians who formed the core of the German military machine. [6]

"I was deeply angered," Churchill wrote. " 'I would rather,' I said, 'be taken out into the garden here and now and be shot myself than sully my own and my country's honor by such infamy.' The President intervened. Not fifty thousand should be shot, but only forty-nine thousand. He hoped, no doubt, to reduce the whole matter to ridicule. But now Elliott Roosevelt made a speech saying how cordially he agreed with Stalin's plan and he was sure the United States army would support it. I got up and left the table, walking off into the next room. I had not been there a minute before hands were clapped upon my shoulders from behind, and there was Stalin with Molotov, both grinning broadly, declaring that they were only playing. I was not then, and am not now, fully convinced that all was chaff and there was no serious intent lurking behind." [3e]

When the guests had risen from the table Stalin walked round chatting animatedly to everyone. "I have been wanting to drink a toast to the Russian fleet," said Admiral Cunningham to him, "but I can find no representative of your navy to assist me." Without hesitation Stalin replied, "I am the Commander in Chief of the Russian navy. You shall drink a toast with me." This was too much for the Prime Minister, who had come up in time to overhear the conversation. As they raised their glasses and Cunningham said, "To the Russian navy!" a well-known voice behind him added drily, ". . . coupled with the health of *Admiral* Stalin!" [6]

On the way home Winston had planned to visit Alexander at his Italian HQ, but when Eisenhower met him at Tunis he was startled at his appearance. "I am afraid I shall have to stay with you longer than I planned," said Winston apologetically and feebly. "I am completely at the end of my tether." He then collapsed in bed and almost died. For a while he was delirious. "The ruins of ancient Carthage," he mumbled. "The sound of the Romans and Hasdrubal . . . What better place can I die than here." [1]

Pneumonia set in, and a scared and anxious world waited for the bulletins reporting his fight for life. [9]

Lord Moran, Churchill's personal physician, and his staff took over. Nurses and specialists began to arrive like magic. Then Mrs. Churchill arrived. Her sudden appearance at his bedside gave him great comfort. From then on he started to come back. The attack was a severe one, but the patient was far tougher than they thought. Despite the fever and weakness, he never relinquished the direction of affairs.

On Christmas Day he insisted on taking part in a conference with Eisenhower and leading commanders at Carthage. [2]

"It was decided he could go to Marrakesh to complete his rest," recalled Inspector Thompson. "We flew at about seven thousand feet, making a large detour to avoid the Atlas Mountains. Churchill seemed to sense this. He insisted on the shorter route over the mountains. He had his way. We increased the altitude slowly, one thousand feet at a time at half-hour intervals. The doctors kept checking his pulse and breathing. On being told by them that he was all right, he roared with gusto, 'Of course I'm all right! I don't need to be told this! I'm announcing it!'

"As he grew stronger, he wanted to get about into the mountains and foothills. Picnics were held daily in picturesque spots. One day we came to a small plateau near a bridge; one hundred feet below a wild stream splashed through rocks in a gorge. After lunch, Churchill, who had been peering down at this cataract, expressed his intention of descending. And down he went, carefully keeping to the narrow path cut out of the cliffside, to the spot where the water pounded through the side of the cliff. When it was time to start up again, I got behind and pushed, but Winston was too tired out. Suddenly Lady Diana Duff Cooper and her husband came hurrying down to meet us, carrying the large tablecloth which had been used for the picnic. Lady Diana suggested we put it round the Prime Minister and use it as a rope, Sergeant Davies on one end and me on the other." [55]

Churchill leaned back against this vast unwound cummerbund as the detectives, one at each end, dragged him slowly upwards while he discoursed on the tenderness of women, their flair for improvisation, and the value of linen. [25]

If there was anyone in Whitehall who imagined that Mr. Churchill would be content to continue his convalescence, slowly gathering the reins as his strength returned, they had a rude shock. From the moment of his arrival back in Downing Street the Prime Minister assumed complete control of the war machine, demanding ACTION THIS DAY on a score of points . . . driving, goading, exhorting. He formed and took personal charge of a committee set up to review the progress of preparations for "Overlord," busying himself with every aspect of the invasion, from the waterproofing of tanks to the intricacies of the naval bombardment plan. He held frequent conferences with General Eisenhower and kept a watchful eye on political developments in Italy as well as in Greece, where the self-styled National Liberation Front was beginning to stir up trouble, and Yugoslavia, where Allied aid had shifted from Mihailovic to the Partisans led by Tito.

These major preoccupations did not prevent him from drawing the attention of the Minister of Supply to an unsightly rubbish dump at Chalfont St. Giles, which he had noticed on his way back from Chequers. And the Minister of Works was surprised to receive an indignant complaint about "a very untidy sack with holes in it and sand leaking out" which the Prime Minister had seen lying "on the grass opposite St. James's Park Lake." [6]

There was an immense love for Churchill in England through these years. The crowds knew every one of his uniforms and hats, his siren suits, the bow tie, the shoes with the zip fasteners, the walking stick, the watch chain. Nothing apparently could ever weary them of the V-sign or the cigar, and the first sounds of the grumpy, reassuring voice on the radio silenced all conversation in any pub or public place.

"He has at least a hundred ideas a day," Roosevelt said, "of which four are good." The good ones included nothing quite so spectacular as the idea for the tank, which he set in motion in 1915; but still, he was responsible for pushing the development of "Pluto," the pipeline under the Channel that carried petrol to France; "Fido," the system of dispersing fog from landing fields; and "Mulberry," the artificial harbor for the landings in Normandy. [42]

He had become, however, more difficult to deal with than ever. There were days when the strain seemed insupportable to Alan Brooke, who, as chairman of the Chiefs of Staff, carried the executive burden for Britain's war effort. His diary entries were marked by an unusual acerbity and he found the difficulties of coping with "that unique old man," the masterful Defense Minister, more than ever wearying. [2]

He was quickly tired, ready to take offense and giving it freely. "I should have to resign at least once a day," Brooke wrote, if he had taken offense each time the old man insulted him, or said that he had lost confidence. When after some minor upset between them, Ismay came to Brooke saying that Churchill thought Brooke hated him, the Chief of Imperial General Staff answered quietly, "I don't hate him, I love him." [54]

"But then," he went on, "he is no ordinary human being and cannot be judged by normal standards. He could drive you to complete desperation and the brink of despair for weeks on end, then ask you to spend a couple of hours alone with him and produce the most homely and attractive personality. All that unrelenting tension was temporarily relaxed, and you left him with the feeling that you would do anything within your power to help him to carry the stupendous burden he had shouldered."

No War Minister can ever have appeared so formidable to his military advisers; none, in reality, ever interfered with them less. A deep-seated humility caused him to recognize, though he might never admit it, that his approach to military problems needed the corrective of cooler judgments. [15]

By now slogans had been chalked up all over the city on boards and pavements demanding the Second Front. Churchill saw these all the time, and on one occasion he said: "Yes, we will start the Second Front when we are ready. But we will not throw thousands of lives away on any project until the time is ripe and our preparations are made. Then our losses shall not be too heavy, God willing." And his eyes filled.

"We went on a mad sequence of visits," wrote Inspector Thompson, "to docks at Southampton and Portsmouth where the enormous concrete caissons, those dramatic improvisations of artificial harbors, were being built. Towed through the Channel in dead of night, floated to location and sunk, they created breakwaters, floating pierheads, pontoon causeways. On D-Day troop carriers of all kinds would be able to bring in combat units and beach them in calm waters.

"At Winchester he inspected a huge parade of U.S.A. paratroopers. The tireless, sternly cheerful Eisenhower showed the new bazooka and American carbine to the Prime Minister. It was suggested they fire at a target. Immediately Churchill seized on the idea of a contest. The troops gathered round by hundreds. Eisenhower, General Bradley and Churchill stood in a row and took aim with carbines on targets ahead. Churchill stood up well against the younger men. He also fired several rounds with the bazooka. At Tidworth, as Churchill passed along the ranks of troops, we encountered a detachment of Eighth Army men of Libyan fame. Every man knew Winston. Many, unable to speak, touched his coat as he passed." [55]

Meanwhile, round-the-clock bombing of warship and factory slowed down German production; in France, railroad centers and bridges were destroyed to create a railway desert through which troops could be moved only with difficulty. [2]

Appalled by the grievous casualties this methodical bombing threatened on French civilians, the Prime Minister raised with the President the advisability of continuing this offensive. "It is not alone a question of humanitarianism. Postwar France must be our friend." With reluctance it was decided that the bombing must continue. [6]

"The officers and men who fought and died in this fearful battle of the air," wrote Churchill, "reached the limits of human valor and sacrifice. In one raid the Americans had sixty of their large Fortress aircraft destroyed out of two hundred and ninety-one, and on another occasion out of seven hundred and ninety-five aircraft dispatched by British Bomber Command against Nuremberg ninety-four did not return. The American Fortresses carried a crew of ten men and the British night bombers seven. Here we have each time six or seven hundred of these skilled, highly trained warriors lost in an hour. This was indeed ordeal by fire. Let us give them our salute." [3e]

In that final month of May, as he journeyed about the country, Churchill moved through an England that had been transformed into a vast military camp: vast munition dumps under the concealing shelter of trees, railroads congested under the strain of transporting supplies from northern ports to troops around the southern beaches. [2]

This concentration of men, ships and matériel was completely protected from German air observation. "We saw the tiny harbors along the south coast," wrote an American officer, "and the big sprawling harbor of Southampton packed with miniature Pearl Harbors, with ships stacked gunwale to gunwale." In all more than five thousand ships and eleven thousand aircraft were engaged and over a million picked troops, organized in thirty-seven divisions, half of them American and half British and Canadian.

Yet the assembly, training and equipment of this vast force had been only the beginning. The Allies had now to do what no one had done since William the Conqueror, and that Philip of Spain, Louis XIV, Napoleon and Hitler had all attempted in vain. In two days they had to transport across the stormy tidal waters of the Channel, without hurt from U-boat, mine, E-boat or Luftwaffe, nearly two hundred thousand armed men and land them with twenty thousand mechanical vehicles on open beaches along a fifty-mile stretch of fortified coast, negotiating a complex network of undersea obstacles and immobilizing shore defenses of immense strength. Ever since November, when Germany's Field Marshal Rommel had been sent to organize the Channel defenses, half a million troops and conscript workers had been toiling to strengthen the "Atlantic Wall." Tidal stretches before the beaches had been strewn with steel and concrete wrecking devices, the sands and roads into the interior had been mined and barred by fortifications and tank traps, while every accessible landing place was enfiladed by the fire of hidden batteries and the level spaces behind the coastline studded with wooden posts to prevent airborne landings.

Thanks to Alexander's persistent troops in the south, the Germans had been unable to transfer troops from Italy to the Channel coast and had been forced to send half a dozen more divisions to that country. But Hitler, acting on intuition, ordered a reinforcement of the crucial sector between the Seine and Cherbourg. Fortunately, advised by the naval authorities that a landing on this coast was almost impossible and deceived by British feints in the Straits of Dover, Rommel continued to believe that the blow would fall north of the Somme. [15]

From May 28 the coastal area was sealed, all troops being confined to their camps. Foreign embassies could no longer communicate with the outside world and passenger traffic with Eire had ceased. [2]

The Prime Minister had made up his mind that he would sail with the forces on D-Day. When Eisenhower heard of this he said firmly that he could not allow it, but Mr. Churchill then pointed out that the General's authority did not extend to the administration control of the British organization, adding blandly, "Since this is true, it is not your responsibility, my dear General, to determine the exact composition of any ship's company in His Majesty's Fleet. By shipping myself as a bona fide member of a ship's company it would be beyond your authority to prevent my going." Fortunately decisive intervention came from an unexpected quarter, the King pointing out that if it was right for the Prime Minister to take part in the invasion then he himself had an even stronger claim as the head of all three fighting services.

On June 3, news came of worsening weather and after a 4 A.M. conference at Eisenhower's headquarters on June 4 the decision was taken to postpone the invasion for at least twenty-four hours. An agonizing dilemma faced General Eisenhower. He knew that if the invasion could not be launched in the next forty-eight hours it would be a full fortnight before moon and tide offered another favorable opportunity. A gale was raging as the vital meteorologists' conference took place in the early hours of June 5, but to everyone's surprise a brief spell of finer weather was predicted and Eisenhower decided to go ahead. The landing would take place on June 6.

Churchill returned to London and spent most of the succeeding hours in the Map Room, much on edge. When Mrs. Churchill joined him for a few moments before retiring he said to her: "Do you realize that by the time you wake up in the morning twenty thousand men may have been killed?" [6]

That night, the opening blows were struck. The night bombers pulverized German batteries. Parachute troops, three divisions of them, were descending on France. Under cover of the darkness the armada of ships came steaming toward Normandy. As the dawn broke, the battleships were in position to take up the hammering of German defenses. The barges moved in. The invasion had begun. Allied armies were returning to the French soil from which they had been driven four years before. The bad weather aided them. The Germans had also studied the forecasts. Their generals had gone to bed comforted by the belief it was too stormy for an attack to be started.

At the end of twenty-four hours, over a quarter of a million Allied troops were ashore in France. By D-Day-plus-3 Spitfires had their own airfields across the Channel. On D-Day-plus-4 the Allied Front was fifty-one miles wide and fifteen miles deep. As a curtain raiser to Normandy, the Fifth Army struck out from Anzio; the Eighth breached the Hitler line. On June 5 Rome was entered, a propitious overture to "Overlord."[2]

Within a week of the descent on Normandy, Churchill himself set foot once again on the French shore and drove in brilliant sunshine to a chateau at Cruelly, five miles inland from the invasion beaches, where Montgomery had established his headquarters. It was four years to the day since he had left on the *Flamingo* after the last fateful meeting with Pétain, Weygand, and Darlan. [6]

20

Crisis in Greece

TWELVE days after the invasion of Normandy, the Germans commenced to send their flying bombs to London and into southern England. This unholy monster was soon known as the "doodlebug." [55]

The first one blocked all lines into the Liverpool Street Station. For three days there was an ominous lull, and then a torrent of high explosive rained down on the capital. Churchill was at Chequers, but Mrs. Churchill, in London, saw one dive on Whitehall. It struck the Guards Chapel in the middle of the morning service, killing scores of the congregation, which included many of the Churchills' friends.

Three thousand of these missiles came over in the first five weeks. Although the men and women of London behaved with their usual stoicism, it was impossible to treat the "doodlebugs" with the same resigned indifference accorded to the bombing in the blitz of 1940-1941. There was a dreadful inevitability about the flying machines controlled by mechanism, for they came in at between two thousand and three thousand feet, a height which prevented the radar screen from giving any adequate warning. Over six thousand civilians were killed and eighteen thousand seriously injured. To a casual observer, however, Londoners went about their business with the same apparent unconcern and when, one lovely summer day, Mr. Churchill walked to the window of the Map Room and stood gazing out across St. James's Park, crowds were sitting on the grass in the hot sunshine eating their sandwich lunches. "If only Goebbels could see this," he said.

A vast redeployment of guns, radar equipment and barrage balloons was necessary. By the end of August few of the flying bombs were penetrating the elaborate network, and soon afterwards the Allied armies, thrusting deep into Belgium, overran most of the launching sites. But London's affliction was not entirely at an end, for in the closing months of the war five hundred V-2's—rocket bombs traveling beyond the speed of sound and therefore impossible to intercept by any means—reached the capital from launching points in Holland. But the development of the V-2 had come too late for the part which Hitler had boastfully predicted for it. [6]

The British, meantime, had struck at Bayeux and Caen, where they met and engaged the main weight of the German forces in northern France. The Americans tackled the neck of the Cherbourg Peninsula and, after cutting across it, swept up to capture Cherbourg itself and then turned south, drove down across Brittany, swung east along the Loire and thrust through the middle of France in a headlong race towards Paris. Finally, on August 25, Paris fell. [9]

The city was given over to a raptuous demonstration. De Gaulle set up his headquarters in the Ministry of War. Two hours later, at the Hotel de Ville, he appeared before the jubilant population for the first time as the leader of Free France, in company with the main figures of the Resistance. Next afternoon, on August 26, de Gaulle made his formal entry on foot down the Champs Elysées to the Place de la Concorde, and then in a file of cars to Notre Dame. [3f]

Churchill visited Paris shortly after the liberation. The French crowds clamored for a speech. British army headquarters at once put their best linguists at Winston's disposal, but he impatiently brushed aside their offers of help and strode out onto the balcony of the Hotel de Ville with measured, determined steps. *"Prenez garde!"* he exclaimed menacingly, and when there was complete silence in the square below, he added in his best conspiratorial manner, *"Je vais parler français."* His audience went delirious. [58]

He journeyed from battlefront to battlefront and from ally to ally, had conversations with the Yugoslavs, toured the Italian front, inspecting British, Canadian, Indian and New Zealand units. [2]

With Admiral Morse as his guide, he took one of his rare days off to visit Ischia, where he swam and then lay contentedly in the sun, letting the gray volcanic sand trickle through his fingers while the hot water from the island's subterranean springs bubbled around him. As he returned to Naples, landing craft were steaming slowly up the bay packed with American troops on their way to Corsica. When they caught sight of the unmistakable figure in the Admiral's barge they cheered wildly.

So far the Italian "holiday" had been more arduous than Churchill's daily round in England. He began to feel the strain of incessant travel in the heat and dust, arduous days in the field and exhausting political discussions with their intensive preparatory briefing. When his plane took off for home he was feeling ill. He had meant to call at Gibraltar, but a shift of the wind made landing there impossible. Affairs at the Rock were on his mind as he flew home, however, and soon after he reached London he asked the Colonial Office to inquire whether the orders given on his last visit there had been carried out. He had made a disturbing discovery. The population of Barbary apes which from time immemorial had roamed the Upper Rock was dwindling alarmingly. Legend prophesied that if the apes ever left Gibraltar British rule there would end; aware of this, Churchill decreed that the monkey colony must be brought up to strength without delay.

Thus, out of the blue came this signal from the Prime Minister to the Governor of Gibraltar: "The establishment of the apes on Gibraltar should be twenty-four, and every effort should be made to reach this number as soon as possible and maintain it thereafter." The Governor passed the problem to the Consul-General in Spanish Morocco, and twenty apes were sent by sea to Algeciras. The boat became becalmed with a broken-down engine; a rescue boat was dispatched with all haste and twenty seasick monkeys reached the Rock without further misadventure. With the Barbary apes once more at full strength, Gibraltar's future was no longer in jeopardy. [6]

In November Churchill crossed to France to take part in the Armistice Day celebrations of France's liberation. There were thunderous cheers as he drove through the Paris streets. [2]

At the Quay d'Orsay a whole floor had been reserved for him and his party. The suite set aside for the Prime Minister had a spectacular attraction—a gold bath which had been specially installed for Goering. [6]

The next morning the Prime Minister, in a Royal Air Force uniform and accompanied by General de Gaulle and Mr. Eden, left the Quay d'Orsay in an open car, preceded by cars filled with French police. Flags were fluttering from the buildings; window frames were jammed with wildly excited men, women and children. On the stroke of eleven, a single gun was fired for silence. The crowd congealed. Another announced the end of the two minutes. Mr. Churchill and General de Gaulle, each carrying a huge wreath, walked side by side to the Tomb of the Unknown Soldier. Then Churchill, de Gaulle and Mr. Eden walked abreast from the Arc de Triomphe down the Champs Elysées through crowds which the French police found almost impossible to control. [55]

At the luncheon which followed, de Gaulle spoke: "We should not have seen a day like this but for our brave ally, Britain, under Winston Churchill's leadership." [2]

As the month ended, the Prime Minister celebrated his seventieth birthday. A present from the officers of his Map Room particularly delighted him: a silver menu-holder which bore a picture, colored on enamel, of the prefabricated harbor at Arromanches. On the reverse side was inscribed his own far-sighted directive: *Piers for the Beaches. They Must Rise and Fall with the Tide.* With this was engraved the date when the directive was written—two years before Mulberry Harbor played its vital part in the invasion of Normandy.

At this moment Churchill found himself with a political crisis on his hands. In the middle of October, as the Germans had retreated, British troops had occupied Athens. [6]

The Greek Government, under its Premier, M. Papandreou, had ordered members of the various resistance movements to lay down their arms, but the E.L.A.S. [the military instrument of the Greek Communist Party] refused to comply. Left-wing Ministers resigned from the Government. Street fighting broke out, developing into civil war. This involved the British forces under General Scobie. Reports reached the Prime Minister in London that the Athens police stations had been seized, their occupants murdered. [2]

"At this moment," wrote Churchill, "I took a more direct control of the affair. Mob violence could only be met by fire-arms. There was no time for the Cabinet to be called. The Foreign Minister and I agreed that we must open fire. At 4:50 A.M. this telegram was dispatched to General Scobie: 'You are responsible for maintaining order in Athens. You may make any regulations you like for rounding up any number of truculent persons. *Do not hesitate to act as if you were in a conquered city where a local rebellion is in progress. We have to hold and dominate Athens. It would be a great thing*

238

for you to succeed in this without bloodshed if possible, but also with bloodshed if necessary.' " [3e]

The press was up in arms. *The Times* and the Manchester *Guardian* accused the Prime Minister of seeking to install a government of Greek reactionaries and to suppress the republicans. American correspondents proclaimed that here was a flagrant instance of Britain's imperialist designs. [2]

A motion of censure on the Government was introduced in the House of Commons. The Prime Minister came down to the House spoiling for the fight. [2]

"The charge against us," he said, "is that we are using His Majesty's forces to disarm the friends of democracy in Greece. The question arises how is the word 'democracy' to be interpreted. My idea of it is that the plain, humble, common man, the ordinary man who keeps a wife and family, who goes off to fight for his country when it is in trouble, goes to the poll at the appropriate time, and puts his cross on the ballot paper showing the candidate he wishes to be elected to Parliament—that he is the foundation of democracy. Democracy is no harlot to be picked up in the street by a man with a tommy gun. I trust the people in almost any country, but I like to make sure that it is the people and not a gang of bandits who think that by violence they can overturn constituted authority. I call upon the House as a matter of confidence in His Majesty's Government to reject such pretensions with the scorn that they deserve." [3f]

The censure motion was defeated by two hundred and seventy to thirty. Meanwhile the position in Athens was growing worse. The British forces were almost cut off. General Alexander, leaving his headquarters in Italy to investigate on the spot, recommended stern measures. A political settlement must be reached, no easy matter. The Papandreou Cabinet was discredited, the King was unpopular. A regency under the Archbishop of Athens was favored by the Greeks, but their King, in exile in London, opposed it. [2]

"It was December 24," Churchill recalled, "and we had a family and children's party for Christmas Eve. We had a Christmas tree—one sent from the President—and were all looking forward to a pleasant evening. But when I had finished reading my telegrams I felt I ought to fly to Athens, see the situation on the spot and especially make the acquaintance of the Archbishop, around whom so much was turning." [3e]

As the plane approached the airfield at Athens, the pilot could see bright flashes all round the airdrome. There was a hurried conference, and it was decided to take the Skymaster down and risk the consequences. Field Marshal Alexander, General Scobie, Harold Macmillan, and the British ambassador, Mr. Leeper, were awaiting them. While a strong R.A.F. detachment guarded the perimeter of the field they held a meeting in the plane. Once the engines were switched off it soon grew bitterly cold. Flurries of snow howled mournfully round the aircraft. Churchill's secretary was summoned to take down a statement. [6]

"Frankly I felt terrified," wrote Elizabeth Nel. "Mr. Churchill, wrapped up in overcoat and scarf, looked flushed; remembering his previous illness, I wondered what on earth we should do if he were to contract a feverish cold—where in this embattled city was to be found a warm and comfortable resting place for him? He dictated a press communiqué. The table was sloping, the light bad; the wind howled and jerked the aircraft up and down; once he stopped and said, 'That was cannon fire.' With cold hands it was hard to type. When the communiqué had been typed, it was decided that the party would be housed aboard the H.M.S. *Ajax*, a cruiser standing by in the Piraeus harbor. The British Embassy, under siege for some days, was without light and with very little food." [45]

Churchill described what followed: "We boarded the *Ajax* before darkness fell, and I realized for the first time that it was Christmas Day. Preparations had been made by the ship's company for a jolly evening: a dozen of the sailors were dressed up in every kind of costume to seranade the officers and warrant officers. The Archbishop with his attendants arrived—an enormous tall figure in the robes and high hat of a dignitary of the Greek Church. The two parties met. The sailors thought he was part of their show of which they had not been told, and danced around him enthusiastically. The Archbishop thought this motley gang was a premeditated insult, and might well have departed to the shore but for the timely arrival of the captain, who explained matters satisfactorily.

"The Archbishop spoke with great bitterness against the atrocities of the E.L.A.S. He told us he had issued an encyclical condemning the E.L.A.S. crowd for taking eight thousand hostages, middle-class people, and shooting a few every day. From what the Archbishop said, I was impressed by the intensity of hatred for Communists in the country, and convinced that he was the outstanding figure in the Greek turmoil." [3e]

When Churchill went ashore the next morning he carried a revolver in his pocket. Armored cars escorted the British party as they drove through the Athens streets to the Embassy to meet with the Archbishop. That afternoon they went into conference in a bare room, ill-lit and cold, at the Greek Foreign Office. [2]

Churchill made his opening speech. He said how glad he was to have brought all the Greek representatives together and how he welcomed the Archbishop's decision—given to him that morning—to act as Regent. Now it was up to the Greek people to settle their differences among themselves; he would take no part in their discussions. Having brought them together, his work was done. [6]

"The conference was intensely dramatic," said Churchill in a telegram to his wife. "All those haggard Greek faces round

241

the table, and the Archbishop with his enormous hat, making him, I should think, seven feet high, whom we got to preside.

"You may have read about the plot to blow up HQ in the Hotel Grand Bretagne. A ton of dynamite was put in sewers by extremely skilled hands and with German mechanism between the time my arrival was known and daylight."

"Bitter and animated discussion between the Greek parties," Churchill wrote later, "occupied all the following day. At five-thirty that evening I had a final discussion with the Archbishop in which he reported the results of his conversations with the E.L.A.S. It was agreed I should ask the King of Greece to make him Regent. He would set about forming a new Government without any Communist members.

"Mr. Eden and I arrived back in London on December 29. The next day the Foreign Secretary and I sat up with the King of Greece till four-thirty. I had a very painful task: I had to tell the King that if he did not agree the matter would be settled without him, and we should recognize the new Government instead of him. 'The Greek King,' I wrote to Roosevelt two days later, 'behaved like a gentleman and with the utmost dignity, and I am sure a private message from you should give him comfort.' " [3f]

King George of the Hellenes then issued a proclamation of his resolve not to return to Athens unless summoned by a free expression of the national will, and appointing Archbishop Damaskinos as Regent. A new Government was formed under General Plastiras, a lifelong republican. [2]

And thus Greece, thanks to Churchill, alone of the Eastern European countries, was liberated by a Western country and did not go Communist. [1]

With the Presidential election concluded and Roosevelt's fourth term inaugurated, the way was clear for a summit approach to settle the problems of the treatment of Germany, reparations, Poland and the war in the East. [2]

Stalin, as before, refused to move far from home. Roosevelt

suggested that they should try Yalta, which he described as "A pleasant resort on the Crimean Riviera." There was some confusion as to whether Roosevelt had meant *Malta* and not Yalta, but Churchill settled it with the phrase: "Yalta, not Malta: don't alter or falter." [31]

When the Prime Minister pressed Roosevelt for a preliminary meeting of the British and American staffs at Malta, Roosevelt felt that discussion at Malta might offend Stalin. Furthermore, he suggested the business of the coming Conference be discharged in five or six days. Churchill, still convinced that some initial problems must be disposed of before the main talks began, telegraphed: "I do not see any other way of realizing our hopes about World Organization in five or six days. Even the Almighty took seven." [6]

Roosevelt gave way so far as to agree to a meeting of the Staffs, but his Secretary of State, he insisted, could not be present, nor could his limited time permit a halt of more than one day at Malta. [2]

Thus, in the forenoon of February 2, the *Quincy*, with the President aboard, arrived at Malta's Grand Harbor where Churchill and the Staffs had been in conference three days. She passed close by *Orion* on her way to her berth and Churchill waved a greeting to the President. As soon as the ship made fast he went on board and plunged into discussion of the staff talks, which had covered much ground: plans for the Rhine crossing, Italy and Greece, and operations in the Pacific. The Prime Minister stayed to dinner, then drove out to the airfield to board his plane for the fourteen-hundred-mile flight to Yalta. The others followed in Skymasters and Yorks, throbbing silver shapes in the light of the rising moon. [6]

21

Capitulation

THE Crimea was a wasteland, burned and blackened by the Germans; thousands of unexploded mines were still embedded on and off the roads. In preparations for their visitors the Russians detailed thousands of Red army soldiers to restore the roads, filling in bomb holes and refurnishing the houses for the three delegations. No less than fifteen hundred railway coaches were run from Moscow—four days' journey north—with supplies of food, drink, bedding, Moscow's best hotel carpets and thousands of panes of glass to make the houses habitable. Saki airfield was little better than a snowy field, rutted and pitted by the wheels of lorries. [31]

From the airfield it took six hours' traveling by car over winding mountain roads heavily guarded by Russian women troops armed with rifles to reach Yalta. "We could not have found a worse place for a meeting," protested Churchill, "if we had spent ten years in search."

With seven hundred visitors to house, as well as the Russian delegation, accommodations fell far short. Generals had to share rooms with generals, and colonels were tightly packed. Admiral King, being assigned the Czarina's boudoir, was the butt of Conference wits.

For the leaders, spacious provision was made: the President in the Livadia Palace, once the summer quarters of the Czar; Stalin in the palace of Prince Yusupov, assassin of

Rasputin; Churchill in the Vorontsov Palace, once the home of a Russian ambassador to England. The arrangements placed the Prime Minister and President twelve miles apart, with Stalin between at the halfway distance. [2]

In the small villas outside, the British staff lived under barrack-room conditions. As many as twenty would be queuing every morning to use one washhouse, while Russian girls, who had arrived with bath brushes to scrub their backs, were surprised that their services were not required.

The Russians were in a mood of elation. Since smashing the thin German lines in Poland three weeks before, their armies had swept westward for nearly three hundred miles and were now only forty miles from Berlin and in possession of almost the whole of East Prussia and Silesia, as well as of Hungary and Slovakia. They were ready to welcome their allies with their usual profuse Oriental hospitality, but they meant to drive the hardest possible bargain. No longer mainly concerned with defeating Germany, but only with dominating as much of Europe as possible, they meant to keep the eastern half of Poland and the Baltic republics that Hitler in 1939 had given them, ignore Britain's and America's pledges for a free Poland, and make similar satellite states of Roumania, Bulgaria, Hungary, Albania, Yugoslavia and, if they could overrun them before their allies, Austria, Czechoslovakia, Denmark, Norway and the eastern half, or even whole, of Germany. [15]

The Yalta conference lasted a week. Roosevelt looked increasingly tired and ill. Stalin played with the greatest skill on his obvious determination to conciliate the Russians whenever a deadlock threatened. [6]

Most of the hard words and brickbats fell on Churchill. The President, whose vanity was flattered by Stalin, did not give Churchill the support he expected in dealing with the Russians. The most grievous mistake was in allowing Stalin to displace and destroy the accredited government of Poland's national resistance. The British gave way—and all the rest followed: the Baltic states, East Prussia, Rumania, Hungary, Czechoslovakia, the Russians entrenched in the middle of Europe. Churchill cannot be blamed for this, though he has to bear some share of the responsibility for what happened: it remains an Anglo-American responsibility, an historic mistake for which the West has to endure the greatest consequences. [7]

The concession which Roosevelt made to Stalin in return for the dictator's promise to enter the war against Japan made Stalin the virtual master of Manchuria and, in effect, the master of North China. Eden begged Churchill not to put his signature to it. The Prime Minister replied that "the whole position of the British Empire in the Far East was at stake" and if he refused to sign he might find himself excluded from any further say on these affairs. [4]

The pact was labeled top secret, preserved in the Presidential safe at the White House, its contents undisclosed even to State Department officials. Some months after Roosevelt's death a startled Secretary of State learned of its existence from a Russian newspaper report. Ironically, the atom bomb that caused the Japanese to capitulate made Soviet participation in the Far East war superfluous, but fulfillment of the pact was still required by the Russians—it contained no escape clause. [2]

"After the formalities," wrote Churchill, "a dozen of us talked together in twos and threes. I mentioned that there would be a general election in the United Kingdom after the defeat of Hitler. Stalin thought my position was assured, 'since the people would understand that they needed a leader, and who could be a better leader than he who had won the victory?' I explained that we had two parties in Britain and I belonged to only one of them. 'One party is much better,' said Stalin with deep conviction." [3f]

The mood of the American delegates, including Roosevelt

and Hopkins, was one of supreme exultation as they left Yalta. "We really believed," said Hopkins later, "that this was the dawn of the new day we had all been praying for and talking about for so many years. We were absolutely certain that we had won the first great victory of the peace—and by 'we' I mean *all* of us, the whole civilized human race. The Russians had proved that they could be reasonable and far-seeing, and there wasn't any doubt in the minds of the President or any of us that we could live with them and get along with them peacefully for as far into the future as any of us could imagine." [51]

Precisely sixteen days later, Stalin—who at Yalta had signed a Declaration of Liberated Europe calling for free elections and the establishment of democratic Governments in all countries occupied by Allied armies—staged a *coup d'état* in Roumania, and a Communist Government took office.

By the middle of March units of Patton's Third Army had dislodged the Germans from their last toehold west of the Rhine, and the scene was now set for the crossing of the great river. The Prime Minister was determined to be present on this historic occasion. When Montgomery realized he was in earnest he sent him a cordial invitation. [6]

On the way, near Aachen, Churchill picked up a piece of mechanic's chalk and printed on a shell in great capitals: FOR HITLER PERSONALLY. Then, as a cheer went up, he fired the 240-mm. gun and sent the shell toward Berlin. [55]

"I am with Field Marshal Montgomery at his HQ," Churchill wrote Stalin on March 23. "He has just ordered the launching of the main battle to force the Rhine." "Throughout the night," he later recalled, "the attacking divisions poured across. In the morning Montgomery arranged for me to witness from a hilltop the great fly-in: two thousand aircraft streamed overhead in formations. I was conducted by motor on a long tour from one point to another.

"The next day we met Eisenhower. There was a house, he said, about ten miles away on our side of the Rhine, which the Americans had sandbagged, from which a fine view of the river and of the opposite bank could be obtained. He proposed that we should visit it and conducted us there herself. The Rhine—here about four hundred yards broad—flowed at our feet. The officers told us that the far bank was unoccupied so far as they knew, and we gazed and gaped at it for a while. With appropriate precautions we were led into the building. Then the Supreme Commander had to depart on other business, and Montgomery and I were about to follow when I saw a small launch come close by to moor. So I said to Montgomery, 'Why don't we go across and have a look at the other side?' To my surprise he answered, 'Why not?' We started across the river with three or four officers and half a dozen armed men, and landed in brilliant sunshine and perfect peace on the German shore." [3f]

"We spent a little time examining the German river defenses," reported Alanbrooke, "and then recrossed the river, got back into the car and motored to the main road bridge over the Rhine at Wesel. The bridge had been broken in several places but partly boarded over. Winston at once started scrambling along it for about forty yards. German shells began to fall about a hundred yards upstream of us. The U.S. General Simpson, on whose front we were, came up to Winston. 'Prime Minister,' he said, 'snipers are shelling both sides of the bridge. I cannot accept the responsibility for your being here and must ask you to come away.' The look on Winston's face was like that of a small boy being called away from his sand castles on the beach by his nurse! He put both arms round one of the twisted girders of the bridge and looked over his shoulder at Simpson with pouting mouth and angry eyes. Thank heaven he came away quietly. It was a sad wrench for him; he was enjoying himself immensely." [15]

That evening from headquarters, Churchill sent a message

of congratulation to the soldiers of the twenty-first Army Group, and made this entry in Montgomery's autograph book:

"The Rhine and all its fortresses lie behind the 21st Group of Armies. Once again they have been the hinge on which massive gates revolved. A beaten Army, not long ago masters of Europe, retreats before its pursuers." [2]

Mannheim and Frankfurt fell, the Russians captured Danzig, the French entered Karlsruhe. On the day following the Prime Minister's return from the Rhine, the last German rocket fired against England fell at Orpington. Within a few hours London's air-raid sirens wailed for the last time. The scent of victory was in the air. It was a time to rejoice. But the Prime Minister saw a different picture. [6]

"This climax of apparently measureless success was to me a most unhappy time," he wrote. "I moved amid cheering crowds with an aching heart and a mind oppressed by forebodings." [3f]

He had urged that the Allies strike for Vienna, for Prague and Berlin, that they grab as much territory as possible and then hold it until the Russians lived up to their agreements—notably for free elections in Poland. [10]

But Eisenhower had telegraphed Stalin, without previously mentioning the subject to the Combined Chiefs of Staff, that after isolating the Ruhr he proposed to make his main thrust along the Axis Erfurt–Leipzig–Dresden line, which, by joining hands with the Russians, would cut in two the remaining German forces. Stalin agreed readily. "The proposal," he said, "entirely coincides with the plan of the Soviet High Command." [3f]

Montgomery placed Berlin as a primary objective, to be reached ahead of the Russians. The previous September Eisenhower had agreed with this view. "Clearly," he had said, "Berlin is the main prize." But now his opinion had changed. "Berlin has become, so far as I am concerned, nothing but a geographical location, and I have never been interested in these. My purpose is to destroy the enemy's forces and his power to resist." Montgomery threw up his hands. The Americans could not understand that it was of little avail to win the war strategically and to lose it politically. [2]

Churchill wrote to General Eisenhower of the latter's proposal to stop at the Elbe: "Why should we not cross the Elbe and advance as far eastward as possible? I do not consider that Berlin has yet lost its military and certainly not its political significance. The fall of Berlin would have a profound psychological effect on German resistance in every part of the Reich. While Berlin holds out, great masses of Germans will feel it their duty to go down fighting. I deem it highly important that we should shake hands with the Russians as far east as possible."

The British Chiefs of Staff, concerned both about the merits of the new plan and the short-circuiting of the highest authorities, both military and constitutional, drafted a lengthy telegram to their colleagues in Washington. "I did not see it till after it had gone," wrote Churchill, "though I was in full agreement in principle. The United States Chiefs of Staff replied that it was for the Field Commander to judge the measures which should be taken; that the United States Chiefs considered his strategic concept was sound and should receive full support and that he should continue to communicate freely with the Commander in Chief of the Soviet army.

"I summed up the position in a message to the President: 'The Russian armies will no doubt overrun all Austria and enter Vienna. If they also take Berlin will not their impression that they have been the overwhelming contributor to our common victory be unduly imprinted in their minds, and may this not lead them into a mood which will raise grave and formidable difficulties in the future?' " [3f]

There was no yielding in Washington. The President, by

then, had grown so weak that the task of replying was entrusted to General Marshall. With his colleagues Marshall rejected the idea of pressing on to Berlin. Churchill was powerless to rouse his great friend in Washington to share a sense of alarm or to secure his support. [2]

On Thursday, April 12, the President was at Warm Springs, Georgia, where he had gone to rest for a few days. That afternoon he died of a cerebral hemorrhage. The news reached the Prime Minister's Map Room at midnight, and Churchill, who was dining out that evening, was told as soon as he returned. [6]

At 3 A.M. the phone rang in the room of Churchill's bodyguard, Inspector Thompson. Churchill wanted him to come quickly. Thompson grabbed his guns and rushed in, to find Churchill silently pacing the room.

"Have you heard the terrible news, Thompson?" he said, his eyes wet, staring at the rug. "It's the President of the United States. Your friend and mine, Thompson. He has passed away." Then he added slowly, "He died on the eve of victory, but he saw the wings of it. And he heard them." [30]

That morning, Churchill went down to the House of Commons and proposed that they pay their respects to the memory of a great friend. This unprecedented step on the occasion of the death of the head of a foreign state was in accordance with the unanimous wish of the Members, who filed slowly out of the Chamber after a sitting which had lasted only eight minutes. [3f]

On April 17, Churchill paid further tribute to the statesman whose passing was, in his words, a bitter loss to humanity. [2]

"Not one man in ten millions, stricken and crippled as he was, would have attempted to plunge into a life of physical and mental exertion and of hard, ceaseless political controversy. To the end he faced his innumerable tasks unflinching. He died in harness, in battle harness, like his soldiers, sailors, and airmen. What an enviable death was his!" [3f]

On the day that Roosevelt died, the United States forces under General Simpson were only about fifty miles from Berlin. Simpson asked for permission to go on to Berlin. The Supreme Commander ordered that he hold on the Elbe. The Russians, after a last fortnight of savage attack and heavy artillery bombardment, forced their way into the center of Berlin on May 2. They had the first somber sense of triumph, the first awesome sight of the ruins, the first parades under the pall of smoke. [24]

Churchill brooded over the consequences. He saw all the great capitals of Middle Europe passing to the Soviets, a catastrophe for which Europe's history could furnish no parallel. With time running out, could he induce the new President of the United States to follow the course Roosevelt had declined? He cabled Truman, urging that action be taken in Czechoslovakia to forestall the Russians. The State Department endorsed Churchill's proposal. By that time, the recurrent warnings of Ambassador Harriman from Moscow were having effect: "The Soviet program is the establishment of totalitarianism and the ending of personal liberty and democracy as we know it." [2]

General Marshall passed this information on to Eisenhower with this comment: "Personally, and aside from all logistic, tactical, or strategic implications, I would be loath to hazard American lives for purely political purposes." Eisenhower agreed and halted his troops on the frontier. Although he received frantic appeals from Prague, then being subjected to severe German attack, he remained stationary; and when, on May 4, the Russians asked him formally not to move forward any further, he agreed. Three days later he received a wire from Churchill begging him to proceed to Prague; instead, he instructed the Czechs to refer their requests for aid to Moscow. The following week Czechoslovakia was liberated by the Russians. [4]

Arrangements for Austria's occupation had yet to be made. She had been omitted from the original occupation plan. When the Russians took Vienna they went about the business of setting up a provisional government to their own liking. The Prime Minister recommended a joint protest to Stalin. Unless a firm stand were taken it would be difficult to exercise any influence over the future of Austria. Here Truman was sympathetic. Cables were sent to Stalin demanding the admission of Allied missions to Vienna. Nothing came of them.

There remained Denmark, a country that carried control of the Baltic. The Prime Minister urged Montgomery forward and faster, anxious to move into Schleswig-Holstein before the Russians. Great was his relief when the report came that the armored spearheads had reached the Baltic at Wismar and Lubeck on May 2. The Danish peninsula was sealed off. Montgomery had won the race by six hours. By air a force was sent in to hold Copenhagen, where Russian parachutists had already been dropped. Fast-moving columns occupied the country. The Danes had been saved from Soviet occupation.

By then, the fighting in Europe was done. The German armies disintegrated. Capitulation followed capitulation. A million Italians surrendered to Field Marshal Alexander, the first of all the capitulations and vindication of the Churchill strategy that had tied down fifty-five German divisions in the Italian peninsula. [2]

Italian Partisans rose against the German forces as they withdrew northward. The Duce himself was captured as he tried to escape into Switzerland in a German convoy. He and his mistress, Clara Petacci, were shot, their bodies strung up, head downward. [6]

Churchill announced this event to guests in his house by

rushing into his dining room and crying, "Ah, the bloody beast is dead!" [8]

In Berlin, the twilight of disaster was falling on the Germans. The end came at Lüneburg, on the blasted heath, where Montgomery received the emissaries of capitulation with his historic queries: "Who are these men? What do they want?"

After five and a half years of fighting the guns had ceased to fire in Europe. It was five years almost to the day since Winston Churchill had become Prime Minister. It was his voice that fittingly gave the signal for the celebrations of V–E Day, the eighth day of May in 1945:

> The cease-fire began yesterday to be sounded all along the front. The German war is therefore at an end. The evildoers are now prostrate before us. We may allow ourselves a brief period of rejoicing but Japan remains unsubdued. Advance Britannia! Long live the cause of freedom! God save the King!

As the Prime Minister drove across to the House of Commons there was a press of crowds in Whitehall. He passed down a cheering avenue. As he entered the House of Commons, Members rose to him. A deep-throated cheer rumbled out on all sides. Members waved papers in salute. He was deeply moved. He read out the formal announcement. Then putting off his glasses, he offered his humble thanks to Members who had sustained him and his Ministers in the long struggle. His voice quavered. He paused to master his emotion. Members waited in silence. He resumed in the very words used at the close of the war against the Kaiser's Germany: "That this House do now attend at the Church of St. Margaret, Westminster, to give humble and reverent thanks to Almighty God for our deliverance, from the threat of German domination." [2]

With bells pealing out overhead, they walked through the

cheering crowds to the ancient church, and from the church the Prime Minister drove to Buckingham Palace for lunch. Afterwards he went in a small open car to the Ministry of Health building in Whitehall, where he spoke from the balcony. It was a lovely sunny afternoon, and London looked at its gayest, with flags and paper streamers everywhere. "This is *your* victory!" he said, smiling happily at the sea of faces below him. "It is the victory of the cause of freedom in every land. In all our long history we have never seen a greater day than this. God bless you all!" [6]

22

Triumph and Tragedy

THAT night Churchill appeared again on the balcony,
now floodlit, with members of the War Cabinet, and
led the singing of "Land of Hope and Glory." [6]

"I wish," he said, "I could tell you tonight that all our toils
and troubles were over. Then indeed I could end my five
years' service happily, and if you thought that you had had
enough of me and that I ought to be put out to grass I would
take it with the best of grace. But, on the contrary, I must
warn you, as I did when I began this five years' task, that
there is still a lot to do to make sure that the words 'freedom,'
'democracy,' and 'liberation' are not distorted from their true
meaning as we have understood them. I told you hard things
at the beginning of these last five years; you did not shrink
and I should be unworthy of your confidence and generosity
if I did not still cry: Forward, unflinching, unswerving, indomitable, till the whole task is done and the whole world is
safe and clean." [3f]

As the peoples of the world continued their carefree celebrations of the fall of Nazism, Churchill's apprehensions
mounted. Was the elimination of Germany to become Russia's opportunity? Europe's future, he wrote to Eden in San
Francisco, was more pressing than the charter of the United
Nations. He invited Eden to consider what was going to
happen when the American forces withdrew from Europe
and when their own men had been demobilized. [2]

"The Allies ought not to retreat from their present positions to the occupational line," wrote Churchill, "until we are satisfied about Poland and the temporary character of the Russian occupation of Germany and the conditions in the Russianized or Russian-controlled Austria and Czechoslovakia. If these matters are not settled before the United States armies withdraw from Europe and the Western world folds up its war machines, there are no prospects of a satisfactory solution and little of preventing a third World War. I propose to telegraph to President Truman about an indispensable meeting of the three major powers." [3f]

In the cable he coined the famous phrase "the Iron Curtain": "In a very short space our armed power will have vanished. What is to happen about Russia? The Iron Curtain is drawn down upon their front. We do not know what is going on behind. A settlement with Russia before our strength has gone seems to me to dwarf all other matters."

With the Presidential advisers in Washington on guard against what were conceived to be Churchill's designs to obtain American backing for British influence in Europe, the "Iron Curtain" cable served to check, not to advance, his purpose. On one point only the President was convinced—the time had come to arrange for a summit conference. On the choice of a meeting place, Churchill had been emphatic that it should not be within the Russian zone of Germany. Ultimately the choice fell on Berlin in the Potsdam Palace, once the home of the German Crown Prince.

In vain Churchill urged that the Big Three hold their meeting before Eisenhower drew back his armies. On June 12, there came a message from Truman, proposing that immediate orders be given for the Allied withdrawal. "This struck a knell in my breast," commented Churchill. "I felt I had no choice but to submit, if the alliance with the Americans were to be maintained." And so the orders went out for the Anglo-American armies to withdraw.

This retreat, which took place in July, established tyranny

permanently in the center of Europe, bringing down, as Churchill put it, "an Iron Curtain between us and everything to the eastward." [15]

While these matters were in the balance, the situation was complicated by developments on the political front. With the end of the war in Europe, the breakup of the Coalition Government could not long be deferred. The Socialists wished to part company and take advantage of the tide of opinion running in their favor. Again Churchill sought Eden's advice. Should the Coalition continue till October, the limit set by the Socialists for their cooperation, or should the break be made forthwith and an election held in June? "A June election would probably be better for our party," replied Eden from Washington, "than an October one, though the Labor Party will no doubt blame us for ending the Coalition, which the nation, I believe, would like to retain for a while."

Accordingly it was decided. The famous Coalition was dissolved. Comrades loyally associated in the partnership of wartime became the strident rivals of the hustings. Churchill formed his Caretaker Government. [2]

With the election set for July 5, the Prime Minister, campaigning enthusiastically, beaming and giving the V sign, seemed supreme, irresistible, utterly confident. True, now that the dust of battle had settled and the four-year political truce had ended, the Tories stood naked before the electorate as the party of Munich which had gotten the nation into the mess in the first place, while the Socialists appeared to be the party of the future, the party which would provide the "homes for the heroes" which Lloyd George had promised the returning soldiers in 1919 and had not delivered.

Incomprehensibly Winston had failed to read the signs. As far back as D-Day there was an incident that might have shattered some of his illusions had he chosen to interpret it correctly. He and Ernest Bevin were watching a line of British troops embarking for Europe. Excitement was in the air. In every mind was the thought that this operation was going to win the war, and afterward the soldiers could go home. As they saw the two great figures of wartime England standing there the soldiers cheered, and one shouted, "See they don't let us down when we come back this time, Ernie."

Ernie? Why not Winston? Who was meant by "they"? The fact was the British soldier had a blistering hatred of everything that had to do with the Tory Party. He had no intention of voting for it under any circumstances, under no matter what leader it presented itself. The figure of Churchill tended consequently to be an irritant. He confused the issue for the soldier who preferred to see everything as deep Tory black and spotless Labor white.

In early July, Churchill asked General Sir William Slim, back from his brilliant campaign against the Japanese in Burma, how he thought his soldiers would vote. Slim was a tough man who did not mince words. "Seventy per cent will vote Labor, sir," he said. Winston was surprised. "What will the other thirty do?" "They will abstain from voting at all, sir, out of affection for you."

Clement Attlee, leader of the Labor party, based his campaign on the nationalization of the mines, the railroads, the Bank of England, the cable and wireless services, medicine, steel. Against these far-reaching and exciting proposals the Tories seemed to be campaigning, as a cynic remarked, with nothing more than a picture of Winston Churchill. [1]

Churchill began his campaign in his own constituency of Woodford in Essex, where he was being opposed by a hopeful farmer. In spite of drizzling, miserable rain he had a tremendous welcome, and wherever he stopped to speak, Clementine held an umbrella over his head. When he avoided its protection an old lady in the crowd called out, "Please sir, do put on your hat. We don't want you to catch cold." On their way to Chequers for a quiet weekend, whole populations turned out to greet them. At Uxbridge, they were almost torn from the car by overenthusiastic crowds, who had waited more than two hours. On went the car to High Wycombe, where fifteen thousand waited outside the Red Lion Hotel from which Disraeli made his first political speech as a candidate in 1832. Winston was puffing away at a new cigar. "Where did Disraeli speak?" he inquired. The spot was indicated to him. He entered the hotel, climbed briskly from a bedroom window to the front of the platform beside the head of the large red lion where Disraeli had stood.

A thousand-mile tour by special train and car carried them through England and up to Glasgow and Edinburgh. They slept in the train and in it Winston continued with official work, constantly busy with Government papers until the early hours of the morning. [25]

Fifty thousand people were waiting to hear him in Manchester, where he spoke from a bombed site near the center of the city. As he left, a craggy veteran stepped in front of the car and shaking his fist in mock rebuke shouted out, "You old bugger!" "What did he say?" asked Churchill. When he was told he grinned delightedly, and, craning round in his seat, he gave the old man a special salute.

At the gardens below Princess Street in Edinburgh, where the Prime Minister made his last speech of more than thirty in four days, he was given the most rapturous welcome of the whole tour. But the strain of the campaign had begun to tell on him. To Brooke he confessed he had never been so tired since the days of his escape during the Boer War. [6]

Then in a radio broadcast, an angry Winston began to make personal attacks on Labor leaders who had served with him in the Coalition Government. He warned that Socialism would result in a "Gestapo." Public opinion began to harden against him. [25]

Back in London he was met by organized preparations to wreck his meetings. At one meeting he was struck by a stone; at Tooting Bec Common a student threw a firecracker at him which exploded almost in his face. The sorriest performance was reserved for the final meeting of the campaign at Walthamstow, where he arrived to find a hostile crowd of twenty thousand who booed, heckled, and jeered until he had difficulty in making himself heard at all. Most of the uproar came from young hooligans under voting age who pursued him at every place he spoke on the way back to Whitehall—a bitter ordeal to face when he was at the limit of his endurance. [6]

On July 5, the people voted. The poll was to remain sealed until the twenty-sixth of that month to enable the complete votes of the forces overseas to be counted. [25]

Churchill was not due to arrive at Potsdam until July 15. He badly needed rest. With a small party, he and Mrs. Churchill and Mary flew to Bordeaux to spend a week at Hendaye near the Spanish frontier. As usual he got through a vast amount of work sent down to him from the British Embassy, but the week that followed was the happiest time he had spent since his days of convalescence at Marrakesh: the daily painting and bathing expeditions, and the chateau itself in its lovely setting above the Bay of Biscay. But the Prime Minister could not drive thoughts of the election entirely from his mind. "The mystery of the ballot boxes and their contents had an ugly trick of knocking on the door and peering in at the windows." And at lunch one day he remarked gloomily, "Soon we shall have to go back to London to see if they've thrown me in the gutter." But from the moment he began to paint again he seemed more relaxed than his friends had seen him for a long time, and he grudged every hour of daylight when painting was denied to him.

His first bath was an impressive occasion. A tent was pitched halfway down the beach. From this he emerged wearing his ten-gallon hat and a pair of large and shapeless drawers. He marched to the water's edge followed by Sawyers, his valet, who removed his cigar and his cowboy headgear.

Then Mr. Churchill took to the water, floating happily to and fro like a contented porpoise. There was thunder in the air and a tremendous electric storm broke over the mountains beyond the Spanish border. During the night a violent gale raged over the Landes Forest, uprooting hundreds of trees.

On the other side of the world a great storm also raged that night over a remote village called Oscuro. Near by, in the New Mexican desert, vivid flashes of lightning ringed a gaunt steel tower which had just been erected. A few hours later, from the top of this scaffolding, there burst a blazing ball of fire which grew and grew until it seemed to the watchers that it would engulf the whole universe. [6]

"President Truman arrived in Berlin the same day as I did," Churchill wrote. "I called on him that afternoon and was impressed with his gay, precise, sparkling manner and obvious power of decision. Next day we made separate tours of Berlin. The city was nothing but a chaos of ruins. No notice had been given of our visit and the streets had only the ordinary passersby. In the square in front of the Chancellery there was, however, a considerable crowd. When I got out of the car and walked about among them, except for one old man who shook his head disapprovingly, they all began to cheer. My hate had died with their surrender, and I was much moved by their demonstrations and also by their haggard looks and threadbare clothes. Our Russian guides took us to Hitler's air-raid shelter. I went down to the bottom and saw the room in which he and his mistress had committed suicide, and when we came up again they showed us the place where his body had been burned. The course Hitler had taken was much more convenient for us than the one I had feared." [3f]

The Palace itself lay on the outskirts of Potsdam. The Russians had planted a courtyard with red flowers in the shape of a huge red star in the grounds; it showed up brightly against the short cropped lawn. Inside was a large room paneled in dark wood, furnished with a crimson carpet over-laid with a red and purple Oriental rug. The room had a twelve-foot circular table and fifteen chairs and desks for secretaries and stenographers. The chairs of the delegates were decorated with carved angels. Three interpreters and nine other subordinates sat at the table with the Big Three, where Truman's mainstays were James Byrnes, his Secretary of State, and ex-Ambassador Joseph Davies. Churchill often consulted Clement Attlee and his Foreign Secretary, Ernest Bevin. Truman, a brisk and affable chairman, did not wander from the point as Roosevelt used to do.

A flight of stairs, designed for an entrance in the grand manner, swept majestically down from Churchill's personal quarters into the fifty-foot-high meeting room. In the eyes of finicky Russian experts of protocol, Churchill could not be allowed to make his stately descent while Truman and Stalin had to enter from below. So the British Prime Minister had to leave the building by a side door, and then reenter by another way, retiring to a small anteroom. Truman and Stalin waited in other anterooms, until a train of complicated signals set all three into coordinated movement. Stalin would roll in with characteristically ursine gait; Churchill entered like John Bull, while Harry Truman almost skipped in with a permissible speed, since his anteroom was slightly farther away than the others. [31]

Potsdam was the inconclusive conference. Session after session the debates proceeded, with Churchill challenging the Russians. When the question of Germany's future came up, Churchill put the question: "What is Germany?" To this Stalin replied: "What is left of Germany." When Churchill raised the religious rights of Roman Catholics in Poland, Stalin reflected a moment, stroking his moustache, then speaking in an even tone he asked: "How many divisions has the Pope?"

On its social side Potsdam did not fall short of its predecessors. "Stalin's dinner was a wow," Truman wrote home, "with caviar and vodka, watermelon and champagne. There was a toast every five minutes." He ate little, drank less, but made his own contribution to the entertainment that produced the battle of the music. [2]

It began when Truman gave the first formal dinner; the musical entertainment featured the talented Sergeant Eugene List, who played the Chief Executive's favorite composer, Chopin. Stalin shared the President's love of classical music and proposed that they drink a toast to the young army sergeant-pianist. When he was host, Stalin, determined to offer better music than that provided by Truman, sent to Moscow for a prize music student and another famous Russian pianist. Also, two excellent female violinists—who made up in ability what they lacked in looks. About 1 A.M., the Prime Minister had had quite enough. Churchill got up and went over to Truman. "When are you going home?" he whispered. The President replied blandly, "What's the matter? I'm having a fine time." "Well," Churchill said grouchily, "I'm bored to tears. I do not like this music, I'm going home." Of course, he didn't. The end, however, did not come until 1:30 A.M.

The Prime Minister hinted that he would "get even" with Truman and Stalin. When he was host, he had the full orchestra of the British Royal Air Force play long and loudly throughout the dinner. And Churchill, with puckish malice, saw to it that the musicians kept going until 2 A.M. The Potsdam Conference set at least one record—it was the most musical of all the nine Allied war councils. [35]

"On July 17," recalled Churchill, "Henry Stimson, Secretary of War, called at my abode and laid before me a sheet of paper on which was written, 'Babies satisfactorily born.' 'It means,' he said, 'that the experiment in the New Mexican desert has come off. The atomic bomb is a reality.'

"The President invited me to confer with him forthwith.

He had with him General Marshall and Admiral Leahy. Up to this moment we had contemplated the terrific air bombing of Japan and the invasion of very large armies; the desperate resistance of the Japanese fighting to the death with samurai devotion, as on Okinawa island where many thousands of Japanese, rather than surrender, had destroyed themselves by handgrenades. To quell the Japanese resistance man by man and conquer the country yard by yard might well require the loss of a million American lives and half that number of British. Now all this nightmare picture had vanished. In its place was the vision of the end of the whole war in one or two violent shocks. The Japanese people, whose courage I had always admitted, might find in the apparition of this almost supernatural weapon an excuse which would save their honor and release them from their obligations of being killed to the last fighting man.

Moreover, we should not need the Russians. The end of the Japanese war no longer depended upon the pouring in of their armies for the final and perhaps protracted slaughter. We had no need to ask favors of them. The array of European problems could therefore be faced on their merits. We seemed suddenly to have become possessed of a merciful abridgment of the slaughter in the East and of a far happier prospect in Europe. I have no doubt that these thoughts were present in the minds of my American friends. At any rate, there never was a moment's discussion as to whether the atomic bomb should be used or not, only unanimous, automatic, unquestioned agreement around our table.

Eventually it was decided to send an ultimatum calling for an immediate unconditional surrender of the armed forces of Japan. This document was published on July 26. These terms were rejected by the military rulers of Japan, and the United States air force made its plans accordingly to cast one atomic bomb on Hiroshima and one on Nagasaki. To give every chance to the inhabitants, eleven Japanese cities were warned by leaflets that they would be subjected to intensive air bombardment. Next day six of them were attacked. Twelve more were warned on July 31 and four were bombed. The last warning was given on August 5. By then the Superfortresses had dropped a million and a half leaflets every day and three million copies of the ultimatum. The first atomic bomb was not cast till August 6, and the second on August 9. The next day the Japanese Government agreed to accept the ultimatum. The Allied fleets entered Tokyo Bay, and on the morning of September 2 the formal instrument of surrender was signed on board the United States battleship *Missouri*." [3f]

On July 25, Churchill arrived back at 10 Downing Street. The famous Map Room at the Ministry headquarters had been temporarily requisitioned to deal, this time, with a political battlefield. In his siren suit Winston sat in the Prime Minister's chair throughout that evening, watching election results coming through and being chalked up on a giant scoreboard on the wall. By the time he went to bed the results were still obscure, but he was convinced the people wanted him to continue his work. But just before dawn he woke suddenly with a sharp stab of almost physical pain. A hitherto subconscious conviction that he had been beaten dominated his mind. [3f]

By noon defeat was a fact. To the astonishment of the whole world, Churchill had been repudiated by his countrymen. Looking at him, Clementine said: "It may well be a blessing in disguise." "At the moment it seems quite effectively disguised," replied Winston. [25]

"The verdict of the electors," he remarked, "had been so overwhelmingly expressed that I did not wish to remain even for an hour responsible for their affairs. At four o'clock, therefore, I drove to the Palace, tendered my resignation to the King and advised His Majesty to send for Mr. Attlee." [3f]

He had been turned out of office by one of the greatest

political landslides of modern parliamentary history. Labor had won three hundred and ninety-three seats, giving them a majority of one hundred and forty-six. The Conservatives and their allies had lost one hundred and ninety-three seats. On his return from the Palace Mr. Churchill reappeared in the Map Room. By now the total votes had been added up and checked and these were read out to him. "Five million against us," he said thoughtfully. Then, turning to Captain Pim, he remarked, "We've had good times together. We've seen great days and traveled in many countries. God bless you always!" [6]

That night he issued his farewell statement to the nation from 10 Downing Street: "The decision of the British people has been recorded in the votes counted today. I have therefore laid down the charge which was placed upon me in darker times. I regret that I have not been permitted to finish the work against Japan. It only remains for me to express to the British people, for whom I have acted in these perilous years, my profound gratitude for their unflinching, unswerving support which they have given me during my task, and for the many expressions of kindness which they have shown towards their servant." [25]

That weekend the Churchills drove down to Chequers. After dinner newsreels of the early stages of the Potsdam Conference and an American documentary film, *The True Glory,* were shown. The program ended all too soon, and as Churchill made his way back from the Long Gallery, he said sadly: "This is where I miss the news . . . no work . . . nothing to do." Before retiring his guests signed the Visitors' Book. Churchill was the last to add his name, and below, at the foot of the page, he wrote the one word—*Finis.* [6]

23

"An Iron Curtain Has Descended"

THE British voters did not mean Churchill's stinging defeat to be personal—in fact many were dismayed to learn that by voting Labor they had caused him to lose his job. But they were fed up with the Tories—and the class system they represented—and they were ready for a change. [10]

The votes of men serving in the Forces were decisive. Such votes are never likely to be on the side of the party in power. To the private soldier the Government is the War Office, and the War Office is the sergeant-major. The exercise of the franchise gives to the private soldier a brief and blessed opportunity of expressing his opinion of the sergeant-major. [19]

Still pondering on his dismissal, Churchill was genuinely puzzled by the warmth of the welcome accorded to him when he appeared in public. He attended a performance of Noel Coward's comedy *Private Lives,* and the entire audience rose and applauded him for several minutes. At the end of the play John Clements made a moving speech from the stage, and again the audience rose and cheered as though they would never stop. When he moved into the flat of his son-in-law Duncan Sandys, crowds gathered night after night in the hope of seeing him, and searchlights were played on the building. At the Savoy, where he dined one evening, every one in the restaurant stood up and clapped and cheered as he passed through the room.

On August 16 the New Prime Minister, Clement Attlee, paid a moving tribute to him in the House of Commons: "In the darkest and most dangerous hours of our history this nation found in my Right Honorable friend the man who expressed supremely the courage and determination never to yield which animated all the men and women of this country. In undying phrases he crystalized the unspoken feeling of all. He radiated a stream of energy throughout the machinery of government—indeed, throughout the life of the nation. His place in history is secure." [6]

On that same day—August 16, 1945—Churchill, rejected by the electorate in his hour of victory and now smoldering in the abyss of defeat, rose in the House of Commons among a storm of jeers and countercheers. He ruefully surveyed the congested benches opposite him and said:

"A friend of mine, an officer, was in Zagreb when the results of the late general election came in. An old lady said to him, 'Poor Mr. Churchill! I suppose now he will be shot.' My friend was able to reassure her. He said the sentence might be mitigated to one of the various forms of hard labor which are always open to His Majesty's subjects."

The laughter on all sides of the House dissolved antagonisms. It was more than a tribute to his mastery as a parliamentarian; it saluted a democrat who, as long ago as 1909, had defined democracy as "the occasional necessity of deferring to the opinions of other people." [22]

Packages began arriving at Chartwell soon after the Japanese surrender. Jamaica came through with five hundred cigars, New Zealand made him a gift of money raised in a shilling fund—Churchill handed it over to St. Mary's Hospital in Paddington. King Ibn Saud gave him a gold and jeweled sword and dagger and a set of ceremonial robes in a hide

269

case. A man in Portugal shipped him one hundred and sixteen gallons of very old port wine, the Stock Owners Association of Australia sent him a kangaroo, and a group of Maoris inquired whether he would like a male or female kiwi. Some African farmers sent a beautiful ebony walking stick and Switzerland a "perpetual-motion" clock guaranteed to run forever. And the French town of Aix-en-Provence officially changed its name to "La Ville Churchill." [8]

Offered the Royal Honor of the Order of the Garter, Churchill declined: "How can I accept the Order of the Garter, when the people of England have just given me the order of the boot?" Soon after, in October, the Churchills moved into their new town house, 28 Hyde Park Gate, a quiet cul-de-sac near Kensington Gardens. [25]

Britons expected, now that Winston was seventy, he would retire to paint pictures, write books and give the world the benefit of his wisdom as an elder statesman. [1]

But Winston had no intention of retiring. The conviction that he could manage things much better than anyone else still burned strongly within him. To those friends who urged his resignation from the party leadership he replied: "My horse may not be a very good one, but at least it's better than being in the infantry." He plunged into the attack against the Labor Government with obvious relish: "I hope you will believe that it is with no personal bias, soreness or conceit that I declare that the vote of the nation at the general election was one of the greatest disasters that has smitten us in our long and checkered history." As for leaving Parliament, that was unthinkable. "I am a child of the House of Commons." [4]

So he led the Opposition during the five eventful years when Labor had power as well as office and gave free play to an invective, witty, ironical, sometimes devastating and without its match in a humdrum House. [37]

When Socialist members constantly interrupted him with jeers, he would make a typical aside in the best House of

Commons tradition: "The crackling of thorns beneath the pot does not disturb me."

The Minister of Fuel and Power, Hugh Gaitskell, once urged the nation to take fewer baths, as a measure for saving coal. It was a piece of advice that Churchill did not allow to pass without comment. "When Ministers speak like this," he said, "the Prime Minister and his friends have no need to wonder why they are getting increasingly into bad odor. I have even asked myself, when meditating on these points, whether you, Mr. Speaker, would admit the word 'lousy' as a parliamentary expression in referring to the administration, provided of course that it was not intended in a contemptuous sense, but purely as one of factual narration."

"The Socialist belief," he growled, "is that nothing matters so long as miseries are equally shared, and certainly they have acted in accordance with their faith," and added, "Sir Stafford Cripps [Labor M.P.] is a great advocate of 'Strength through Misery.' " [4]

Churchill admired Cripps's intellect but otherwise had little affection for him. He said of him, "Neither of his colleagues can compare with him in the acuteness and energy of mind with which he devotes himself to so many topics injurious to the strength and welfare of the state." And there were times when he seemed to have difficulty in pronouncing the name, which came out sounding something like "Sir Stifford Crapps." [1]

During one Churchill speech, Piratin, the Communist, cried out, "Shame." Quickly came the retort, "The Honorable Member is a good judge of shame." During exchanges in debate, Hartley Shawcross shook his head to indicate dissent from one of Churchill's assertions. "The Attorney General," remarked Churchill, "shakes his head at Bolshevism, of which he was such an admirer only two years ago." Later Sir Hartley ventured a muttered interruption. "What," asked Churchill, "did the Attorney General say?" "I said, 'Rubbish,' " replied Sir Hartley. "That," interjected Churchill, "may be what the Right Honorable and learned gentleman has in his head, but it does not carry conviction." [2]

Once while Hugh Gaitskell, Minister of Fuel, was delivering a speech on economic affairs, Churchill suddenly sat up very straight on the Opposition front bench instead of remaining in his usual indifferent slouch. He looked about distractedly, went through all his pockets, then started looking on the floor of the House, seemingly impervious to the fact that he had by now stolen the interest of all Members on both sides of the House. Gaitskell was so thoroughly rattled that he even lost the last thread of his speech and hesitated. Winston looked up in surprise and explained in his famous mumble, "I was only looking for my jujube." The story was carried in the press under the headline 'The Fall of the Pastille.' " [29]

Ernest Bevin tangled frequently with Winston. When Bevin launched into an attack on the Communists and the Soviet Union with crushing impact, the two Communist Members writhed and squeaked, "Cheapskate." At the end Bevin lost his thread and automatically, it seemed, found himself attacking Churchill instead. Winston leaned forward and said, inaudible to all but a few, "Don't spoil a good speech." Bevin stopped, stammered, resumed the thread and went off again without another reference to Churchill.

But they never forgot the debt they owed to each other as they had fought together in the Coalition. At six o'clock one morning in September 1947, Bevin was awakened by a telephone call from New York; Andre Vishinsky of Russia had attacked Winston Churchill in the U.N. and called him "as bad as Hitler." Bevin hurried from his bed, called an early morning conference of Foreign Office officials and drafted a reply for the British delegate to make. The draft stated, among other things, that Mr. Churchill had done more to fight Fascism than any Communist in the world, that he had worked in London while German planes, fueled with Soviet oil, were shoveling bombs on the capital. [1]

On foreign affairs, Churchill's voice carried more weight than that of any man in England, and perhaps in all the free world. His speech at Fulton, Missouri, in March 1946, was a watershed, the beginning of recognition that the cold war was on. [10]

"When I wrote the invitation to Mr. Churchill to come to us to speak," said Dr. F. L. McCluer, Westminister College president, "I took the letter to the White House where Truman scrawled a footnote: 'This is a fine little school. If you will come, I will go with you to Fulton and introduce you.'

"It was certainly a significant day. Truman and Churchill were seated on top of an open limousine which started down the hill into Fulton. I was cushioned between them lower down in the seat, when Churchill nudged me with his knees to get my attention. 'I can't light my cigar in this wind,' he said, 'and I know the people will be expecting it.'" [40]

At the convocation, Churchill spoke words that roused the world:

"*A shadow has fallen upon the scenes so lately lighted by the Allied victory. From Stettin in the Baltic to Trieste in the Adriatic, an Iron Curtain has descended across the Continent. Behind that line lie all the capitals of the ancient states of central and eastern Europe, Warsaw, Berlin, Prague, Vienna, Budapest, Belgrade, Bucharest, and Sofia, and all these famous cities and the populations around them lie in what I must call the Soviet sphere, all subject to Soviet control. This is certainly not the liberated Europe we fought to build up.*

"*I do not believe that Soviet Russia desires war. What they desire is the fruits of war and the indefinite expansion of their power and doctrine. From what I have seen of our Russian friends and allies during the war I am convinced there is nothing they admire so much as strength and there is nothing for which they have less respect than weakness, especially military weakness.*

"If we adhere faithfully to the Charter of the United Nations . . . if all British moral and material forces and convictions are joined with your own . . . the high roads of the future will be clear, not only for our time but for a century to come." [3j]

So far ahead was Churchill of prevailing opinion that he caused surprise and indignation on both sides of the Atlantic, and he was reproved for his "imprudence" and "irresponsibility." The Democratic Senators described the speech as "shocking." "Mr. Churchill," said Henry Wallace, then Secretary of Commerce, "is not speaking for the American people and their Government." At home in Britain, the Prime Minister was asked to confirm that the Government "entirely disapproves of the tone and temper of the speech." The Government, replied Attlee, was not called upon to express any opinion on a speech delivered in another country by a private individual.

By midsummer the breakdown in collaboration between East and West was plain to see. Ernest Bevin presented a somber indictment of the men of the Kremlin and the Soviet campaign of vilification accorded to the Western Allies. The language of Fulton had become the policy of the governments of the United Kingdom and the United States. Fulton was followed by the Marshall Plan and the setting up of NATO.

In home affairs, septuagenarian Churchill displayed a vitality youth might envy. As leader of His Majesty's Opposition, he provided the government a solution for their problem in Palestine.

Terrorists had blown up a wing of the King David Hotel in Jerusalem used as British military headquarters, killing ninety-one persons and injuring forty-five others. Public opinion was gravely shocked. In August the House debated the impasse. Stafford Cripps and Herbert Morrison made the Government's defense, but it was Churchill the Leader of the Opposition who presented a policy to meet the occasion. He reminded his fellow members that he spoke with the authority of one who, as Colonial Secretary in 1922, had defined the British obligations when the mandate for Palestine was accepted from the League of Nations. These obligations, with the delicate balancing of the opposing claims of Jew and Arab, had been faithfully fulfilled during the years that followed.

"I think the Government should say," observed Churchill, "that if the United States will not come and share the burden of the Zionist cause, as defined or as agreed, we should now give notice that we will return our mandate to the U.N.O. and that we will evacuate Palestine within a specified period."

On May 15, 1948, the British mandate in Palestine was terminated, whereupon the independent Jewish State of Israel was proclaimed. There had been an inevitable delay before the Ministers brought themselves to accept the proposals of their opponent.

Under Lord Mountbatten, last of the Viceroys of India, meanwhile, the final arrangements were being pushed through to hand over power to the Indian people. At midnight on August 14, 1947, King George VI ceased to be Emperor of India and the two new states of India and Pakistan came into being. In the closing stages of the negotiations between the Viceroy and the Indians, Churchill spoke with foreboding of the handing over of the Government to Nehru with consequences that will darken ("and redden") the coming years. But when all negotiations ended and the necessary bill was presented for Parliamentary approval, he announced his acquiescence. What had been done reflected credit not only on the Viceroy but on the Prime Minister who had appointed him. [2]

The full-time job of remaking a beaten and dispirited party represented only a tiny fraction of Winston's endeavors in this bright twilight period of his life. Beginning in 1948 the six majestic volumes on *The Second World War* appeared one by one. Each one had a special theme. The first, *The Gathering Storm,* told "How the English-speaking peoples through their unwisdom, carelessness and good nature allowed the wicked to rearm." The second, *Their Finest Hour,* "How the British held the fort ALONE till those who had been half blind were half ready." The third, *The Grand Alliance,* "How the British fought on with Hardship their Garment until Soviet Russia and the United States were drawn into the Great Conflict." The fourth, *The Hinge of Fate,* "How the power of the Grand Alliance became predominant." The fifth, *Closing the Ring,* "How Nazi Germany was isolated and assailed on All Sides." The sixth and last, *Triumph and Tragedy,* tells with a stinging pain "How the great democracies triumphed and so were able to resume the follies which had so nearly cost them their life." The moral of the whole work was, "In War: Resolution; In Defeat: Defiance; In Victory: Magnanimity; In Peace: Goodwill." [1]

For the production of this vast compilation, he again assembled a team of secretaries, historians, technical experts, research workers and editorial assistants. They rolled forward through forests and prairies of wartime documents like a large reaping and binding machine, rejecting, codifying and sorting. There were times when secretaries were working in shifts all through the night, and often eight or nine thousand words would be dictated in a single day. [42]

Not even politics and literature combined satisfied his vast energy. He purchased five hundred acres of land around Chartwell and began serious farming. At the same time he developed a strong desire to own a racing stable. He acquired a gray three-year-old, Colonist II, which started off with a win at Ascot in 1949, went on to win £13,000 in prize money. He had taken his father's racing colors, chocolate and pink, as his own. In the weighing room Winston was as wide-eyed as a child, watching everything. [1]

Once when Colonist finished fourth (in the Gold Cup at Ascot), Churchill had his own excuse. He said that he had had a very serious talk with the horse just before the race. "I told him, 'This is a very big race and, if you win it, you will never have to run again. You will spend the rest of your life in agreeable female company.'" Then Churchill added, "Colonist II did not keep his mind on the race." [21]

He worked at painting with furious concentration, sometimes from early morning until late in the afternoon, sitting there in his siren suit and sombrero, hunched like an enormous egg, put out only if someone whistled or was bold enough to try looking over his shoulder. The paintings gathered and overflowed. They hung on the walls at Chartwell and stood in piles in spare rooms, for he made it a principle that none was to be offered for sale. Every year at least one of his pictures was hung in the Royal Academy and, as he had begun submitting his work under the name of "Mr. Winter," it could not be said that his illustrious name had influenced the committee. [1]

Churchill showed a group of his canvases to a friend. "Tell me," said the friend, "why do you paint only landscapes and never portraits?" "Because," said Winston, "a tree doesn't complain that I haven't done it justice." [40]

"I remember," wrote Lady Violet Bonham-Carter, "when we were both staying in a country house, set in a monochrome of dull, flat country, I went out to watch him painting. I saw on his canvas range upon range of mountains, rising dramatically behind the actual foreground. I inquired where they came from and he replied: "Well—I couldn't leave it as dull as all that." [39]

Three days before his seventy-fourth birthday, he donned jodhpurs, fortified himself with rum punch and galloped off to the hounds astride a borrowed horse. His square-crowned Russell hat was jammed well down on his head, his inevitable cigar clenched firmly between his teeth. Later, his birthday and the hunt behind him, Churchill stood up in the House of Commons and demanded from Prime Minister Clement Attlee an account of the Labor Government's stewardship over the nation's moldering defenses. [56]

For his seventy-fifth birthday, congratulations came in from friends and enemies alike. Nothing, perhaps, put England's feelings toward Churchill more perfectly than Low's cartoon on that occasion. It showed two Churchills, one magnificent with one hand on a pile of books, his other on a sword, and near him his painting palette and brushes. It was labeled, "Dear Old Winston, the Nation's pride." The other Churchill was labeled, "Winston, Naughty Old Party Politician." An average British citizen was pushing the second away and crying, "Stand aside, sir. Not even you will stop me paying my respects." [1]

But in the Conservative party there began to be discontent. Perhaps things would be better, they whispered, if Winston resigned and Eden took his place. *Picture Post* ran an article entitled: "Is Churchill a Liability to the Tories?" and Lord Beaverbrook's *Sunday Express* stoutly replied: "When Churchill is in his seat, the Opposition breathes fire. When he is not, the Tory front bench has the venom of a bunch of daffodils."

Although Churchill was well aware of the agitation in favor of Eden he clung firmly to his saddle, unperturbed. "When I want to tease Anthony," he remarked slyly to a friend, "I remind him that Gladstone formed his last administration at the age of eighty-four." Winston was right to remain unruffled. For when the results of the 1950 general

election were known, Conservative criticisms abruptly ceased.
[4]

The huge Labor vote had a bare majority of six, and it was
patent that before long there was bound to be another election. It was clear that Churchill was coming in with the tide.
[42]

The Socialist leaders were exhausted. Bevin died in April,
1951, a month after his seventieth birthday. Cripps was
dying, Attlee and Morrison were sick men. [1]

In an hour of gathering darkness and discouragement the
people of Great Britain turned again to a leader who had
served them well before. There was reassurance in the old
familiar, dogged smile beneath the square black hat, and in
the sight of Churchill making the V sign from his big, black
Humber, and the red, blue and gold flag of his honorary
title—Lord Warden of the Cinque Ports—bravely flying from
its fender and the deep blue ribbon of Conservatism decorat-
ing its hood.

At seventy-six, Churchill was not the man he had been ten
years before. His shoulders were rounder, his jowls hung
looser beside his bulldog jaws. But his step was still springy,
and under his beetling brows his eyes could still smolder and
twinkle with their old fire. Friends and enemies alike had
noticed in Churchill's speech a tendency to slur and meander,
but in the heat of this latest campaign, with victory once
more within his grasp, the old leader gave no sign of such
deterioration. In a speech at Plymouth, he begged for a
chance to lead his country again to greatness and to peace.
"It is the last prize I seek to win," he said.

The voting itself was quiet; the excitement came after the
balloting. On October 26, 1951, Clement Attlee went to Buckingham Palace to hand King George VI his resignation. The
message, "Winston is back!" flashed through the world. [57]

The country held its breath waiting to see how and where
the master of the sensational and unexpected would direct

the Ship of State. But Churchill surprised his audience. His policy was one of amelioration. Ruffled tempers were to be smoothed down, angry hands joined in friendship. He was determined to put an end to the class war which had been mounting during the Socialists' tenure of office, and to lower the tension between the two parties.

"We are met together here," he told Parliament in his first speech as Prime Minister, "with an apparent gulf between us as great as any I have known in fifty years of House of Commons life. What the nation needs is a period of tolerant and constructive debating on the merits of the questions before us. [4]

In the Smoking Room of the House of Commons Churchill passed a small group of members. He stopped and beamed, and then his glance fell on Richard Stokes, the Socialist for Ipswich, who all through the war had attacked Churchill fearlessly, continuously. Now the Prime Minister came back and put a hand on his shoulder. "Of course, I've forgiven you," he said. He moved away a few paces and said, as if they might be surprised by what he had said: "Such hatred as I have left in me—and it isn't much—I would rather reserve for the future than the past." [21]

24

The Last Fling

O N the last day of the year the Prime Minister departed in a gale for America. [7]

The Washington visit was looked on, at home and in America, as a begging mission, with another American loan as its objective. The Prime Minister, it was suggested, was coming cup in hand for dollars. Churchill repudiated this notion in a broadcast to the nation three days before Christmas: "We are resolved to make this island solvent, able to earn its living and pay its way. We have no assurance that anyone else is going to keep the British lion as a pet."

In Washington collaboration for peace was the overall topic—or preparations to resist aggression. The agenda included such topics as air bases in Britain for the United States; enlisting the support of West Germany in European defense; the North Atlantic Treaty Organization; standardization of rifles and ammunition; affairs of the Middle East.

Churchill was delighted to be made a member of the Society of Cincinnati, an organization of men descended from officers who served under George Washington in the Revolution. He qualified through his mother, for Jennie Jerome was great-granddaughter of Reuben Murray, who had served in Washington's Continental Army. The wheel had turned full circle when the successor of the Prime Minister who lost the American colonies for Britain was admitted to the fraternity formed in honor of officers of the insurgent Americans who achieved their independence.

The following day (January 17), for the third time in his career, he addressed a joint session of the United States Congress: "I have not come here to ask you for money to make life more comfortable or easier for us in Britain. Our standards of life are our own business, and we can only keep our self-respect and independence by looking after them ourselves. I have come here to ask of you not gold but steel, not favors but equipment; that is why so many of our requests have been so well and generously met."

He spoke of the change in the world scene since last he had addressed the Congress. Former allies had become foes, former foes allies. Russia, eight years previously our brave ally, had cast away the goodwill and admiration her valiant soldiers had gained for her. "The sooner strong enough force can be assembled in Europe under a united command, the more effective will be the deterrent against a third world war. The sooner also will our sense of security and the fact of our security be seen to reside in valiant, resolute and well-armed manhood rather than in awful secrets science has wrested from nature. If I may say this—Members of the Congress, be careful above all things not to let go of the atomic weapon until you are sure, and more than sure, that other means of preserving peace are in your hands." [2]

A reporter asked him whether he had any plan for retirement. "Not until I am a great deal worse," said Churchill, "and the Empire a great deal better." [30]

The urgent necessity for an understanding with Russia, some assured basis for peace—these were the thoughts that obsessed his mind. He longed to bring about a meeting of the three leaders at the summit, to end his career, not as a "warmonger" but as a harbinger of peace to the nations. Time pressed—certainly for him. He strained every nerve to bring it about, but American opinion was consistently unfavorable; nor were the Russians willing. [7]

No secret matter of state was ever so pleasing to Winston Spencer Churchill as the one he kept to himself in April 1953. The secret: he was about to be knighted. The Prime Minister told no one about it, but observers of the Churchillian character should have taken warning of untoward events from the vitality of his bearing and his high good humor. At a St. George's Day dinner with the Honorable Artillery Company, he told the gunners what would happen if St. George were alive today: "St. George would be armed not by a lance, but by several flexible formulas. He would propose a conference with the dragon. He would lend the dragon a lot of money. The maiden's release would be referred to Geneva or New York, the dragon reserving all rights meanwhile."

Returning to the House in white tie and tails, Churchill was all sweetness. "I was hoping we should find ourselves in a friendly atmosphere tonight," he cooed with a wicked twinkle. "Nonsense!" shouted the dragons of Labor—but eventually his good humor spread to them. "Good night!" yelled the Laborites as the Prime Minister waddled out. He turned and blew them a kiss.

The following afternoon, the secret was out. At Windsor Castle, while Mrs. Churchill looked on, the seventy-eight-year-old Prime Minister knelt before his twenty-seven-year-old Queen. Taking the ceremonial sword, Elizabeth II touched Churchill, first on the right shoulder, then on the left, and bade him, "Rise, Sir Winston." Then she presented him with the insignia of the Order of the Garter. [56]

King George VI had died in 1952, still a comparatively young man, but worn out by work, the strain of the war years. Now, in May 1953, came the Coronation of Queen Elizabeth II, and that moment coincided with a recovery of the country's spirits. Not until then did the mood of weariness and war exhaustion lift from the people; everybody noticed a new buoyancy, a return to the old English gaiety and cheerfulness after too long an endurance.

The Coronation junketings helped. One saw Churchill at that marvelous spectacle in the Abbey, leading the procession of the Commonwealth Prime Ministers, pausing to say a word to Lady Churchill in the pew in front before taking his place in his stall in the choir, a billowing figure in the plumes and robes of a Knight of the Garter. On his way out from the astonishing hieratic scene—its poignancy multiplied a hundredfold for those in whose minds reechoed the memories in that place of Victoria, of Anne and Sarah and Marlborough, of Elizabeth I and the medieval kings going right back to the Conqueror—one saw him hang back surveying the scene on which the improbable sacrament had taken place, then moving on in the procession and out. [7]

The strain of the Coronation told on Churchill, and he went down with a severe stroke which paralyzed him down one side and kept him out of the Commons for four months. He was given a great reception on his return, and the Socialists gallantly declared that "the House had been a duller place in his absence." [1]

"Would the Old Man prove to be his old self again?" His speech provided a triumphant and a moving affirmative: "If I stay for the time being, bearing the burden at my age, it is not because of love for power or office. I have had an ample share of both. If I stay it is because I have the feeling that I may, through things that have happened, have an influence on what I care about above all else—the building of a sure and lasting peace." [7]

In October he was awarded the Nobel Prize for literature "and his brilliant oratory in which he has always stood forth as the defender of eternal human values." [2]

"I am proud indeed to receive an honor which is international," he said. "I notice that the first Englishman to

receive the Nobel Prize was Rudyard Kipling and that another was Bernard Shaw. I cannot attempt to compete with
either of them. I knew them both quite well. My thought was
much more in accord with Mr. Kipling than with Mr. Shaw.
On the other hand Rudyard Kipling never thought much of
me, whereas Bernard Shaw often expressed himself in most
flattering terms." [4]

Two years and exhausting strains had taken their toll, but
in the cut and thrust of debate, his repartee had lost none of
its barbs. With the blandness of Mr. Pickwick, he disposed of
the parliamentary picadors. [2]

Arthur Lewis (Labor M.P.): Is the Prime Minister aware
of the deep concern felt by the people of this country at the
whole question of the Korean conflict?

Prime Minister: I am fully aware of the deep concern felt
by the Honorable Member in many matters above his comprehension.

Hector Hughes (Labor M.P.) asked the Prime Minister if
he would reconsider his refusal to separate the Ministry of
Agriculture from the Ministry of Fisheries.

Prime Minister: It would not, I feel, be a good arrangement to have a separate department for every industry of
national importance. These two industries have been long
associated departmentally; and, after all, there are many
ancient links between fish and chips. [28]

One day a political opponent delivered a tedious, long-
winded address. After a half hour, Churchill slumped into his
seat and closed his eyes. Irritated, the speaker walked over to
him and said in a loud voice: "Must you fall asleep when I
am speaking?" Without opening his eyes, Churchill replied:
"No, it is purely voluntary." [23]

In June Churchill spent a weekend at Washington with
President Eisenhower. "I come from my fatherland to my
mother's land." [7]

Questioned at a luncheon given by the National Press

Club, he replied to the crucial point of relations with Russia: "I am of the opinion that we ought to have a really good try for peaceful coexistence. I have a feeling that there must be a wish among the mass of the Russian people to have a better time and more fun. Nothing is more likely to bring about a modification of the rigid Russian system than contacts between the Russian people and the Western world—cultural contacts and trade contacts." The phrase "peaceful coexistence," coined by Eden, was adopted by the President himself. In the peaceful coexistence of Communist and non-Communist countries, Eisenhower said, lay the hope of the world.

To relieve France's fears, Churchill and the Cabinet committed Britain to the maintenance of a force of one hundred thousand men in Europe, an undertaking no British Prime Minister had previously been prepared to contemplate. Churchill and Eden ended Britain's centuries-old isolation behind the Channel ditch. British troops would be stationed permanently in Europe in peace for the first time since Mary Tudor lost Calais. Eisenhower called it one of the greatest diplomatic achievements of our time. [2]

Churchill's eightieth birthday, in November 1954, was a tremendous occasion. Lords and Commons gathered in Westminster Hall to do him honor. When he rose, slowly now with his years, his listeners were seized by that old tingling of the senses which they used to feel while waiting for him to speak during the dark days of the war. They were not disappointed. "I have never accepted," he said modestly, his s's slurring in the old way, "what many people have kindly said, namely that I inspired the nation. Their will was resolute and remorseless, and, as it proved, unconquerable. It fell to me to express it, and if I found the right words you must remember that I have always earned my living by my pen and by my tongue. It was the nation and the race dwelling all round the globe that had the lion's heart. I . . ."—and now the great

Churchillian boom was heard again with the resounding echo of 1940—"had the luck to be called on to give the r-o-a-r." [1]

He was presented with a Birthday Book in green leather, inlaid with the pattern of his racing colors, chocolate and pink. Inside were the signatures of the Members of Parliament, with the dedication: "We, the elected Members of the House of Commons, representing all political parties and all the people within Her Gracious Majesty's realm of the United Kingdom of Great Britain and Northern Ireland, do hereby join in one accord to show our deep affection to your person and our abiding gratitude for your incomparable service to the Parliament and the peoples of this realm, and to the causes of justice, freedom and peace during more than fifty years." [4]

There were two birthday cakes weighing ninety pounds each—one for cutting after the ceremony in the hall, the other for the private luncheon party at Downing Street. Iced in pale amber, the first cake had eight giant candles and colored badges depicting milestones in the Prime Minister's career—Harrow, Sandhurst, the Order of the Garter, the Nobel Prize medal, the crest of Pink and Brown with a jockey's cap. In gold set in a circle was the phrase: "A thousand years hence free people will say this was our finest man."

The second cake had eighty candles and measured a yard across; sugared in pink and white with white roses raised above the pink it also bore a quotation: "He is a man, take him, for all in all, we shall not look upon his like again." [25]

There was one false note. The distinguished portrait painter Graham Sutherland was commissioned by the House to paint Churchill for the occasion. It was a clever but inappropriate picture in mustards and purples, showing Churchill powerful but gluey-eyed and senile. "It is disgusting," said a Tory leader flatly. Churchill was politely ironic, but hurt. "A remarkable example of modern art," he said. Aneurin Bevan, Winston's old enemy, purred, "a beautiful work." [1]

Still Churchill did not resign. He evidently enjoyed the comedy of keeping people guessing; his colleagues might be on tenterhooks, but the Opposition relished the situation—they had become fond of their old enemy and were loath to let him go. [7]

During a series of debates Churchill was being attacked savagely by Aneurin Bevan. The final day of the debate the whole six hundred and seventy-five Members of Parliament were there to see the battle between the two lions. Aneurin Bevan did not turn up. As he was leaving at the end of the debate, walking through the lobbies of the House of Commons, Churchill said to an aide, "And where was he?" And the aide replied, "Don't you know, sir? Mr. Bevan is ill." "Nothing trivial I trust," snorted Churchill. [16]

Still, as if by some dispensation, a remarkable improvement had overtaken British affairs almost from the moment Churchill took office. The Korean War had ended, and with the building up of the North Atlantic Treaty Organization the fear of a sudden Russian onslaught across Europe was removed for the first time since the 1940's. When during the summer of 1954 an armistice was arranged in Indochina, there was less open conflict in the world than at any time since the day when Churchill first mobilized the British Grand Fleet against the Kaiser, precisely forty years before. [42]

In March 1955, newspaper readers were startled to learn that Churchill was at last to step aside in favor of his successor-designate, Sir Anthony Eden. The wits had made play over Sir Anthony's supposedly deferred hopes, and friends, according to the current gibe, had been heard to remark: "You know, Winston, if you don't retire soon, Anthony will be too old for the job." But the report was received with reserve. Was it no more than the latest variation on a timeworn rumor? Sphinxlike and bland, Churchill gave no indication that he was or was not moving on. So matters passed in suspense up to the last.

But, on the night of Monday, April 4, there was an occasion without precedent at 10 Downing Street. To do honor to her Minister, Queen Elizabeth attended a dinner given by Sir Winston and Lady Churchill. Leading members of the Cabinet and of the famous Coalition were present, and, a graceful recognition, Mrs. Neville Chamberlain. [2]

In proposing the Queen's health, he was able to say that he had enjoyed drinking that toast as a cavalry subaltern "in the reign of your Majesty's great-great-grandmother, Queen Victoria." [7]

Not until the following afternoon did rumor of his resignation resolve into certainty. The door of No. 10 opened to reveal Winston in black frock coat, with shiny top hat, goldheaded cane, zippered shoes, and cigar in mouth. Behind him in the doorway was the smiling Clementine. He waved his hat to acknowledge the cheers, got in his car and drove to Buckingham Palace. At 5:12, Winston's car drove out. People outside, strangely silent, suddenly went mad. Hundreds surged forward cheering and singing, "For he's a jolly good fellow." At 5:21 the official announcement of his resignation was issued from Buckingham Palace. [25]

25

The Elder Statesman

AT Chartwell the sun burst through the skies as the Churchill car hurried through the lanes. To the little groups of people, most of whom had waited from noon to greet him, he laughed and waving his hat shouted, "Come in the grounds all of you and see my goldfish." Asked whether he had any last message as Prime Minister, he smiled, hesitated, then said, "Yes—it is always nice to come home." [25]

There had been much speculation as to how he would spend his days. In what fashion should a man conduct himself on stepping down from the highest place? Should he become the elder statesman, offering oracular pronouncements from afar to the embarrassment of his successors and to the detriment of his own fame? Or should he withdraw completely? Neither course was his. Characteristically, he chose to remain a parliamentarian—Churchill, M.P. Above all, he was a House of Commons man. His place, in which he became the distinguished ornament of the Chamber, was the corner seat on the front bench below the gangway—adjacent to the Ministers of the Crown, but not one of them. [2]

He also took up again his work on *History of the English-Speaking Peoples,* which he had set aside twenty years earlier under the pressure of politics. A review noted Winston's preoccupation with historic battles and his affection for the Cavaliers. Attlee suggested amiably that the book might

better have been called, "Things in history which have interested me." But this and similar criticism did not dim its great
success. [1]

When told that Field Marshal Viscount Montgomery's
Memoirs earned more than Sir Winston's *History of the English-Speaking Peoples*, Churchill replied: "I'm not at all surprised that the Field Marshal lived up to the finest tradition
of Englishmen, by selling his life as dearly as possible." [49]

On social occasions Sir Winston and Lady Churchill were
given tremendous cheers by Londoners watching them step
from their car to keep dinner and theater appointments.
Sometimes they would visit the Old Vic to see Laurence
Olivier or Richard Burton. This was not altogether an un-
qualified honor for the actors. [1]

"One night," recalled Burton, "I got into the theater and
was making up when in came the director of the theater. 'Do
be good tonight,' he said, 'because the Old Man's out there in
the front row.' In Britain the Old Man is only one person, and
that's Winston Churchill. I panicked. But I went on the stage
and started to play Hamlet. I heard this dull rumble from the
front row of the stalls and I thought, what on earth is that—
well, it was Churchill speaking the lines with me, and I could
not shake him off. I tried going fast, I tried going slow, we did
cuts. And every time there was a cut an explosion occurred.
He knew the play absolutely backwards—he knows perhaps a
dozen of Shakespeare's plays intimately. Generally you can't
keep him for more than one act. I looked through the spyhole,
he got up from his seat, and I thought, that's it, we've lost
him. But indeed there he was suddenly coming backstage
and he said, 'My Lord Hamlet, may I use your bathroom?'
And he did." [16]

He showed no more disposition in his old age to grow up
than he had ever done, and his love for dumb animals and
living things grew even greater. Telephoning home, Churchill
would never fail to inquire after his dogs or his other "dear

little animals." He had a due appreciation for an animal's self-respect and was not at all amused when a friend suggested an insignificant name for a new dog he had been given. "This is an important dog," he said severely. Feeding his tropical fish became an adventure fraught with significance and emotion, a gastronomic discourse, a philosophical estimate on marine mentality. The fish were not simply fed; they were wooed with endearments.

Winston was a happy man, happy in his life's record, happy in his home. He played six-pack bezique for hours with Lady Churchill, happy as a child every time he won. In his garden he tended special flowers until he considered them beautiful enough to present to his wife. He still attended the House occasionally, listening carefully and politely, his hand cupped over his ear, especially when one of the younger Members was talking, and although he never attempted to take part in the debate, his presence gave it a new urgency and tension. [1]

In November 1958, he stood face to face in Paris with General de Gaulle. They had not met for fourteen years. There had been times when they had not found it possible to exchange speech. That day the amity of allies alone remained as Sir Winston Churchill was admitted to the proud fellowship of the Companion of the Liberation. Under the plane trees in a Paris garden, de Gaulle bent to affix the bronze medal of the Companions, embossed with a sword and superimposed with the Cross of Lorraine. "Sir Winston," said de Gaulle, "we acknowledge you as our Companion for the Liberation of France in honor and by victory." There was a brief pause and the two men regarded each other, Churchill looking up with a smile. Then, bending, de Gaulle gave the faint brush of a kiss on either cheek. [2]

In May 1959, Churchill visited Washington—a melancholy occasion—to see those aging fellow warriors George Catlett Marshall and John Foster Dulles at Walter Reed Hospital. He celebrated his eighty-fifth birthday that November with a visit to the House of Commons and with a dinner of oyster, pheasant and champagne. [10]

Asked by a reporter whether he had any fear of death, Churchill answered, "I am ready to meet my Maker. Whether my Maker is prepared for the great ordeal of meeting me is another matter." [30]

He still exercised his right to be unpredictable. He dedicated the ground for Cambridge's new Churchill College, a recent addition to the study of sciences in Britain. All the intellectual Establishment was there. Sir Winston symbolically planted a tree. In the casual conversation that followed, he agreed it was all mighty impressive. Every one glowed. "But that's a damn small tree," he said. Consternation was evidenced. "I like 'em big," he added as he stumped away. [46]

Sir Winston's eighty-seventh birthday brought him bulging mailbags of greetings from admirers the world over. Queen Elizabeth, touring Sierra Leone, sent her good wishes and so, too, did President Kennedy, voicing, as he wrote, the deep admiration and respect of his fellow Americans. At Westminster it was made a parliamentary occasion. The Commons rose to him as his Pickwickian figure was seen to advance into the Chamber. As he made his way to his place below the gangway they cheered him and waved their order papers. Sir David Eccles (Minister for Education) observed: "I am sure all Members of this House wish to give their good wishes to the Member for Woodford." Members accorded their endorsement with a deep-throated cheer. Then, the leader of the Opposition rose. "As a supplement to that," said Mr. Gaitskell, using the time-honored phrase of the parliamentary questioner, "may I ask the Right Honorable gentleman if he appreciates the pride and pleasure we all feel on his eighty-seventh birthday and of his presence amongst us on this historic occasion?"

A brief pause and the House was hushed. Then the familiar figure stood up slowly. They cheered him loudly but cut short their greeting to listen to him. They would have been delighted had he committed a major infringement of the rules, but, mindful as ever of the requirement, he permitted himself no more than seven words. "I am very grateful to you all," he said in a low but clearly heard voice, the last speech in the House made by Sir Winston Churchill.

In the summer of 1962 he was staying at Monte Carlo when he fractured a leg in a fall. A spasm of apprehension followed the announcement on the world's radio stations. They patched him up and with his limb encased in plaster from hip to ankle, the R.A.F. flew him home. Worldwide attention focused on the Middlesex Hospital. By mail, telegraph and cable, messages of goodwill came pouring in. The bulletins told of daily progress, followed by reports of the patient sitting up, dining on chicken and reading what the newspapers had to say about him. Slowly he fought back phlebitis and bronchial infection. His temper returned with his strength. He was fractious, rebellious. He demanded to go home. At last on the fifty-sixth morning since he was borne in, the hospital doors opened and the figure few had expected to see again emerged before them.

That August day a crowd packed the street so that no vehicle could move. As Churchill came into view a united thundering cheer came from a thousand throats. His eyes, eager as ever, looked out on the people crammed between the buildings on either side of the street. "Good old Winnie!" [2]

On April 9, 1963, President Kennedy proclaimed Sir Winston Churchill the first honorary citizen of the United States. The colorful and dramatic ceremonies were held in the White House rose garden, precisely timed so that the British Broadcasting Corporation could bounce it off the orbiting relay satellite and Sir Winston could watch it on television in Great Britain.

The official proclamation read:

In the dark days and darker nights when Britain stood alone—and most men save Englishmen despaired of England's life—he mobilized the English language and sent it into battle. The incandescent quality of his words illuminated the courage of his countrymen. Given unlimited powers by his fellow citizens, he was ever vigilant to protect their rights. Indifferent himself to danger, he wept over the sorrow of others. A child of the House of Commons, he became in time its father. Accustomed to the hardship of battle, he has no distaste for pleasure. By adding his name to our rolls, we mean to honor him—but his acceptance honors us far more. For no statement or proclamation can enrich his name—the name Sir Winston Churchill is already legend.

Sir David Ormsby-Gore handed the President a letter from Sir Winston, and Mr. Kennedy gave it to Randolph Churchill to read:

I have received many kindnesses from the United States of America, but the honor which you now accord me is without parallel. I accept it with deep gratitude and affection. It is a remarkable comment on our affairs that the former Prime Minister of a great sovereign state should thus be received as an honorary citizen of another. I say "great sovereign state" with design and emphasis, for I reject the view that Britain and the Commonwealth should now be relegated to a tame and minor role in the world. Our past is the key to our future, which I firmly trust and believe will be no less fertile and glorious. Let no man underrate our energies, our potentialities and our abiding power for good.

Mr. President, your action illuminates the theme of unity of the English-speaking peoples, to which I have devoted a large part of my life. I would ask you to accept yourself, and to convey to both Houses of Congress, and through them to the American people, my solemn and heartfelt thanks for this unique distinction, which will always be proudly remembered by my descendants.

George Ball, Under Secretary of State, presented to Randolph Churchill for his father an honorary citizen's passport and described it as "the only one of its kind in existence. It is a unique document for a unique citizen." [49]

When Churchill learned of President Kennedy's death his response was immediate and the ringing words were unmistakably Churchill: "This monstrous act has taken from the United States a great statesman and a wise and valiant man. The loss to the United States and the world is incalculable. Those who come after Mr. Kennedy must strive the more to achieve the ideals of world peace and human happiness and dignity to which his presidency was dedicated." [46]

February 27, 1964: "Sir Winston Churchill [reported Edwin Roth in the Vancouver *Sun*] has announced that he will not run for Parliament again. But in his last weeks as Right Honorable Member for Woodford, he comes as often as he can to his beloved House of Commons.

"The big swinging doors opposite the press gallery are opened wide by two tail-coated messengers. Just behind the wide open swing doors stands a wheelchair. Two Tory Members of Parliament, conscious of the great honor, help Sir Winston Churchill rise to his feet. As always he wears an elegant black jacket with striped trousers, and his famous black butterfly tie with white spots. A large white handkerchief protrudes from his breast pocket, and a golden watch chain curls across his waistcoat. His bald head with its wisps of snowy hair still seems enormous, and his wrinkled face is rosy.

"Slowly, one short step at a time, the two members help the Father of the House into the Chamber. His right hand clutches a stick on which he leans heavily. He pauses and bows respectfully to the Speaker, as all Members do when they enter, then very shakily walks to his seat at the corner of the first row of Conservative benches. All eyes in the Chamber watch this proud, brave and poignant walk until the moment when Sir Winston sinks down on the green leather, grateful that the walk is over again—and pleased that he has made it.

"The Tory Member sitting beside Sir Winston hands him the order paper on which the day's questions to Ministers are printed, and points out the question which is being answered. Despite Sir Winston's great age, his hands are steady. The order paper never shakes as he holds it. Prime Minister Sir Alec Douglas-Home leaves his seat to shake hands with Sir Winston, and sits down for a few minutes on the carpet-covered gangway step to talk to him.

"When Sir Winston has had enough he begins to pick up his stick. Immediately two Members walk over to help him up. If he is not too tired Sir Winston growls proudly that he wants to walk alone—and he walks alone with his stick. Sometimes his left leg, still held by a surgical pin, cannot take the strain, and helping hands must support him.

"At the Bar of the House, Sir Winston turns slowly, and bows to Mr. Speaker. For long moments, he looks at the Chamber, as though he were reviewing his life. As the two tail-coated messengers open the big swing doors, the waiting wheelchair is seen. The arch beneath which Sir Winston walks out of the Chamber is made from broken stones deliberately left ruined when the Chamber, which was destroyed by bombs in 1941, was rebuilt after the war. It is called the Churchill Arch." [49]

July 28, 1964: A packed House of Commons [reported James Fearon in the New York *Times*] paid a rare and warm tribute today to the most famous Member, Sir Winston Churchill. The seat usually occupied by the 89-year-old Sir Winston was virtually the only one empty in the historic chamber as Members rose to pay homage. Sir Winston had spent what was probably his last hour in the Commons yesterday. Today, to the relief of his colleagues, who thought the emotional strain might be too great, he stayed home.

As Randolph Churchill, Sir Winston's son, watched from

the gallery, Sir Alec Douglas-Home moved a formal motion honoring the war leader and world statesman.

Sir Alec's predecessor, Harold Macmillan, came closest to touching the nostalgic mood of the House. He recalled that "great administrators in times of peace, like Walpole, and great leaders of the nation in the hour of peril—Chatham, Pitt, Lloyd George—have nearly equaled but not surpassed Sir Winston's immense span of Parliamentary and public life. There have been debaters and orators of equal resource and power but few with that gift of puckish and mischievous humor which so endears him to us. The oldest among us can recall nothing to compare with him, and the younger ones among us, however long we live, will never see the like again. If I were to try to sum up his whole character, I can think of no words more appropriate than those which he has himself written on the flyleaf of each volume of the history of the Second World War:

> *In War: Resolution*
> *In Defeat: Defiance*
> *In Victory: Magnanimity*
> *In Peace: Goodwill*

"In effect," Macmillan concluded, his voice trembling, "these words are the story of his life."

There was a pause and then the Chamber was filled with a roar as members shouted their approval. [47]

Since the twelfth century a Church of St. Mary Aldermanbury has stood at the junction of Love Lane and Aldermanbury Street in London, resting on a corner of the wall which defended the city in Roman times. Shakespeare worshiped in it. The present church was built by Sir Christopher Wren following the Great Fire of 1666. In the blitz of London in 1941 it was totally gutted by an incendiary bomb. Destined for destruction, since it no longer serves a parish in the old City of London, this church will now live again as a house of

God. As a memorial to Churchill's prophetic "Sinews of Peace" speech at Fulton on March 5, 1946, funds have been raised to dismantle the outside shell and rebuild it on the ground where he made what he himself regarded as his most significant speech. On the twentieth anniversary of that speech it will stand as a chapel of Westminster College in the small Missouri town, reconstructed and rededicated as the Churchill Memorial Chapel. The walls, the belltower and interior columns of the church survived the ravages of fire. The stones, a gift from the Diocese of London, will be dismantled one by one and marked so they can be put again in their right places on Missouri soil.

President John F. Kennedy assumed the honorary chairmanship of the committee sponsoring the memorial, and upon his assassination, President Lyndon B. Johnson was named to carry on the project.

When told about the memorial plans, Churchill said he was "honored that Westminster College should wish to commemorate the speech I made at Fulton. The removal of a ruined Christopher Wren church, largely destroyed by enemy action in London in 1941, and its reconstruction and rededication at Fulton, is an imaginative concept. It may symbolize in the eyes of the English-speaking peoples the ideas of Anglo-American association in which rest, now as before, so many of our hopes for peace and the future of mankind." [40]

Shortly after Churchill went into retirement in 1955, Field Marshal Viscount Montgomery proposed a toast to him. The occasion was the presentation of a portrait to Sir Winston as Lord Warden of the Cinque Ports, one of the almost endless honorary titles he received. The words Montgomery spoke might well stand as the free world's toast to Winston Churchill.

"This is one of the occasions, I think, on which it is right and proper to break through the reserve of the English heart, and to say in that tongue of which he is so unquestioned a master why it is that his portrait exists in the souls of free men throughout the world, and in the souls of many not so free.

"First, because he is a Man. There is not one of us who has had the privilege of sharing his work and his thoughts who cannot say with Mark Antony: 'He was my friend, faithful and just to me.' Never has any land found a leader who so matched the hour as did Sir Winston Churchill. When he spoke—in words that rang and thundered like the Psalms—we all said, 'That is how *we* feel and that is how we shall bear ourselves.' Let me conclude with the words which Cromwell used about the men whom the state chooses to serve her: 'So that they render good service, that satisfies.'

"Sir, you have rendered good service. Sir, we are satisfied. I give the toast of: Sir Winston Churchill, Knight of the Most Noble Order of the Garter, Lord Warden of the Cinque Ports, the greatest Englishman of all time." [41]

EPILOGUE

"Requiem for Greatness"

CHURCHILL'S last illness began with a cold. In this, his last, loneliest battle, that defiant vow—*We shall never surrender*—seemed graven on Sir Winston Churchill's soul. Hour after hour, day after day, the world stood vigil as the medical bulletins became ever more grave. But Churchill fought on with almost unbelievable tenacity. Finally, after days of drifting in and out of consciousness, the old warrior sank into peaceful sleep. The battle was over, the lion heart stilled forever.

As the curtain of grief descended over Britain, the nation's life slowed almost to a halt. Queen Elizabeth, who was notified of Churchill's death before it was officially announced to the public, took the unprecedented step of requesting Parliament to accord her former Prime Minister a state funeral, the first such tribute to a commoner since Gladstone's death in 1898. Churchill would be buried in a tranquil Oxfordshire graveyard beside his parents: Lord Randolph Churchill and his beautiful American wife, Jennie Jerome.

Typically, with his incomparable sense of history and theater, Churchill had years ago issued directions for his own funeral. He insisted: "I want lots of soldiers and bands." As the solemn leavetaking was acted out on January 30, a great drama and a great work of art in every ceremonial detail, Sir Winston had everything he desired—and more.

Dawn broke cold and gray. Calm in its majesty beside the

Thames, the palace of Westminster emerged from the drifting mist. Across the river stood the starkly modern outline of Festival Hall, its garden windows catching the first pale light. Far downstream, the dome and finial of St. Paul's Cathedral were faintly etched against the wintry sky. Between these two points, Westminster and St. Paul's, gathered a million men and women and the children they brought with them to capture the scene in memory. Via Telstar and television, millions the world over watched the obsequies of Churchill, a man who would have been great in any century, and who was, beyond doubt or envy or animosity, one of the greatest men that Britain—and the West—had ever produced.

At 9:45 A.M., as Big Ben struck the quarter-hour and cannon boomed, a gun carriage emerged from Westminster Hall, where Churchill's body had lain in state for three days and nights. The coffin on the gun carriage was shrouded with the Union Jack, on which rested a black velvet cushion bearing the diamond and gold regalia of the Order of the Garter. More than one hundred sailors of the Royal Navy—Churchill's favorite service—drew the gun carriage and its burden forward at a measured 65 paces to the minute. Each minute, the cannon boomed their soldierly lament.

Ahead of the gun carriage marched platoons from all the arms and services, their arms reversed. Here, also, were Lord Mountbatten, Chief of the Defense Staff, and the other service chiefs, followed by eight officers of the Queen's Royal Irish Hussars—Churchill's first regiment—bearing Sir Winston's medals. Behind the gun carriage strode the top-hatted men of the Churchill family, led by his son Randolph. In a carriage lent by the Queen were Lady Churchill and her two daughters Sarah and Mary. The march was accompanied by music of the Drum Horse and State Trumpeters in their velvet jockey caps and gold-laced jackets. Band after band—ten in all—appeared at appointed intervals in order to keep the pace steady and slow all down the long line of marchers.

Up Whitehall, past Nelson's monument in Trafalgar Square, by the National Gallery, where the flag hung at half-mast, and into the Strand moved the gun carriage, which had borne the regal corpses of Queen Victoria, Edward VII, George V and George VI. Along the way the pavements were thronged with silent watchers, and the white topees of Royal Marines dotted the route like snowdrops.

At Temple Bar, the boundary between Westminster and the City, the gun carriage entered the ancient section of London that had been heavily bombed by Nazi planes and was heartened on those long-ago, smoky, red-eyed mornings by the inspiring Churchill presence poking defiantly among the ruins. The cortege moved on through Fleet Street, home of London's press, and then up Ludgate Hill to the strains of Chopin's *Funeral March.*

St. Paul's was meticulously packed with heads of state and government, with famous men and old colleagues of Churchill's. They came in powdered wigs and capes and frocks of office, in morning clothes sprayed with medals and sashes, set off by black ties and armbands. Here sat Charles de Gaulle and Dwight D. Eisenhower, the kings of Norway, Greece and Denmark. One hundred and thirteen nations had been invited to send representatives to the funeral. Only one—Red China—refused. Unwatched and unheralded, Queen Elizabeth and Prince Philip drove to St. Paul's by a circuitous route—leaving the panoply and glory of the day to Sir Winston. The Queen could scarcely help remembering how she first knew and admired the wartime Prime Minister when she was a girl, and how later, on her accession to the throne, he guided her in her first steps of statecraft.

As Churchill's coffin was carried up the nave, the choir intoned "I Am the Resurrection and the Life." There were no flowers, but many flags and banners from old campaigns.

Between the bier and the altar rested Churchill's tokens of office: his black-draped sword, the great carved lion that is the Churchill family crest, sashes bearing the medals and honors of a lifetime of great achievement. The pallbearers— Churchill's old wartime colleagues and chiefs of staff— moved quietly to their seats.

As the regular, short Anglican funeral service proceeded, the first hymn to be sung was John Bunyan's

> *Who would true valour see,*
> *Let him come hither;*
> *One here will constant be,*
> *Come wind, come weather . . .*

After a special prayer read by the Dean of St. Paul's, organ and choir burst into Churchill's favorite American anthem,"The Battle Hymn of the Republic." It was sung at his express command and in homage to the honorary U.S. citizenship granted him in 1963. It was also symbolic of his lifetime dream of a closer union between the two nations whose blood flowed in his veins. The martial thunder of the old abolitionist hymn, with its stern New England pieties, may at first have sounded startling in Christopher Wren's graceful English Renaissance church, but it was one with the Churchillian spirit—militant, sonorous, confident of being in the right. The church that symbolized the survival of the British nation and the hymn that symbolized the endurance of the American Union—the suddenly mingled echoes of Agincourt and Antietam—served to remind the world of a kinship that goes deeper than shifting alliances and new patterns of power.

The funeral had really begun days earlier in the House of Commons. Preeminently, Churchill was a child of the House, in which he spent full fifty-three years of his long life. In fact, he was the last man to have served in Parliament under Queen Victoria.

In speaking of Churchill to the House, after a slight nod

to the empty seat of the Member for Woodford, Prime Minister Harold Wilson suddenly seemed touched with the Churchillian magic. "Where the fighting was hottest, he was in it." Wilson recalled, "sparing none, nor asking for quarter. The creature and possession of no one party, he has probably been the target of more concentrated parliamentary invective than any other member of any parliamentary age, and against each in turn he turned the full force of his own parliamentary oratory." Churchill, said Wilson, "was a warrior, and party debate was war. It mattered, and he brought to that war the conquering weapon of words fashioned for their purpose: to wound, never to kill; to influence, never to destroy."

As Churchill lay in state in Westminster Hall, the three party leaders, Labor's Wilson, the Conservatives' Sir Alec Douglas-Home, and the Liberals' Jo Grimond, stood together in reverent silence before the catafalque. They must have recognized the rightness of the scene, for in this very hall and on the very spot where Churchill lay, Simon de Montfort had called together Britain's first Parliament seven hundred years before almost to the day.

For twenty-three hours a day, a two-mile-long queue stretched from Westminster Hall along Millbank, past Horseferry Road and across Lambeth Bridge, then along the South Bank as far as County Hall. In the queue people chatted and swapped war stories of Winston, or told the younger ones what those days had been like. The atmosphere was not so much of sadness as of gratitude for what Churchill had done to save England. There were all sorts: working-class parents carrying their children, housewives and commuter husbands, young fellows and their girl friends, men in dinner jackets and women in evening wraps. Some took nips from hip flasks against the intense cold; others poured hot tea from Thermos bottles. It was almost like the old days of the Blitz, when stranger talked to stranger as if they were neighbors.

But on entering the great, drafty hall with its canopy of ancient oak, a great silence enfolded them. Footsteps were muffled by brown carpet, and the crowd divided into two lines, which passed on both sides of the catafalque. At the four corners stood tall candles and, nearly as rigid as the candlesticks, the honor guard, which solemnly changed every twenty minutes. As the people of Britain passed the casket, they dropped flowers—snowdrops, white carnations, daffodils. Before going out into Palace Yard, each one paused and looked back.

At St. Paul's, as the funeral service drew to a close with "God Save the Queen," there was a long pause; and then from high in the Whispering Gallery a Royal Horse Guards trumpeter sounded the Last Post, its plaintive notes ascending and echoing round the dome itself. In answer, from across the cathedral, came the bugle call of Reveille played by a Royal Irish Hussar, a hearty and heartening last trump that would have stirred the old warrior's blood.

The great bells of St. Paul's pealed out as the coffin was returned to the gun carriage. Cannon again reverberated. Sixty salutes had already been fired; now came thirty more— one for every year of Churchill's life. Sixty Highland bagpipers from different Scottish regiments piped the coffin down to the wharf at the foot of Tower Hill where Beefeaters in full uniform stood guard. Against the backdrop of Tower Bridge the vast Pool of London lay as still as an inland lake. Across the river great cranes bowed low in touching, mechanical precision. To the piping of a bosun's whistle, the coffin went aboard the *Havengore*, a Royal Navy launch.

With this action, the state funeral closed and the private one began. Churchill's body crossed the Thames, once London's great avenue of trade and triumph, under a massed fly-past of fighter planes, which dipped to five hundred feet in tribute. At Festival pier, the coffin was placed in a private hearse and driven slowly to Waterloo station. There were no more parades or bands or flags or muffled drums. Accompanied by his family, Churchill's body was carried by special train some sixty miles into the heart of Oxfordshire, to rest beside the graves of his English father and his American mother in the small parish churchyard at Bladon.

Winston Churchill's countrymen quickly turned back to present realities and future problems. Yet everywhere people paused to wonder what Churchill might teach the world he left behind. The mere fact that he happened, said historian Will Durant, "silences the grumbling of a thousand pessimists." Said Adlai Stevenson: "Like the grandeur and power of masterpieces of art and music, Churchill's life uplifts our hearts and fills us with fresh revelation of the scale and reach of human achievement." Yet, he concluded, "our world is thus the poorer, our political dialogue diminished and the sources of public inspiration run more thinly for all of us. There is a lonesome place against the sky."

Many were mourning not only an exceptional figure but an era and a society that was able to produce exceptional figures. There is a feeling that, as Harvard historian H. Stuart Hughes puts it, today's world has "little tolerance of greatness," and that in an era of computers, expert teams and government by consensus, the Churchillian kind of leadership may never again assert itself. With Churchill's passing, the world was diminished and felt it. Amid all the public outpourings of tribute and grief, however, no words struck a nobler note than the heartsick message that Winston Churchill himself broadcast to the people of defeated France in 1940:

Good night, then: sleep to gather strength for the morning, for the morning will come. Brightly will it shine on the brave and true, the kindly, on all who suffer for the cause, and gloriously upon the tombs of heroes. Thus will shine the dawn. [57]

Key to Contributors

1. BOCCA, GEOFFREY. *The Adventurous Life of Winston Churchill*
    [Reprinted by permission Julian Messner, Division of Pocket Books,
    Inc., © Copyright 1958 by Pocket Books, Inc., New York]

2. BROAD, LEWIS. *Winston Churchill: The Years of Preparation*
    [Copyright © 1958 by Hawthorn Books, Inc., New York]
    Winston Churchill: The Years of Achievement
    [Copyright © 1963 by Hawthorne Books, Inc., New York]

3. CHURCHILL, WINSTON S.
    a. *The Gathering Storm*   (1948)
    b. *The Grand Alliance*   (1950)
    c. *Their Finest Hour*   (1949)
    d. *The Hinge of Fate*   (1950)
    e. *Closing the Ring*   (1951)
    f. *Triumph and Tragedy*   (1953)
    [Reprinted by permission of Houghton Mifflin Company, Inc.,
    Boston]

    g. *My Early Life: A Roving Commission*   (1949)
    h. *World Crisis*   (1951)
    i. *Amid These Storms*
    [Reprinted by permission of Charles Scribner's Sons, Inc., New
    York]

    j. Churchill's Speech, "Sinews of Peace," given at Westminster
    College, Fulton, Missouri, in March 1946.

4. COWLES, VIRGINIA. *Winston Churchill, the Era and the Man*
    [Reprinted by permission of Harper & Row, Publishers, Inc., New
    York, and Curtis Brown, Ltd., London]

5. DE MENDELSSOHN, PETER. *The Age of Churchill*
    [Reprinted by permission of Alfred A. Knopf, Inc., New York, and
    Thames and Hudson, Ltd., London]

6. PAWLE, GERALD. *The War and Colonel Warden*
    [Reprinted by permission of Alfred A. Knopf, Inc., New York, and
    George G. Harrap & Co., Ltd., London]

7. ROWSE, A. L.   *The Later Churchills*
    [Reprinted by permission of Harper & Row, Publishers, Inc., New
    York, and Macmillan & Co., Ltd., London]

8. TAYLOR, ROBERT LEWIS *Winston Churchill: An Informal Study in
    Greatness*

9. THOMSON, MALCOLM. *The Life and Times of Winston Churchill*
   [Reprinted by permission of Odham's Press, Ltd., London]

10. ARMSTRONG, RICHARD. *Finest Hour—1962*
    (*USA–1*, June 1962)

11. ASQUITH, EARL OF OXFORD AND. *Memories and Reflections*
    [Reprinted by permission of Little, Brown and Company, Boston, Mass., and Cassell & Co., Ltd., London]

12. ATTLEE, CLEMENT. "Across the House"
    [From *Winston Churchill—A Tribute by Various Hands;* edited by Sir James Marchant. Reprinted by permission of Cassell and Co., Ltd., London]
    See also No. 39.

13. BIBESCO, PRINCESS MARTHE. *Sir Winston Churchill: Master of Courage*
    [Copyright © 1957 by Princess Marthe Bibesco and Robert Hale, Ltd. Reprinted by permission of the John Day Company, Inc., New York]

14. BLAKE, ROBERT. *Unrepentant Tory*
    [Reprinted by permission of St. Martin's Press, Inc., New York, and Eyre and Spottiswoode, Ltd., London]

15. BRYANT, ARTHUR. *Turn of the Tide*
    [Copyright © 1957 by Arthur Bryant. Reprinted by permission of Doubleday and Company, Inc., New York, and William Collins, Sons and Company, Ltd., London]

16. BURTON, RICHARD. From *The Jack Paar Show* of May 8, 1964
    [Copyright © 1964 by Richard Burton]

17. CHURCHILL, JOHN SPENCER. *A Churchill Canvas*
    [Copyright © 1961 by John Spencer Churchill. Reprinted by permission of Little, Brown and Company, Boston, and Odhams Press, Ltd., London]

18. COLLIER, RICHARD. *The Sands of Dunkirk*
    [Reprinted by permission of E. P. Dutton & Co., Inc., New York, and William Collins, Sons & Co., Ltd., London]

19. COOPER, DUFF. *Old Men Forget*
    [Reprinted by permission of E. P. Dutton & Co., Inc., New York, and Rupert Hart-Davis & Co., Ltd., London]

20. DRAWBELL, JAMES. *An Autobiography*
    [Reprinted by permission of Random House, Inc., New York, and William Collins Sons & Co., Ltd., London]

21. EADE, CHARLES, editor. *Churchill by His Contemporaries*

Guy Eden, "Churchill in High Office"
Geoffrey Gilbey, "Churchill and Racing"
Professor A. M. Low, "Churchill and Science"
Paul Reynaud, "Churchill and France"
Sir Gerald Wollaston, "Churchill at Harrow"
[Reprinted by permission of Simon & Schuster, Inc., New York]

22. EDELMAN, MAURICE. *The Member for Woodford*
[From *The Listener*, London, August 6, 1964]

23. EDGAR, E. E.

24. FEIS, HERBERT. *Churchill, Roosevelt and Stalin*
[Reprinted by permission of the Princeton University Press, Princeton, N.J.]

25. FISHMAN, JACK. *My Darling Clementine*
[Reprinted by permission of the David McKay Company, Inc., New York]

26. GUEDALLA, PHILIP. *Mister Churchill*
[A. P. Watt and Son, London. Reprinted by permission of Mrs. Philip Guedalla]

27. GUNTHER, JOHN. *Roosevelt in Retrospect: A Profile in History*
[Reprinted by permission of Harper & Row, Publishers, Inc., New York]

28. HANSARD, LONDON. [from May 21, 1952 (column 531); November 18, 1952 (column 1585); June 17, 1954 (column 2289)]

29. HARRIS, LEON. *The Fine Art of Political Wit*
[Reprinted by permission of E. P. Dutton & Co., Inc., New York]

30. HARRITY, RICHARD and MARTIN, RALPH G. *Man of the Century: Churchill*
[Reprinted by permission of Duell, Sloan & Pearce, New York]

31. HOLLIS, GENERAL LESLIE and LEASOR, JAMES. *War at the Top*
[Reprinted by permission of David Higham Associates, Ltd., London]

32. HUGHES, EMORY. *Winston Churchill: British Bulldog*
[Reprinted by permission of The Exposition Press, Inc. New York]

33. ISMAY, LORD HASTINGS L. *The Memoirs of General Lord Ismay*
[Copyright © 1960 by the Viking Press, Inc., and the Trustees of the Ismay Literary Trust. Reprinted by permission of the Viking Press, Inc., New York, and William Heinemann, Ltd., London]

34. KRAUS, RENE. *Winston Churchill*
[Copyright 1941 by Rene Kraus. Published by J. B. Lippincott Company, Philadelphia]

Young Lady Randolph
[Reprinted by permission of Longman's Canada Limited, Ontario]

35. LEAHY, REAR ADMIRAL WILLIAM H. *I Was There*
[Published by the McGraw-Hill Book Company, New York]

36. *Life* magazine. [from March 13, 1964]

37. LOCKHART, J. G. *Winston Churchill*
[Reprinted by permission of Gerald Duckworth Co., Ltd., London]

38. MAGNUS, PHILIP. *Kitchener, Portrait of an Imperialist*
[Reprinted by permission of E. P. Dutton & Co., New York, and
John Murray Publishers, Ltd., London]

39. MARCHANT, SIR JAMES, editor. *Winston Churchill—A Tribute by
Various Hands*
A. P. Herbert, "The Master of Words"
Robert Menzies, "Churchill and the Commonwealth"
Bernard Baruch, "A Birthday Letter"
[Reprinted by permsision of Cassell and Co., Ltd., London]
See also No. 12.

40. Milwaukee *Journal*. [Leo Soroka, © 1964 by United Press Inter-
national]

41. MONTGOMERY, VISCOUNT SIR BERNARD. *Memoirs of Field Marshal
The Viscount Montgomery
of Alamein*
[Reprinted by permission of the World Publishing Company, New
York, and William Collins Sons & Co., Ltd., London]

42. MOOREHEAD, ALAN. *Winston Churchill in Trial and Triumph*
[Reprinted by permission of Laurence Pollinger, Ltd., London]

43. MORTON, H. V. *Atlantic Meeting*
[Copyright 1943 by Dodd, Mead & Company, Inc. Reprinted by
permission of Dodd, Mead & Company, Inc., New York, and
Methuen and Company, Ltd., London]

44. MURPHY, CHARLES J. V. and DAVENPORT, JOHN. *The Lives of Winston
Churchill*
[Charles Scribner's Sons, 1945]

45. NEL, ELIZABETH. *Mr. Churchill's Secretary*
[Reprinted by permission of Putnam's & Coward-McCann, New
York]

46. New York *Herald Tribune*. [from April 10, 1963; December 1, 1963]

47. New York *Times*. [James Feron, July 29, 1964]

48. O'BRIEN, E. D. "Winston Churchill the Man"; an 80th Year Tribute
to Winston Churchill
[*Illustrated London News*, edited by Burse Ingram (1954)]

49. READER'S DIGEST

50. SHERIDAN, CLARE. *Naked Truth*
    [Reprinted by permission of Harper & Row, Publishers, Inc., New York, and Eyre and Spottiswoode, Ltd., London]

51. SHERWOOD, ROBERT E. *Roosevelt and Hopkins*
    [Reprinted by permission of Harper & Row, Publishers, Inc., New York]

52. SOUTAR, ANDREW. *With Ironside in North Russia*
    [Reprinted by permission of Hutchinson & Co., Ltd., London]

53. SPEARS, SIR EDWARD T. *Prelude to Dunkirk*
    [Reprinted by permission of Hill and Wang, Inc., New York, and William Heinemann, Ltd., London]

54. THOMPSON, R. W. *The Yankee Marlborough*
    [Copyright © 1963 by George Allen & Unwin, Ltd., London. Reprinted by permission of Doubleday & Company, Inc., New York]

55. THOMPSON, INSPECTOR WALTER H. *Assignment Churchill*
    [Copyright by Walter H. Thompson]

56. *Time* magazine. [From January 5, 1942; January 2, 1950; November 5, 1951; May 4, 1953; January 29, 1965; February 5, 1965]

57. WHEELER-BENNETT, JOHN W. *The Nemesis of Power*
    [Reprinted by permission of St. Martin's Press, Inc., New York]

58. WILLANS, GEOFFREY and ROETTER, CHARLES. *The Wit of Winston Churchill*
    [Reprinted by permission of Miss Irene Josephy, London]

INDEX

317

INDEX

To Eric on the 5th
of November 1967

with all my love

Mother